SPEECHREADING
(LIPREADING)

To the memory of

Don Barley

*for his patience and forebearance
during the time we were engaged
in writing this book.*

(Second Printing)

SPEECHREADING
(LIPREADING)

─────────*By*─────────

JANET JEFFERS

Professor in Audiology
Department of Special Education
California State College at Los Angeles
Los Angeles, California

and

MARGARET BARLEY

Instructor in Speechreading
California State College at Los Angeles
Teacher of Adult Lipreading Classes
Alhambra and Pasadena, California

CHARLES C THOMAS • PUBLISHER
Springfield • *Illinois* • *U.S.A.*

Published and Distributed Throughout the World by
CHARLES C THOMAS • PUBLISHER
BANNERSTONE HOUSE
301–327 East Lawrence Avenue, Springfield, Illinois, U.S.A.

© *1971, by* CHARLES C THOMAS • PUBLISHER

ISBN 0-398-02185-6

Library of Congress Catalog Card Number: 72–157288

First Printing, 1971
Second Printing, 1974

Printed in the United States of America

N-1

PREFACE

Speechreading (lipreading) means understanding a speaker through a combined look and listen technique. The speech-reader observes such articulatory movements as are visible and at the same time hears the message. Vision is used to supplement an inaccurate or partially received auditory pattern. Because of this useful congruence of sight and sound, most hearing impaired individuals* are able to function in an almost normal fashion and in a way that would be difficult, if not impossible, if they were to rely only on the auditory channel. A basic knowledge of language is considered to be a requisite to the acquisition of any useful degree of competence. The individual learns to recognize, in part through vision, the language with which he is already familiar. However, speechreading can also be used as a basic tool or visual aid in the initial development of language comprehension, as with the profoundly deaf child. This latter use is touched upon, but not developed in any comprehensive fashion in this text. While the basic philosophy and principles found herein should be useful to the teacher of the young deaf child, the methodology and materials have been designed primarily for the teacher of hearing impaired, but not deaf, children and for the teacher of hard-of-hearing and deaf adults. Much of the practice material assumes that the student possesses a basic understanding of language.

Speechreading has been taught to the hard-of-hearing in the United States for nearly one hundred years. In the early 1900's and later on in the thirties, various texts were published dealing with methods of instruction. A critical examination of such texts reveals more similarities than differences. The differences are largely differences in emphasis. Some authors stressed visual clues; others, association; still others pointed up the importance of

---

* An exception to this statement is the profoundly deaf child who has limited auditory information at his disposal.

vii

rhythm, stress, tactile clues, etc. Almost all of them followed the part to whole approach, from phoneme to syllable, to phrase, to sentence, to paragraph.* Sounds were organized with respect to the speechreading movements which identified them. As each movement was introduced, it was analyzed with respect to its visible features and associated sounds. Next, words or phrases were practiced which contained the movement in question. They were followed by sentences incorporating the sounds illustrative of the movement, and finally associative material loaded with the sounds, and hence, movement or movements for the day. Yet we find that the best teachers have quickly learned to disregard the texts and to teach in a holistic fashion. It is this holistic and eclective method that we present in this text. While superior teachers have long taught in this fashion, their approach has never been adequately recorded.

The belief that one could speechread through an additive approach undoubtedly stemmed from a confusion between speechreading and speech development in the minds of the early teachers of deaf children who were also the first persons to teach speechreading to the hard-of-hearing. Only much later, long after the time that the part to whole method had become established as *the way* to teach speechreading, was there any recognition that many sounds were not visible and that much of the information must come either from the ears or from educated guessing. The legacy of teaching in this fashion is still with us and has a number of ramifications. For example, from the beginning it was assumed that hard-of-hearing pupils could not associate lip movements with speech sounds without conscious awareness of how each sound appeared on the lips. In practice, one finds that this knowledge has almost always been absorbed in the process of learning to talk. Much wasted time and effort has been traditionally spent in teaching the hard of hearing what they already know—in making conscious what should be, and must become, an unconscious process. In addition, we find that materials intended for training in word association and idea association have evolved from materials designed for training

---

* A notable exception is Morkovin-Moore, *Life Situation Speech Reading,* where the basic units for study are skits.

in visual proficiency. There has often been an unnatural loading of sentence and paragraph material with particular speech sounds. The result is stilted, artificial material that is not representative of colloquial speech.

The impetus for writing this book arose from a need for a college text that would recognize and correct the errors of the past, described above, while retaining many of the fine suggestions and techniques that have been proved to be helpful, specifically: (a) Training in visual proficiency was to be retained, but divorced from training in association and flexibility. Identification and fast perception of speechreading movements were to be achieved through visual contrast—not through explanation or conscious recognition of their characteristics. (b) Associative material would be representative of everyday colloquial speech. Beginning materials would be structured, and enough visual and associational clues would be provided to insure easy understanding. There would be a gradual transition from the easier to the more difficult materials. Associational materials would not evolve from specific speech movements and would not be loaded with them.

In addition, the authors had other objectives in mind. Much of what is known about speechreading is not in the currently available speechreading texts, or not, at least, in one principle source. And while much good practice material has appeared from time to time, it has, for the most part, been published separately from the texts and has rapidly gone out of print. There appeared to be a need for a comprehensive text on speechreading. Included, in addition to methodology, must be chapters on principles of instruction; basic knowledge regarding the formation and visible characteristics of speech sounds; a chapter on the history and development of speechreading, including explication and evaluation of the recognized methodologies; a chapter containing tests of speechreading ability; and a special chapter covering the research literature. This last chapter was to be not just a grouping of research studies but instead an organization of the findings with respect to a theoretical model of the skills believed to be inherent in the speechreading process. Hopefully from this treatment might emerge new insights with respect to what is already known and what is yet to be determined or verified experimentally. And finally, in the belief that "many" illustrations are worth a thousand words, we planned to include in the text a large section of pretested speechreading materials, coordinated with the methods chapter and illustrative of the suggested techniques.

This text should serve at least three basic purposes: (a) as a basic text for a course on speechreading, (b) as a resource book on speechreading in a seminar on hearing, (c) as a source book for teachers of speechreading. When used for either of the first two purposes, the instructor may not care to assign all of the materials. A basic course might consist of Chapters 1 through 3, Chapter 5, and Chapter 6. These are the chapters entitled "Principles of Speechreading," "Visibility," "History and Development," "Methodology," and "Materials for Instruction." The chapters on the research literature and on tests of speechreading could be omitted from a beginning course. If the students have had basic courses in speech correction and phonetics, much of the material in the chapter entitled "Visibility" will be familiar to them. It is included for their review and to enable beginning students to understand the material presented herein without having to refer to other texts. Seminar assignments might include such chapters as "History and Development," "The Process of Speechreading," and "Tests of Speechreading." For teachers, the chapters on methodology, materials, and tests should prove to be of most value.

CONTENTS

Contents

SPEECHREADING
(LIPREADING)

Chapter 1

PRINCIPLES OF SPEECHREADING

Because of the nature of speech sounds and the limited visual information available, speechreading can rarely suffice to bring to the individual the information he must have to function effectively. In practice, speechreading is always combined with hearing—in life situations and even in practice periods. Why then a text on speechreading? Is this not outmoded? Should not the title, as well as the content, imply a combined eye-ear approach? Our answer is simply this. To achieve maximum skill in utilizing a sensory channel, it is necessary during practice periods to attend to it with minimal distraction or help from other sensory modalities. Voice is used in giving speechreading instruction, but not so much that close attention and observation are no longer essential.* The ultimate aim is improved comprehension. We are not interested in training people to be good speechreaders or good listeners per se, but, instead, to combine these skills in the interest of good comprehension. But in order to achieve this goal, maximum facility in both areas is desirable. It is believed that this can best be achieved through the separation initially of speechreading training and auditory training. When maximum skill in both areas is achieved, training in speechreading or in auditory training, as such, will no longer be indicated. Ultimately the individual will, without conscious effort, combine the information from the two sensory modalities. He will not know whether he is depending more on hearing or more on vision. He will only know that he understands.

---

* An exception to this general rule is made in teaching the profoundly deaf individual. Full voice is always used. Because of his limited hearing there is little chance that he will fail to attend fully to visual stimuli, although the reverse may very well be true.

1. WHAT IS SPEECHREADING?

1.1. Definitions

Speechreading (lipreading) was defined by Nitchie[8, p. 341] as "the art of understanding a speaker's thought by watching the movements of his mouth."* To this we might well add, "and his facial expression."† Another definition of speechreading is a paraphrase of a definition of reading. Reading has been defined as the gross process of looking at, perceiving, and interpreting written symbols. The definition is considered a good one because it obviates such involved phrases as "reading with meaning," or "understanding the printed word." In like manner, if we define speechreading as the gross process of looking at, perceiving, and interpreting spoken symbols, we have by our definition made it clear that we are speaking of the total process which involves three steps: (a) *sensory reception* of the motor or movement pattern, (b) *perception* of the pattern, and (c) *association* of the pattern with meaningful concepts. It should be noted, however, that whereas the reader of printed symbols is receiving the complete sensory pattern, the reader of speech movements is receiving only limited visual information.

Actually, a fourth step is required of the speechreader. He must mentally replace or "fill-in" information that he has not received in order to complete both steps two and three.

1.2. Terminology—Speechreading or Lipreading?

Both of these terms, *speechreading* and *lipreading*, are used today to describe the art of gaining information about what is being said by watching the lips and facial expression. *Lipreading* is the better established term and was used almost exclusively from the 1900's up to the 1930's or perhaps even later. Since that

---

* This is a paraphrase of an earlier definition used by A.G. Bell which was, "the art of understanding a speaker's thought by watching his mouth."

† Evidence of the importance of full facial expression versus lips only has been provided both by Stone[15] and by Greenberg and Bode.[10] Stone found that the visual intelligibility of sentences increased with increase in facial expression. Greenberg and Bode found that consonant discrimination was more accurate when subjects viewed the talker's entire face than when they viewed only his lips.

time, there has been a conscientious effort by a large number of teachers to change the generic term to *speechreading*. Because the term speechreading is considered by some to be a new term and one largely foisted upon us by that energetic organization, The American Speech and Hearing Association, it is interesting to note that it was first used in the late 1860's or early 1870's. Sarah Fuller,[4, p. 127] an early teacher of hard-of-hearing adults, published a pamphlet entitled *Speech Reading: A Guide for Self-Instruction When Trained Teachers are not Available.* Later, Alexander Melville Bell[4, p. 130] wrote a small book called *Speech Reading and Articulation Teaching.*

The term *lipreading* has the advantage of being well established. Almost everyone has heard of lipreading and understands that it connotes the skill of watching the lips in order to improve comprehension. The term *speechreading* is still not generally understood by the public at large. One of the authors had a college student elect her speechreading class because he assumed that he would be reading great speeches! He had heard of lipreading, but not speechreading. Since he was an accommodating fellow, he stayed on to learn how to teach speechreading. It was explained to him that, since the class was small, his presence was sorely needed in order to keep it from being cancelled!

The advantage of the newer term, or the newly rediscovered term, is that it more explicitly connotes the process. The speechreader is literally reading speech or, at least, speech movements. He observes lip, jaw, and tongue movements that are made by the speaker, as well as his facial expression. The term *lipreading* implies observation of just the lips. Since a decision had to be made, the authors have elected to use the term *speechreading* throughout this book. We admit to using the two terms interchangeably in our daily work.

2. TYPES OF INSTRUCTION

2.1. As a Recognition or Decoding Skill

There are essentially three types of speechreading instruction. The basic form is *teaching the skill.* The pupil learns to use his eyes in conjunction with his ears. He is taught habits of attention and rapid focusing. He must learn to recognize all visible speech movements, even when the speech is quite rapid. He must also learn to piece together bits of information into a related whole and mentally to "fill-in" information that is missing. This kind of instruction presupposes the student's knowledge of the basic language structure and a vocabulary upon which the lessons can be based. The student is taught, for the most part, *to recognize what he already knows.* Instruction of this sort is typical of that given to the deafened: adults who have had normal hearing during their developmental years and have established a basic knowledge of the language through auditory channels.

2.2. Skill Plus Vocabulary Enrichment

The second kind of instruction can be categorized as *speechreading-vocabulary development.* It combines teaching the skill with vocabulary development and tutoring in specific subject matter areas, when the need is indicated. This is the kind of special instruction provided for hard-of-hearing and severely hard-of-hearing children who are *enrolled in regular classrooms.* These children are different from deaf children in that they have mastered most of the essential features of the grammar of their language. They recognize and use correct sentence patterns and word order and understand structural as well as lexical meanings, though they may manifest both receptive and expressive deficits with respect to unheard morphemes (e.g., /t/ in picked; /z/ in leads, etc.). They are also unlike deaf children in that they have more advanced vocabularies. But in comparison with normally hearing children of the same age and intelligence, they are retarded in vocabulary acquisition, often as much as from one to three years. Hard-of-hearing children are first taught speechreading as a skill. But because of their vocabulary lag and because the process of education, in an analytical sense, is largely a process of acquiring a larger and larger vocabulary, the task does not end with the development of the basic skill. It has often been said that the special needs of the hard-of-hearing child consist of speechreading instruction and speech correction. This statement is true only if we define speechreading instruction as being more than recognition of known material and include under this heading instruction aimed at locating and closing gaps in vocabulary and knowledge. When the child has reached school age, lessons should be closely correlated with the subject matter of the classroom. Once the basic skill has been established, the content of speechreading lessons should be based on new or difficult words and concepts that the child is in the process of acquiring or will soon be expected to acquire in the course of his regular classroom instruction. When speechreading is conceived of and taught in this fashion, and when amplification is used and instruction started as soon as the loss is detected, we find that many hearing handicapped youngsters are able to fit into normal classrooms. They have the ability to develop within the limits of their native endowments, largely unhampered by their sensory deficits. But in order to do so such children will need from two to five hours of special instruction per week.

2.3. Concurrent Development of Skill and Language

The third type of teaching could be labeled *language-speechreading* or *concurrent instruction*. It aims at developing language (word meanings, structural meanings, morphemic aspects, and syntax), along with developing speechreading skill. In this kind of instruction speechreading can be said to be used as a *basic tool, along with other tools, such as visual aids and silent reading,* to develop the child's ability to understand language and to permit him to acquire a knowledge of word order and a large enough vocabulary to think in terms of language. This is the kind of approach that is used with the profoundly deaf child. Initially, speechreading is generally learned word by word, though some attempt is made from the first to teach simple phrases and sentences as a whole. Once a word is understood, it should rarely be presented except in a meaningful sentence. Words seen on the lips are associated with the objects or ideas they represent. The child sees the speech patterns and the correct grammatical pattern on the lips over and over again until he associates these movements with the idea the speaker is wishing to convey. But because motor movements are limited and do not convey the complete message, learning is enlarged and reinforced with almost simultaneous presentation of visual aids (such as objects, pictures, and actions), along with the printed word. The child must develop a knowledge of structural as well as lexical meanings at the same time that he acquires the skill of visual recognition of oral language.

The way the deaf child learns through *seeing* the words and correct sentence structure over and over again in a meaningful situation—through speechreading and silent reading—is somewhat analogous to the way the hearing child develops his language through hearing words and sentence structure over and over again in meaningful situations. The small child with normal hearing does not immediately make the correct associations. That it takes him a good many years to master the socially approved tense and word relationships is evidenced by his own garbled version. For example, he may say, "Who do it?" "I do it me own." "He drived his bicycle on the grass." "I'll win you a game," etc. But the chief and very important difference between the normal child and the deaf child is that the latter does not receive enough sensory information through vision and amplified hearing to develop spontaneously a basic knowledge of language.

3. WHO NEEDS TO SPEECHREAD?

Everyone, at times, needs to speechread. Anyone who is not receiving enough auditory information to enable him to understand, needs to speechread. The deprivation can be either environmental or organic. Those of us who have normal hearing need to speechread in an excessively noisy environment, such as a cocktail party or when sitting at the back of a church or lecture hall. Moreover, we unconsciously do so, and in the "back of the hall" situation, are most annoyed if an intervening hat or head prevents our *seeing the speaker*. With the advent of the wearable hearing aid, the hard-of-hearing population became less dependent on speechreading. Because speechreading was less important, some people rushed to the conclusion that speechreading was no longer of any importance. They failed to realize that hearing aids are limited in frequency range and clarity. Most hearing aids do not reproduce accurately the high frequency sounds (s, sh, f, th, p, k, t), and many of them are so limited as to make discrimination of the voiced consonants (d, z, g, b, etc.) impossible without speechreading for those with sensorineural impairments. *All hearing handicapped individuals* need to speechread, some of them only part of the time, while others never receive enough information through hearing alone to piece the message together and must always rely on a dual channel system —ears and eyes—for receiving the necessary sensory stimuli. The important question, then, is not who needs to speechread, but who needs speechreading instruction?

4. WHO NEEDS SPEECHREADING INSTRUCTION?– VARIABLES WHICH WILL INFLUENCE NEED

In general, speechreading instruction is needed by any hearing handicapped child and all hearing handicapped adults who, though wearing hearing aids, find that at times they are having difficulty following the spoken word. The *need* for speechreading instruction will depend upon and vary with the following factors: the amount of *self-teaching;* the adequacy of the hearing aid or aids; the extent, configuration, and nature of the hearing loss; individual differences in ability in mastering the skill; knowledge of the language; and the nature of instruction.

4.1. *Amount of Self-Teaching*

Speechreading does not always have to be taught, though the individual's skill can usually be improved through instruction. Numerous hearing handicapped individuals, both children and adults, have developed a fair degree of proficiency without formal instruction. Usually, this has been an unconscious process; it is apparently "natural" for many people to use their eyes as well as their ears. The hearing handicapped person may react to his sensory deficit, just as the normal person does to an environmental auditory deficit, by watching the speaker. He is not aware that he is doing so, and is often surprised when presenting himself for instruction to discover that he is already a speechreader, and, indeed, may be a rather good one. Despite this assurance, he often remains in the class, for he may wish to become even more skilled. In addition, there are other important values to be secured from speechreading instruction. The class serves to bolster his confidence in himself. Because the material is structured and visible, he can follow with ease. He has the solace of being around others who are so handicapped, receives assurance from not being different, and finds ready and sympathetic ears when he needs to tell of his problem and express his anxieties and frustrations.

Occasionally a hard-of-hearing child may become, through self-teaching, so proficient in speechreading that his loss is not suspected by either his parents or his teachers. Faulty articulation and difficulties in learning phonics and spelling are attributed to other causes. Richard, age five, was such a child. The parents suspected that his younger brother had a hearing loss, but had no idea that Richard might also be similarly involved. His speech was excellent for his age, and his comprehension and recall vocabularies, larger than average. His loss was discovered through a whim of the audiometrist who decided that she might as well check Richard's hearing at the same time that she was testing his brother. Richard was found to have a binaural hearing loss of 42 dB, average level 500–2000 cps (A.S.A. 1951; see Fig. 1) and to be severely hard-of-hearing (60 dB or greater) for a good part of the consonant range. A year later his first grade teacher evinced complete disbelief regarding the loss and almost convinced the parents that a misdiagnosis had been made. On a test of speech intelligibility without speechreading given at normal conversational level, he made a score of 48 percent, which would indicate great difficulty in understanding. With speechreading, his score was 84 percent, indicating good comprehension.

4.2. The Adequacy of the Hearing Aid or Aids

The need for a high degree of proficiency in speechreading, and hence for instruction, will also vary with the help received from a hearing aid. When speech can be restored to normal loudness level and *clarity* through the use of a hearing aid, the hard-of-hearing adult will not usually be in need of *speechreading instruction*. He will still *need* to *speechread* because all hearing aids have certain physical limitations. With even the best hearing aid, he will not perceive accurately all of the consonant sounds.

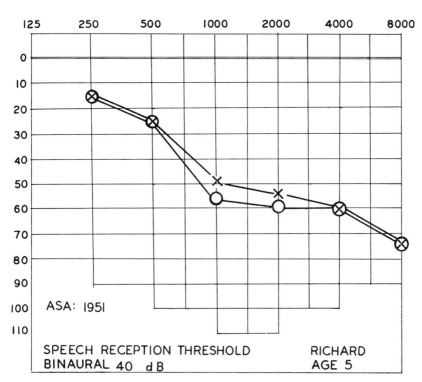

FIGURE 1.

However, his knowledge of the language will enable him to fill in the missing gaps in most listening situations, and in all likelihood, he will train *himself* to *look* as well as to listen when he has a need to do so.

The foregoing is not true of the *hearing handicapped child*. His is a world of constant vocabulary growth and expansion. He must learn the language *before* he will be able to fill in missing information.

4.3. The Extent, Configuration, and Nature of the Hearing Loss

These are the factors which may prevent good hearing aid use.

4.3.1 EXTENT OF LOSS. The individual, be he a child or an adult, with a severe sensorineural hearing impairment (70 dB or greater, I.S.O.: 1964 for the 1000–4000 Hz range), cannot usually depend on incidental or self-teaching. Even with the best wearable hearing aid or aids, he will confuse many speech sounds or miss them altogether. He must always look as well as listen and must be as expert with his eyes as with his ears. For him speechreading is essential. At the far end of the continuum, we find the profoundly deaf individual with only islands of hearing who will not be able to understand a single word by hearing alone and is dependent upon good speechreading.

4.3.2 PATTERN OF LOSS. The configuration of the hearing loss has an important bearing on the need for speechreading instruction. While much can be done with a properly selected hearing aid, if there is an exceedingly sharp fall off in hearing at 1000 Hz and above the person may need to combine speechreading with hearing in order to understand. If the loss is too precipitate, the aid may not be able to reverse the contour of the hearing loss and to restore the higher frequencies to normal or near-normal levels. The vowels will be heard accurately; the voiced consonants, less well, and the voiceless consonants may not be heard at all.

4.3.3 NATURE OF LOSS. Hearing aids can do much to correct discrimination problems due to an extensive loss or to a moderate imbalance in acuity for low and high tones. But if the difficulty in discrimination is retrocochlear, the confusion can only be straightened out through speechreading. Difficulties of this sort occur much more frequently in the adult population and, because of this, have been labeled *phonemic regression* (Gaeth[9]). The person has lost his ability to distinguish among many of the speech sounds even when speech is amplified and he is receiving adequate sensory information. Such a loss cannot be attributed either to the extent of the hearing impairment or its configuration.

4.4. Individual Differences in Ability in Mastering the Skill

Some people are not eye-minded and will not automatically look as well as listen; when trained to look, they will have more than the average amount of difficulty in putting two and two together.

The two following cases are illustrative: (a) Male—age fifty; hearing impairment since age twenty; had used hearing aids continuously for thirty years; normal eyesight; above average intelligence and economic status; responsible position. He presented himself for speechreading instruction at the point when he could no longer understand the speech of those around him. It had never occurred to him to watch the lips of the speaker, and he had not acquired any degree of speechreading skill. (b) Child —age ten; had used hearing aid for three years; loss incurred at age five; precipitate drop-off in higher frequencies; difficulties in learning to read and spell; had had general tutoring in language development in a speech and hearing clinic, but no specific training in speechreading. Observation made it clear that he never focused on the lips of the speaker. He did not hear and, before instruction in speechreading, was unable to recognize any of the high frequency consonant sounds. (See Audiogram, A.S.A. 1951, Fig. 2.)

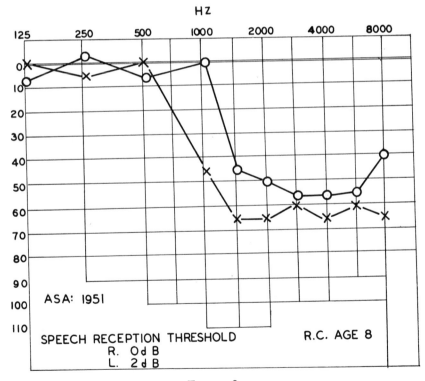

FIGURE 2.

4.5. Knowledge of the Language

Understanding always involves more than hearing, if we limit the term *hearing* to mean the reception and discrimination of auditory sensory stimuli. To understand, one must have associated sound patterns with meaningful concepts; he must have a fairly large recognition vocabulary, and he must have mastered the verb tense system and syntax of his language. (See Section 7.3.2 in this chapter for a more detailed exposition.) Understanding is dependent not only on hearing, but on learning. Because languages are redundant, patterned, and rhythmical, the individual who "knows" the language need not *hear* all of a message in order to understand it. His brain will fill in the missing gaps for him. All normally hearing individuals have this experience when listening over the telephone. We are not aware that we are receiving an imperfect sensory pattern and that our brain is filling in for us. All we know is that we have no trouble understanding. We are only brought up short when a proper name or address is introduced into the conversation. We find ourselves saying, "I didn't hear you. Will you please spell it?"

In most situations, then, we do not have to hear accurately in order to understand. This is why a good number of hearing handicapped adults with *mild* or *moderate* losses of hearing *and good hearing aids* do not need speechreading instruction and only speechread under adverse listening conditions. The mind fills in the information that is not received and does so rapidly and at an unconscious level.

The child with a mild or moderate loss finds himself in no such easy position. He must speechread if his vocabulary is to expand and develop in the normal fashion.

The acquisition of each new word requires both hearing and speechreading. For example, let us say that he is learning about elephants for the first time or is being asked to follow a story about elephants. He will hear el-a-an or el-a-am, and if he is not speechreading, he may wonder what it is all about. The moment he uses his eyes, the message will be clear. He will speechread the *f* and recognize the nasal sound as *n* and not *m*. Now the pattern will be el-a-fun—still not enough for good *spelling*, but sufficient for comprehension.

4.6. The Nature of Instruction

It is not uncommon in our public school programs to find hard-of-hearing children who hate their speechreading class and finally refuse to attend. When this occurs, it is often due to the nature of the instruction. The teacher has failed to ascertain the children's true needs and has continued to teach the beginning skill of recognizing visible sound movements and known vocabulary and ideas to children who are already maximally proficient. The speechreading instruction period for all but beginning pupils should be used to expand the child's recognition vocabulary, to broaden his intellectual horizons, and to tutor him in the areas where he is falling behind in his classwork. When taught in this fashion, speechreading becomes a vehicle for vocabulary development and educational tutoring or enrichment, and is an important supplement to the regular classroom instruction.

5. HOW TO DETERMINE AN INDIVIDUAL'S NEED FOR SPEECHREADING INSTRUCTION

Adults. Any adult with a good hearing aid who still finds that he is not understanding the conversation of those around him needs instruction. He will usually be aware of this himself, or if he is not, his family will be, and he will be urged to seek instruction.

Children. To determine if a child has mastered the basic skill, it is usually necessary to test his ability in some straight-forward fashion. Tests of speechreading ability will be presented in a later section.

If he has mastered the skill, he will still need special instruction, but the instruction should center around *making use of his speechreading ability* in helping him to develop new vocabulary and to catch up in knowledge with his peers. In the process of learning the meaning of words that are new to him, he will also learn to speechread them. Such tools as the Peabody Vocabulary

Test* and the Full Range Picture Vocabulary Test† are of
considerable help in assessing the child's language level.

6. LIMITATIONS OF SPEECHREADING
THE IMPORTANCE OF COMBINING HEARING AND VISION

Speechreading, whenever possible, must always be subordi-
nated to hearing. It can supplement hearing, but it cannot substitute for hearing. If vision were a natural avenue for speech
comprehension, we would have no need for special classes or
schools for the deaf or even for speechreading instruction.
Children with deficient hearing would develop in a completely
normal fashion and adults would not be aware of any difficulty
in understanding attendant upon a hearing loss. As a matter of
fact, they would probably be unaware of the loss itself. Our
language is an auditory phenomenon; one designed for hearing,
not viewing. As a vehicle for visual communication, it is severely
limited. The limitations comprise at least six.‡ They are low
visibility of speech sounds, homophenous sounds, rapidity of
normal speech, transition effect, individual differences in sound
formation, and environmental limitations.

6.1. Low Visibility of Speech Sounds

Speech sounds are made through modulations or changes in
either a vibrating or non-vibrating air stream. These changes are
effected chiefly through positioning the tongue and changing
the size of the mouth cavity by lower jaw movements. Most of
the motor (muscular) movements involved in sound formation
occur within the mouth and cannot be detected by the eye. The
lip movements play a relatively minor part in the formation of
sounds. Yet, all that the speechreader has to guide him are movements of the lips and jaw and, occasionally, of the tongue. Many

---

* Dunn, L.M.: *Peabody Picture Vocabulary Test.* George Peabody College
for Teachers, Nashville 5, Tennessee.

† Ammons, R.B., and Ammons, H.S.: *The Full Range Picture Vocabulary
Test.* Psychological Test Specialists, Box 1441, Missoula, Montana.

‡ Items 1,2,3 and 5 can be found listed in a somewhat comparable fashion in
Kinzie, Cora: *Lipreading for Children:* Grades I, II, III, revised 1947.

of the speech sounds do not require a characteristic movement of either lips or jaw (e.g., t,d,n,l,k,g,ng,h).

In a study designed to assess the relative visibility of consonant sounds, Woodward and Barber[17] found only four sets of consonants which could be considered visually contrastable. They were the following: unit 1: p,b,m; unit 2: w,hw,r; unit 3: f,v; and unit 4: the remainder of the consonant sounds, /t,d,n,l,s,z,j,k, g,h,ʃ,ʒ,tʃ,dʒ,θ,ð/.* And under *usual viewing conditions* it is estimated that approximately 60 percent of the speech sounds are either obsure or invisible. This count includes over half of the vowels and diphthongs and three fifths of the consonants.

Visibility will be discussed in greater detail in Chapter 2.

6.2. *Homophenous Sounds*

Alexander Graham Bell coined a word to describe words which look alike.[4, p. 118] It is *homophene.* Examples of such words are the following: /bat, mat, pat/; face, vase/; /chew, shoe/. The term *homophene* must not be confused with a similar word, *homophone,* which means a word which sounds the same as another, but is different from it in meaning and in spelling, such as /write, right/; or /to, too, two/. Homophones are, of course, homophenes since the sound pattern and hence the movement pattern is identical regardless of spelling or meaning, but the reverse is not true. *Homophenes do not sound alike; they look alike.* We shall extend the original meaning of homophene to include sounds that look alike as well as words that look alike. One of the major problems confronting the speechreader is that *there is not a single consonant sound that has a characteristic lip or jaw movement of its own and hence can be recognized on the basis of vision alone!* The speechreader must always guess as to the sounds which he actually saw. For example, the lips together movement in indicative of /p/, /b/, or /m/. The lip to teeth movement indicates that either an /f/ or a /v/ has been made. The teeth approximate in making either /s/ or /z/. When the tongue is seen between the teeth, the speaker may have said the voiceless sound as in *thin* or the voiced sound in *them.* A forward movement of

---

* The consonant (ŋ) was not included in the study. Only one speaker was used.

the lips may indicate any one of four sounds and a puckering, any one of seven!

6.3. *Rapidity of Normal Speech*

Normal speech is rapid speech. Nitchie[12] estimated that ordinary speech averages about thirteen speech sounds per second and noted that the eye is capable of consciously seeing only eight to ten movements per second.* Speechreading is not a conscious process, but even so it is unlikely that the average speechreader sees all of the information available to him. Speech was filmed with a motion picture camera taking sixteen frames per second. An analysis of the film showed many of the speech sounds to be missing. It was concluded that these sounds were quicker than $\frac{1}{16}$ of a second. Some of the vowels took as long as $\frac{2}{16}$ to $\frac{3}{16}$ of a second. On the whole, the consonants were spoken more rapidly than the vowels, but some vowels were spoken as quickly as the consonant sounds.

Since the average rate of conversational speech is fairly rapid, it becomes especially difficult to speechread the talker who speaks at above average rate. Indeed, it is possible for the speaker to talk so rapidly or with so little lip and jaw movement, that all information is lost to the viewer. There is reason to believe that it is not the speed per se that is so detrimental, but rather the dimunition in visible contrastive movements that occurs.

To converse with a deaf child it is necessary to use a *normal* but slightly below average rate of speech. Unless speech is slowed, most of the movements that serve to differentiate the vowels are lost as well as many of the distinctive consonant movements. Deaf children are usually expert speechreaders within the limitations of their knowledge of vocabulary and sentence patterns. To understand they must, however, speechread vowel as well as consonant sounds. If the teacher wishes to talk to a visiting adult in their presence, all he need do is increase his speech rate. It is not necessary for him to lower his voice or turn his face away. He can say at a fairly rapid clip, "Mary is

* Miller estimates the maximum rate to be 12.5 speech sounds per second. Miller, G.A.: Speech and Language. In Stevens, S.S.: *Handbook of Experimental Psychology.* New York, Wiley, 1960, p. 793.

driving me crazy today. I'll certainly be glad when this day is over." Mary may be watching intently, and yet she will never discover that she has been so maligned.

6.4. The Transition Effect

The formation and, hence, the appearance of sounds can be altered by those that precede or follow. For example, the speech-reader depends on a forward movement of the lips to identify the *sh, zh, ch,* and *j* sounds. IPA: /ʃ/, /ʒ/, /tʃ/, and /dʒ/; but this movement is often missing or obscured when the consonant is followed by a high front vowel as in *jeep, chip,* or *shape.* The speaker is set to make a vowel sound which calls for extension of the lips and does not need to protrude his lips in order to make the preceding consonant sound.

On the other hand, the backward movement for the ē sound, IPA: /i/, may be confused with the normal return of the lips to a relaxed position when the beginning sound in the word is /w/. For this reason the words *weed, word,* and *wood* all look alike. Fortunately, we more often exclaim, "My word!" than "My weed!" or "My wood!"

Still another example can be found in the word, *Seattle.* IPA: /si-ætl/. The speechreader does not see separate movements of the tongue for the /t/ and /l/ sounds for they do not exist. Only one movement is necessary when these two sounds are adjacent.

6.5. Individual Differences in Sound Formation

We do not all talk alike! We learn to make speech sounds and to speak through listening and imitating. Any series of movements that produce the correct sound pattern is correct, regardless of how it is done. Two people may produce the same auditory entity, but the articulation patterns may not be identical. For example, it is possible to make the sound /t/ by putting the tongue in a variety of positions. Try it! But even more discouraging so far as the speechreader is concerned is the number of individuals who speak clearly and well but with minimal movement of the lips and jaw. An extreme example is the ventriloquist. While certain lip movements are usually considered to be associated with given phonemes, it is not always necessary or expedient to make them. Many people make a perfectly good /th/ sound without protruding the tongue. Most of us do not noticeably pucker or protrude the lips when /sh/ is followed by a high front vowel such as in *she* or *ship*. And yet anyone who must understand through his eyes is dependent upon seeing just such movements. One cannot speechread without information. Unfortunately, there will always be speakers whose speech cannot be read. Too often, they turn out to be a parent, a teacher, or a spouse!

6.6. Environmental Limitations

Not only is the speechreader handicapped by insufficient sensory information, but often this limited information is not available to him. It is possible to hear, but not to speechread, someone whose back is turned. When the speaker looks away or turns his back momentarily, information may be lost to the speechreader. Information is also lost if the speechreader is not aware that someone is talking and has his attention focused elsewhere. There must be ample light. The time honored rule is, the light must be on the speaker's face and not in the eyes of the speechreader.

The overall picture is, however, not as dismal as it might appear from the foregoing. While vision is not a good substitute, it is a marvelous supplement to hearing. When we make full use of the residual hearing through the best possible auditory trainers and wearable hearing aids, the help from speechreading often makes the difference between confusion and fear, and easy, effortless understanding.

7. TASK ANALYSIS—FACTORS CONSTITUTING SPEECHREADING SKILL

7.1. Overview—Theoretical Construct

Some people appear to be naturally better speechreaders than others.* There is no such thing as a beginning speechreading

---

* Taaffe was able to isolate a general lipreading factor in a study which, in part, analyzed the speechreading ability of three groups of normal hearing subjects. The better speechreaders were better at all tasks (words, phrases, sentences) and at understanding all speakers (good, moderate, poor) than those with less ability. Taaffe, G.: An investigation of the cognitive domain of lipreading. In *Final Report, Project No. 7-E-048.* Office of Ed., U.S. Dept, H.E.W., March, 1968.

class, whether the group be composed of individuals with normal hearing or the hearing handicapped. One is always dealing with a heterogeneous population. We conclude that speechreading is a skill, amenable to training, to be sure, but a skill for which one may or may not have a natural aptitude.† But granting that there are native or inherent differences in ability to speechread, it is still worth while to speculate as to these differences.

How are good speechreaders different from poor speech-readers? What are the physical, intellectual, educational, and emotional variables? If we can isolate these factors, we can decide to what extent they are amenable to training and what the best techniques and procedures may be. At this stage of the art, much of our analysis must be based upon experience and intuitive knowledge. *Such a statement is not intended as a disparagement of either experience or intuitive knowledge.* There has long been concensus among teachers, and speechreaders themselves, on the importance of two major factors—visual proficiency and the ability to put two and two together.

Our speculations with respect to the factors important to speechreading lead to the development of a theoretical model or construct presented in Table I. It is presented here for the first time. You will find that the methods chapter and the chapter on research are both organized in relationship to it. The model divides the factors which appear to determine speech-reading ability into primary and secondary factors. The primary factors are derived from an analysis of the task requirements—of what the speechreader does—and in essence constitute the processes encompassed by the skill.

There would appear to be three major subfactors or subskills under this heading. They are visual perceptual proficiency, synthetic ability, and flexibility. Speechreading is first of all a visual skill. The speechreader must identify speech movements accurately and rapidly. The second skill is that of synthesis and association. The speechreader must mould the fragmented infor-

---

† See the research of Coscarelli and Sanders, Chapter 4, Section 5.1, "Relationship of Skill to Training." Their second best speechreading score was obtained by two subjects, one with normal hearing and one with a hearing loss but no formal training.

mation he has received into a meaningful message. But because the same limited information may yield various associative patterns, a third skill is required—flexibility. In this context flexibility is defined as the ability to make rapid shifts in either perceptual or cognitive associations if the first decisions do not result in both a meaningful and appropriate message. The secondary factors are the "back-up" factors. They include training, knowledge of language, and emotional attitudes or sets that facilitate the acquisition of speechreading skill.

TABLE 1-I

THEORETICAL CONSTRUCT

Factors Which Appear to Determine Speechreading Ability

I. *Primary Factors*

A. Perceptual proficiency
1. Visual perception
The ability to identify speech sounds or elements
2. Speed of perception
The ability to perceive speech elements rapidly
3. Peripheral perception
The ability to gain information from face and setting when the focus is on the mouth
Ancillary to these processes are *visual acuity* (1); *visual attention* (1 and 2); *speed of focusing* (2); and *peripheral vision* (3).

B. Synthetic ability
1. Perceptual closure
The ability to identify parts and patterns (words and phrases)
This process consists of:
(a) Organization and grouping of elements
(b) Conjectural perception—mentally filling in missing elements
(c) Identification of pattern—tentative

2. Conceptual closure
The ability to identify the message
This process consists of:
(a) Association of ideas
(b) Conjectural closure—mentally filling in missing words
(c) Identification of the message—tentative or final
Ancillary to these processes are *abstract inductive reasoning* (1); *rhythm* (1); *verbal inductive reasoning* (2); *social awareness—abstract deductive reasoning* (2).

C. Flexibility
The ability to revise tentative closures if the first decisions do not result in a meaningful and appropriate message.
The process consists of two interrelated parts:
1. Revision of perceptual closures, followed along with or immediately by
2. Revision of conceptual closures
Ancillary to these processes are *visual memory* (1); *abstract inductive reasoning* (1); *rhythm* (1); *verbal inductive reasoning* (2); *social awareness—abstract deductive reasoning* (2).

II. *Secondary Factors—"Back-up" Characteristics*

    A. Training
        1. Amount—Indices for deaf children are age, grade placement, and years in school.
        2. Kind
            (a) Deaf children
            (b) Hard of hearing

    B. Language comprehension
        1. Structure—morphology and syntax
        2. Lexicon
        3. Idiomatic expressions
        Common educational indices of language comprehension are reading level and educational achievement.

Factors ancillary to A and B are *intelligence; extent and pattern of hearing loss; auditory discrimination; age of onset;* and *duration of loss.*

    C. Emotional attitudes or sets
        1. Self concept—personal adjustment
        2. Reaction to frustration and failure
        3. Motivation

7.2. Primary Factors

We shall discuss first the primary factors—visual proficiency, synthetic ability, and flexibility.

7.2.1 VISUAL PROFICIENCY. Included under this factor are the subfactors of visual perception, speed of perception, and peripheral perception. The good speechreader is believed to possess a high degree of visual proficiency. His visual perception is above average. He has good eyesight or eyesight which can be corrected through glasses to within the normal range. More important than good near and far vision is the ability to focus sharply, one is tempted to say easily, and also the ability to focus rapidly. The speechreader must see fine detail. He must also see fine detail at a rapid rate. He cannot reread what he has missed. He sees it the first time, or it is forever lost to him. There are no second chances, unless one can persuade the speaker to repeat. He must also be able to maintain this sharp focusing over relatively long periods of time. The good speechreader is believed to be an observant person, the kind of person who can leave a room and describe in detail the furniture, the colors, the *objects d'art*, etc. Admittedly this talent requires good memory and an interest in detail, but it is unlikely that memory or interest in detail could exist independently of ease and rapidity in focusing. It has often been said that Ted Williams' prowess as a baseball player was probably in good part attributable to his superior and unusual eyesight as well as his penchant for practice. Pictures taken by Hy Peskin show that Williams, Stan Musial, and Jerry Lynch all kept their eyes glued on the ball during its entire flight from the pitcher to the home plate.* Similar pictures of other players found them looking out into the outfield. Several big league managers, when queried about this, said that they were aware that some hitters did not watch the ball and attributed their failure to follow to the eye's inability to shift fast enought as the ball speeds down the alley at ninety miles per hour.

It is probable that there are unheralded Ted Williams of speechreading as well as the heralded one of baseball. The unusually skilled speechreader appears to *see more* than the person with average skill, needs to depend less on logical associations, and is less dependent upon aids to association, such as knowing the topic of conversation. If one speechreads vocabulary he does not know, he does so on the basis of unusually fine ability to see minimal speech movements. It is well known that some deaf children can speechread words they do not understand, including words of a foreign language. It is also probable that good peripheral vision is an aid in enabling the individual to gain information from the face and setting while still focusing on the mouth of the speaker.

An example of unusual speechreading skill, one requiring a high degree of visual proficiency, was reported by the *Reporter Magazine* a few years ago (in order to tease *Life Magazine*), and entitled, "A Scoop, A Palpable Scoop."† Queen Elizabeth when visiting in this country attended a football game at the University of Maryland. She was flanked by the Governor of Maryland and the President of the University. No reporters were within earshot, and there was no way of knowing the conversational topics. Yet the next issue of *Life* carried almost verbatim the ensuing conversation.‡ Elizabeth was reported to have said. "Why are the goal

---

* Lieber, L.: The most surprising baseball pictures of the year. *Los Angeles Times* (*This Week Section*), July 14, 1957.

† *The Reporter*, December 12, 1957, p. 4.

‡ *Life*. October 28, 1957, p. 30.

posts behind the line at the ends of the fields? In Rugby the goal posts are right at the end." In reference to a huddle, "Why do they gather that way?" Later, "My it's exciting! Oh, that was some spill." And finally, and perhaps plaintively, "What is the duration of the game?" It turned out that *Life* had employed an expert speechreader, Robert Panara, from Gallaudet College, a college for the deaf.* Panara was at least two hundred yards from the Queen's Box, but he had used a high-powered telescope to enable him to pick up the conversation.

The basic physical and psychological attributes believed to underly visual perceptual proficiency are those of visual acuity, visual attention, speed of focusing, and peripheral vision. It is speculated that visual acuity and visual attention are ancillary or basic to the identification of speech sounds; that visual attention and speed of focusing result in perceptual speed; and that peripheral perception will be related to and limited to some extent by one's peripheral vision.

7.2.2 SYNTHETIC ABILITY. The word synthesis is defined by Webster as "Composition or combination of parts and elements, etc., so as to form a whole; also the whole thus formed."† But, when the word is used with respect to speechreading, the meaning is modified to include within the connotation the idea that, because of the dearth of sensory information, speechreading is not a simple combination of elements or parts, but requires guessing and mental filling in as well. Synthetic ability has been defined by Kitson (p. 471) as "the ability to construct meaning by combining isolated fragments into a meaningful whole . . ." It can also be described as the ability to do an unconscious jigsaw puzzle and to do it, moreover, when parts of the puzzle are missing. The speechreader sees a part of the message; he puts it together and then makes an educated guess as to the whole. A more formal definition might be "the ability to make associations and to arrive at perceptual and conceptual closures when a good part of the sensory information is either missing or not perceived."

---

* Robert Panara is currently Director of Academic Affairs at the National Technical Institute for the Deaf, Rochester, New York.

† Webster's New Collegiate Dictionary, Springfield, G. and C. Merriam Co., 1961, p. 862.

As can be seen from the last definition, synthesis is conceived of as consisting of two parts. The speechreader must first make a tentative identification of words and, since words flow together, of phrases. Another way of stating the foregoing is to say that he must first make a number of *perceptual closures* or conclusions. "What was it?" "What did I see?" *Perceptual closure* can be defined as the identification of parts and patterns (words and phrases). In order to make the identifications the speechreader must first *organize or group series of speech elements or movements*. And in the process he must mentally fill in sounds or elements that he did not see. He must make a number of *conjectural perceptions*, which he adds to his visual perceptions, in arriving at the perceptual closures. The formation of perceptual closures is, or course, not a conscious process. It is not clear whether the speechreader literally fills in missing elements or simply infers their existence on the bases of the decisions he has made.

The second part of the synthetic process is the formation of *conceptual closures*. By the phrase, *conceptual closure*, is meant the identification of the message in its totality. This part requires the speechreader to organize and group the words which have been perceived into a tentative idea and to supply missing words. The latter phase, the supplying of missing words, we have dubbed *conjectural closure* in contradistinction to perceptual closure, described above.

The first portion (perceptual closure), "What was it?" "What did I see?" is followed immediately and almost simultaneously by the second portion (conceptual closure), "What did he say?" To illustrate, let us imagine that the speaker said, "My son got a bicycle for Christmas." He said it in this way. Maɪsʌn—gɑtə-baɪsɪkl-fɔɚkrɪsməs. Our speechreader can hear the vowel sounds. He was looking elsewhere, but thought he heard "Mayan" or "myum" and was momentarily set to hear about the Mayan civilization or a trip that his friend had made. He quickly focused on his friends lips and saw and heard the following (virgules are used to enclose the sounds speechread):ɑə-/b/ɑɪ/s/ɪ-l/—/f/ɔɚ-/r/ɪ/s/mə, (ah-a-by-sih-ul for ris-muh): In forming his *perceptual closures* he makes a number of *conjectural perceptions*, mentally filling in the /g/ and /t/ in "gota;" the /k/ in bicycle;

and the /k/ and final /s/ in Christmas. He now knows a good part of the message, "got a bicycle for Christmas," and is cued with respect to the necessary *conjectural closures.* "Mayan" must have been "my son!" The *conceptual closure* or conclusion as to the total message, "My son got a bicycle for Christmas," follows easily in this example.

Associative or inductive reasoning is believed to be basic to synthetic ability. Abstract inductive reasoning, the ability to associate forms and patterns, is believed to be more closely linked to the formation of perceptual closures, and verbal inductive reasoning, the ability to associate words and ideas, to the formation of concepual closures. It is also probable that sensitivity to and awareness of the rhythm of the language are of help in making the synthetic associations, and it is almost certain that social awareness is of considerable value. By social awareness is meant the ability to size up quickly the social situation, to guess as to the topic of conversation, to anticipate what may be said, and perhaps even who may say it. This faculty, in turn, may be dependent upon good peripheral vision and powers of deductive reasoning. The speechreader depends upon many social cues to aid him in making the proper associations. For this reason speechreading test scores (based on words or unrelated sentences) are often low and serve better as comparative devices than as measures of the amount of information the individual obtains through speechreading. On a test where the material was a series of unrelated sentences the following errors were noted:

Intended Meaning	*Mistaken Meaning*
What's new?	What to do?
It's raining.	He's writing.
Breakfast is ready.	Prophets say rain.

The mistaken statements all *look like* the true statements, yet it is unlikely that these errors would have been made in true social situations. As your friend greets you, you expect him to say, "What's new?" and not, "What to do?" If it is breakfast time and the cook speaks to you, you are set to hear, "Breakfast is ready," not, "Prophets say rain." If it's an overcast day with no one around who is writing, the correct association of, "It's raining," will be automatic.

The word "synthesis" has still another connotation when used with respect to speechreading. Its usage is reflected in such phrases as a "synthetic speechreader," or "synthetic type of mind," as opposed to an "analytic speechreader" or an "analytic type of mind." It refers to the *way* in which one builds from elements and parts to the whole. Some people appear to be more proficient at synthesizing than others. Nitchie,[2, p. 28-29] placed individuals roughly into two categories: (a) those with predominantly synthetic habits of thinking, and (b) those with predominantly analytic habits of thinking. The synthetic type of mind is characteristic of the person who is able to grasp ideas in their entirety. He is the person who wants to know the answer, not how he arrived at it, or he is the person who has the intuitive ability to piece together the whole from perceived fragments. While this is an intellectual or mental faculty, it is not necessarily related to high intelligence. As a matter of fact, there is some evidence that highly intelligent people often tend to be analytic in their thinking and so tend to be the poorest speechreaders. These are the people who wish to understand the process. They may want to be able to describe each sound movement, even to practice them individually, and to add one sound at a time. Such a person is bound to fail because good speechreading is based on instantaneous recognition of symbolic patterns and cannot be achieved through a conscious process of either analysis or synthesis. The best speechreader known to the writer had an IQ of not over 85! This is not to say that low intelligence is a help in speechreading, on the contrary, but is intended to stress the fact that fast association and lack of insistence on the "how's" and "why's," on the part of the speechreader, may well be one of the most important contributing factors.

Contrasted with the "synthetic" type of mind, is the person with predominantly analytic habits of thinking. The analytic type of mind was considered by Nitchie[2, p. 20] to be synonymous with a literal or unimaginative mind, and was presumed to be the way of thinking of the speechreader who demands verbal accuracy before attaching meaning to an impression. Apparently the word "analytic" was taken from its use with respect to silent reading to indicate the breaking up of phrases into words and words into their constituent elements and was extended from this referent to speechreading. But it should be pointed out that the speechreader's task is different from that of the reader of printed symbols. *No analysis is possible.* In speechreading the sound symbols (motor movements) are not preorganized into words and phrases ready for quick identifications as wholes. Moreover, the elements which make up the words are not presented simultaneously, but succeed each other in time. The speechreader is forced to read symbol by symbol, comparable to fixating on each letter. The willingness (or ability) to guess and to close is, it would seem, what separates the "synthetic" from the "analytic" speechreader. But the word "analytic" is a poor choice to describe the opposite of what is meant by a "synthetic" speechreader. Speechreading is a combining or synthetic process, not an analytical one. Analysis implies starting from a whole and dividing it into its constituent parts; synthesis, starting from the elements and building to the whole. All speechreaders *must* synthesize. One can have an analytic mind, which, as was noted earlier, may interfere with the attainment of a high degree of success in speechreading, but *one cannot be an analytic speechreader.* The poor or so-called analytic speechreader is different from the "synthetic" speechreader in that he requires more information, i.e. more certainty, before he is willing or able to identify elements, parts, patterns, and wholes. His identifications are slow and uncertain. He tends to reason rather than react and does not have the fast apprehension characteristic of the intuitive mind. In order to clarify our thinking, we should probably use terms different from "synthetic" and "analytic." It is suggested that we use the term "intuitive" with the idea of fast apprehension in place of "synthetic" when the word is used in this connotation. Unfortunately, there is no single word that accurately conveys what is meant in the speechreading literature by the word "analytic." The nearest we can come to describing it is through the use of three words, "Think about it." This phrase is not wholly satisfactory, either, because the "intuitive" mind reasons too, but at an unconscious level, and hence at lightning speed. The distinction is essentially between conscious and unconscious associative reasoning. But for want of a better description we shall refer to the two types of mental processes as the "intuitive type of mind," and the "think about it" type of mind, and when ascribed to speechreaders, as "intuitive speechreaders," and "think about it speechreaders."

7.2.3 FLEXIBILITY. Because so many sounds are homophenous and so much information is missing, the speechreader must be flexible. We have defined flexibility in this context as the ability to revise tentative closures if the first decisions do not result in a message which is both meaningful and appropriate. It consists of two closely interrelated parts, (a) revision of perceptual closures, followed immediately by (b) revision of the conceptual closure. In fact it can be argued, and perhaps is often the case, that the revision of the conceptual closure precedes or occurs simultaneously with the revision of the perceptual closures. Actually the order of revision probably varies from moment to moment and depends on the task at hand. If the perceptual closures—words and phrases—do not "add up," the speechreader must revise them in order to arrive at a conceptual closure. Conversely, if the conceptual closure, while meaningful, is nonetheless not appropriate in light of the topic or situation, the revision is based on a cognitative change in the interpretation of the information and the two types of revision occur simultaneously.

The speechreader's first decisions as to words and phrases may be incorrect or even incongruous and often cannot be moulded into an acceptable message. We reason that in order for him to revise erroneous perceptual closures he must be able to retain, however briefly, the visual imagery on which they were based. This concept is perhaps a new hypothesis. We were not able to find references to it in the literature. However, in interviewing "expert" speechreaders we found that a number of them laid claim to this ability. The research literature appears to give additional confirmation. A number of research workers have correlated skill in speechreading with skill in the retention of visual digits and digit symbols. (See Chapter 4, "The process of Speechreading.") Eleven of the fifteen studies indicated an association between speechreading skill and short term visual memory as measured by these tests. The percent contribution to the total task was estimated to be from 18 to 35 percent.

Conceptual flexibility is of equal importance. Even when the first synthesis is meaningful, it may not be appropriate. The same overall movement pattern can usually be interpreted in more than one way. For example, "How do you spell your name?" and "How do you spend your time?" will look exactly alike to the speechreader. It has been the authors' observation that poor speechreaders are astonishingly rigid. Once they have a mental set they cling to it determinedly like a bulldog to a bone. The following example may serve as an illustration. In viewing a production of "South Pacific" such a person speechread, "Her skin is tender as imagined love." The correct version is, "Her skin is tender as Di Maggio's glove." True, the two versions look alike, but the viewer knew the story and knew that the song was about Bloody Mary. A good speechreader would have quickly discarded the absurd association, after a momentary inward chuckle, and moved on to the true one.

Believed basic to perceptual flexibility, in addition to short-term visual memory, are such factors as abstract inductive reasoning and a sense of rhythm. The two latter factors are related to the ability to perceive pattern and form in a series of sequential motor movements.

Verbal inductive reasoning and abstract deductive reasoning as it relates to social or situational awareness should, on the other hand, be more closely related to conceptual flexibility. There well may be also differences in emotional set, in the degree of emotional rigidity, which differentiate the flexible from the non-flexible speechreader.

7.3. *Secondary or Back-Up Factors*

The primary factors are believed to *determine speechreading ability* because taken together they constitute the task. Secondary factors, on the other hand, are considered to be subservient to the primary factors. They are credited with being most importantly related to synthetic ability though they may influence flexibility and visual proficiency to some extent. The influence of the secondary factors is indirect—they are stepping stones—*the essential foundation* requisite to the development of speechreading ability. They are training, language comprehension, and positive emotional attitudes. Training facilitates learning and enables the individual to achieve his maximum potential. A basic knowledge of language, or level of language comprehension, is obviously necessary in order to understand conversational speech, and certain desirable emotional attitudes and sets make for more efficient learning. Because these factors constitute the foundation upon which the skill is built, *and not the skill itself*, their effect on ultimate attainment can be minimized and sometimes eliminated entirely through training and the development of greater self-confidence and self-esteem.

7.3.1 TRAINING. Training is important in achieving maximal skill in speechreading. Some degree of improvement in visual proficiency is possible for almost everyone. Students learn to associate meaning with fine movements that they had heretofore ignored; speed of perception is improved, and visual memory, enhanced. Synthetic skill and flexibility are also amenable to training. As the result of training, the student more readily identifies words and phrases and can more quickly call to mind multiple associations. When he does not understand, he learns to "wait for information" with which to build associations and to be alert to and make full use of situational cues. Maximum improvement in speechreading as a skill-subject is usually attained in from one to three years of training. But to maintain his skill the individual must continue to speechread. Unlike many other skills, facility is quickly lost if not used.

The effect of training on improvement for the individual can be obscured if group trends are studied. Despite this, its importance has been indicated by a number of research studies. (See Section 5.1.1, Chapter 4, "Process of Speechreading.")

7.3.2 LANGUAGE COMPREHENSION. In order to comprehend a language one must have: (a) a knowledge of the grammar or structural system of the language, (b) a knowledge of vocabulary or the lexicon of the language, and (c) a knowledge of colloquial and idiomatic expressions.

In recent years linguists have given us many exciting new insights, relevant to speechreading, into the importance of understanding structure in comprehending a language. Language is conceived of as a code by which meanings are signalled. According to the structural linguists, there are two layers of meaning. They consist of (a) lexical meanings signalled by words, and (b) structural meanings signalled by the contrastive arrangements and forms of these words. Words are formally marked as belonging to one of a small number of form classes (referred to in traditional grammars as nouns, verbs, adjectives, and adverbs). "For English (these) four major form-classes and a very small number of function words, (e.g., the, an, more, some, etc.) make up the units of the contrastive patterns that signal the whole range of structural or grammatical meanings."[7, p. 668] It is the markers, not the lexical meanings, that signal the form classes and, hence, the structural meanings. For example, "*Woggle* becomes a 'thing' word with such markers as 'a woggle . . . ,' 'two woggles.'" "With other markers *woggle* becomes an action word such as, 'Two woggles *woggled* another woggle.'" (Fries, p. 668.) In addition to these formal markers, an important structural signal of meaning in modern English is a contrast of position within the utterance. "In 'The man killed the bear,' the contrastive position alone signals whether the man or the bear is the performer of the killing." (Fries, p. 668.)

Language comprehension is the *essential* secondary factor in the attainment of speechreading skill—the foundation upon which the skill is built. Speechreading can be defined as the visual recognition (aided by partial hearing) of known language. From this definition it is evident that a basic understanding of language must precede its recognition. The individual must have a knowledge of vocabulary and idiomatic expressions extensive enough to permit him to understand what is said to him. But of the three major aspects of comprehension—knowledge of structure, knowledge of lexicon, and knowledge of idiomatic expressions—it is perhaps evident that the first one is of paramount importance. In a very real sense it is, in many instances, what makes speechreading possible. The unconscious mastery of structural meanings and word sequences makes it possible for the speechreader with quite limited hearing to fill in mentally information that he has not received either through hearing or vision. It enables him to organize motor movements into words, to judge the proper word form or verb tense (e.g., pretty or prettier; like or liked), to fill in words that are not seen or only partially seen, and to anticipate the words that will follow.

Frisina,[8, p. 199] in an excellent review of the literature on research in speechreading, has said: "Theoretically, the greater knowledge one has concerning the probabilities of occurrence of word sequences in language, the greater the mathematical chances of his speechreading connected discourse presented by a speaker." And he added, "It would, however, be less than candid to assume that knowledge of one's native language guarantees that one can learn to speechread efficiently."

The size of the vocabulary which a given individual must learn to recognize is dependent upon the kinds of conversations he has, which in turn are dependent on his age, intelligence, environment, education, and interests.

Language comprehension is normally not a factor in the training of the hard-of-hearing or deafened adult and should not interfere with his attainment of maximum skill in speechreading. On the other hand, skill in speechreading for hearing impaired children can be expected to vary to some extent with their growth in language. The relationship between skill in speechreading and language development is particularly evident when considering the prelingually deaf child. As Craig[3, p. 284] has pointed out, his speechreading skill cannot exceed his rate of language growth. Evidence of this contention can be found in the research literature. Positive correlations were found between the speechreading skill of deaf children and such indirect indices of language comprehension as reading ability, educational achievement, and vocabulary level in twelve out of thirteen research studies. (See Tables 4-IV, 4-V, and 4-VI, Chapter 4, "The Process of Speechreading.")

Subfactors which can have an effect both on the efficiency of training and on the development of language comprehension are age, age at which the loss was incurred, duration of loss, extent and pattern of loss, auditory discrimination, and intelligence.

7.3.3 EMOTIONAL ATTITUDES OR SETS. In teaching speechreading it has often been observed that the pupils who are relatively free from fear of failure are apt to be those who learn most readily. Such persons do not demand perfection of themselves. Instead they have patience and tolerance for their own foibles as well as those of others. They are able to relax and learn, and have confidence that they will improve with practice. They are able to laugh at their own mistakes and are not easily disconcerted. To garble a message is for such a person a hilarious rather than a shameful experience. This kind of person is willing to gamble, to take a chance of being wrong, to be wrong, and to try again. He does not block when he misses something, but continues speechreading until he catches on to the trend of the conversation. He also shows little hesitation in admitting that he did not understand and asking for repetition and clarification. He is motivated and is able to concentrate on the task at hand.

It should be emphasized that the foregoing should not be interpreted to mean that all good speechreaders are well adjusted people, but only that such adjustment facilitates learning. The person with strong primary aptitudes will succeed regardless of his overall self-evaluation. Individuals with low self esteem do well in many skill areas. The person who is at first fearful of making mistakes gains confidence as he becomes more adept and as he learns that the social consequences of failure are not as great as he had anticipated. Motivation is also an important subfactor which can affect progress. It is probably fair to say, however, that the fact of the hearing loss itself usually provides adequate motivation. If motivation is lacking, it is usually because of feelings of inadequacy and discouragement. An exception to this may be the person trained manually.

8. USE OF VOICE IN TEACHING

8.1. *Importance*

The essential aim of speechreading instruction is improved comprehension of speech, not speechreading instruction per se. We are not interested in developing champion speechreaders of silent speech, for there is little need or opportunity for this kind of skill, and it should be added, few individuals are capable of good understanding if all sound is denied them, regardless of the amount of instruction. Speechreading should serve as a supplement, not as a substitute for hearing. We do not live in a silent world. The hearing handicapped person's task is that of unconsciously integrating auditory and visual information. In terms of instruction this means that we teach speechreading in the way in which it will be used in a hearing world, *with voice*. We do not teach silent recognition and hope for transfer of training to a real life situation. As a matter of fact, there is some evidence that people so trained are distracted by voice and unable to make use of their speechreading ability when they most need it. Another reason for using voice is that silent speechreading instruction imposes undue physical and psychological strain. The unnatural attention and focusing of the eyes will result in severe eyestrain for many people, enough for some to result in fatigue and drowsiness. The speechreader finds he can no longer keep his eyes open, let alone focus them! And if eyestrain is not a major problem, the emotional strain is almost bound to be one. Too much is missed. A word is caught now and then, but not enough to understand what is being said. He is in the unhappy and frustrating position of the individual who is trying to read a sign in a foreign language with inadequate knowledge of the language. Every third or fourth word is recognized but not enough to be able to piece it together into a meaningful whole. In addition, voice is recommended to insure that the teacher will use normal articulatory and stress patterns. Most of us when speaking silently automatically tend to mouth our words, to use exaggerated lip movement, and to forsake normal rhythm and stress patterns, patterns upon which the speechreader is dependent for good understanding. To be sure, the instructor can train himself to speak naturally when not using voice, but many teachers have not done so.

8.2. Amount of Voice

The essential problem for the teacher is to use enough voice to make integration of hearing and seeing possible, but not so much that speechreading is unnecessary. In general, instruction is given with *reduced voice*. The students will hear some of the voiced sound energy, vowels, diphthongs, and voiced consonants, but not enough to understand by hearing alone. The pupils are usually grouped in a semicircle at approximately six feet from the instructor. They are then asked to close their eyes or look at the floor. The teacher then tests each pupil in turn by making a statement or asking a question. If the response is, "I can hear you, but I can't understand what you are saying," a proper level has been effected.

In order for a given level to be satisfactory for the entire class, certain pupils will have to reduce the volume and others to increase the volume of their hearing aids. In giving the test statements or questions, the teacher must avoid such common expressions as "How are you?" or "How old are you?" or even "When is your birthday?" These constitute overlearned material and can usually be pieced together on the basis of vowel energy alone plus the accompanying familiar rhythm and stress patterns. Test sentences should contain material that cannot be easily anticipated. Examples of such sentences are, "Basketball was first played with a soccer ball;" "Our cow gives two quarts of milk every day." Reduced voice is used when teaching the hard-of-hearing. By hard-of-hearing we mean those individuals whose average hearing level for 500–2000 cps is from 30dB-90dB (I.S.O., 1964). When teaching deaf children or adults with hearing levels of 90 dB or greater, the use of full voice is recommended. These individuals recognize so few speech sounds, even with the best possible amplification, that one need not be concerned for fear they will not use their eyes to maximum advantage.

9. RATE OF PRESENTATION

In general, the greater the loss, the slower the rate of speech for maximum comprehension. Speechreading material must always be given at a very slow rate to anyone who must speechread the vowel and diphthong sounds. Specifically, this means a very slow rate for the profoundly deaf individual and a slow rate for the severely hard of hearing child (70dB-90dB level, I.S.O., 1964), until such time as he has mastered language syntax and developed a working vocabulary.

The deaf individual depends on his eyes for 80 to 100 percent of received information. The severely hard-of-hearing child initially receives approximately half through speechreading. After considerable training, his need for speechreading decreases. By the time he is eight or nine years of age (assuming 3 or 4 years of instruction), he will depend on speechreading for approximately 30 percent and hearing for 70 percent. This same ratio, 30 percent speechreading and 70 percent hearing, will usually be the *beginning ratio* for the child with a moderate loss. As he acquires knowledge of the language, he will become more expert at filling in missing information and have less need for speechreading. Eventually he will need to speechread only under difficult listening conditions or when acquiring new vocabulary.

In teaching the hard-of-hearing, the teacher must keep in mind that one of the aims of instruction will be to increase speed of speechreading. As the students progress, the teacher will gradually speed up his rate of speech. From the very beginning, he will vary his rate of speech, using quite rapid speech for easy, highly visible or overlearned material and slowing down, sometimes to a "snail's pace," when it is necessary for the students to depend more on their eyes and less on the mind's ability to fill in.

The more rapid the speech, the less visual information that can be transmitted. Sounds will be missed, not because they are not visible, but because the eye cannot focus rapidly enough to receive the information.

To summarize: The rate of speechreading instruction varies with and is limited by the extent of the loss and the proficiency of the pupil.

10. SPEECH CHARACTERISTICS OF THE TEACHER

A person who wishes to teach the hearing handicapped must, in most instances, be willing to modify his own speech habits. If he has not used much lip or jaw movement before, he must learn to use more. If he has always talked at a rapid clip, he must learn to slow down. If he has never protruded his tongue when making *th,* puckered his lip for *sh,* or put his teeth together for *s*, he must learn to do so. If he "normally" has a dead-pan expression, he must learn to use more facial expression. And in acquiring all these new speech habits, he must be sure that his speech is still looking natural and that he is maintaining normal rhythm and stress pattern.

The speechreader expects and depends on normal rhythm and stress and has real difficulty following exaggerated or mouthed speech.

The good teacher may sometimes exaggerate the normal articulation in teaching a speech sound (e.g., t, d, n, l) to a small hearing handicapped child, but will rarely use exaggeration in talking to the child or in teaching speechreading. To modify one's speech habits is not as difficult as one might assume. All one needs is the desire and will to do so and considerable practice in front of a mirror. The mirror practice is not only helpful, but necessary. The teacher usually discovers that he can use a great deal more lip and jaw movement without looking strange. Considerable, *but not exaggerated,* lip and jaw movement are essential. Especially important is adequate jaw movement. Many speakers, in attempting to make their speech more visible, increase the amount of lip movement, but ignore the equally important factor of jaw movement. Tongue-tip and tongue-back sounds cannot be seen, and high and low vowel sounds cannot be differentiated, unless the mouth is opened fairly wide. Equally important is the willingness to modify one's articulatory movements in forming sounds if the ones used are not the general pattern. Some information can be obtained from all speakers, but very little from those who do not make the conventional articulatory movements. Initially the new habits will feel strange to the speaker, but fortunately will not appear so to the viewer.

In order to summarize and put the foregoing in a positive fashion, it is possible to list the desirable speech characteristics of the teacher. They are (a) mobility of lips and jaw, (b) normal (i.e. conventional) articulatory movements, (c) good facial expression that will convey the emotional tone and nuances of the message being conveyed, (d) normal rhythm and stress pattern.

REFERENCES

1. Bruner, J.: *The Process of Education.* Cambridge, Harvard University Press, 1960, chap. 4, pp. 54–68.
2. Cherry, C.: *On Human Communication.* New York, Science Editions, 1961.
3. Craig, W.N.: Effects of preschool training on the development of reading and lipreading skills of deaf children. *Amer Ann Deaf, 109:* 280–296, 1964.
4. Deland, F.: *The Story of Lip-Reading, Its Genesis and Development,* Washington, D.C., The Volta Bureau, 1931.
5. Franks, J.R.: Focus on linguistic factors in lipreading. Paper presented at the 44th Annual Convention of the American Speech and Hearing Association, Denver, Colorado, November 16, 1968.
6. Fries, C.C.: *The Structure of English.* New York and Burlingame, Harcourt, Brace, 1952.
7. Fries, C.C.: Structural linguistics. In *Encyclopaedia Britannica.* 1966, vol. 10, p. 668.
8. Frisina, D.R.: Speechreading. *Rep Proc Int Congr Educ Deaf (Doc. No. 106),* pp. 191–207, 1954.
9. Gaeth, J.: A Study of Phonemic Regression Associated with Hearing Loss. Unpublished Ph.D. Thesis, Northwestern University, 1948.
10. Greenberg, H.J., and Bode, D.L.: Visual discrimination of consonants. *J Speech Hearing Res, 11:*869–874, 1968.
11. Kirk, S.A.: A model of a communication process. *Rep Proc Int Congr Educ Deaf (Doc. No. 106),* pp. 450–457, 1964.
12. Nitchie, E.B.: *Lip-Reading, Principles and Practice.* Philadelphia and New York, Lippincott, 1930.
13. *The Reporter.* December 12, 1957.
14. Samuelson, E.: Notes from lectures. Teachers College, Columbia University, 1947.
15. Stone, L.: Facial cues of context in lip reading. In Lowell, E.L. (Ed.): *John Tracy Clinic Research Papers.* Los Angeles, John Tracy Clinic, 1957, no. V.
16. *This Week,* July 14, 1957.
17. Woodward, M.F., and Barber, C.G.: Phoneme perception in lipreading. *J Speech Hearing Res, 3:*212–222, 1960.

Chapter 2

VISIBILITY

1. INTRODUCTION

1.1. Overview

What kind of visual information is available to the speech-reader? How trustworthy is it? Under what conditions is it useful? How much information can be obtained from the eyes alone? What percent information can be obtained from the eyes as contrasted with the ears? How much information must be filled in through hearing or through knowledge of the probability of sound or word sequences? How are the speechreading movements related to the formation of speech sounds or to the transitions from one sound to another? What is the information carrying content of specific movements? How does this vary with the number of sounds with which they are associated and with the relative frequency of occurrence of the sounds in the spoken language? How may the formation of speech sounds and hence their appearance be altered by the speaking habits of the talker? Can the speaker if he wishes provide more than the ordinary or usual amount of information to the viewer?

These are the questions that are of concern to the teacher of speechreading. Our answers are based on the opinions of prior writers, on our own experience, on knowledge concerning the formation of speech sounds, on data regarding the frequency of occurrence of the various speech sounds in the spoken language, on the limited experimental literature available, and on what might best be called informal experimentation. When the appearance or the relative visibility of a movement was in doubt, nonsense syllables were formed, and the movement in question was contrasted with other movements.* Our answers to many

---

* In these experiments two talkers and two viewers were used. See Section 2.7 for description.

of the questions posed above are tentative; hence they should not be interpreted as hard facts but instead as representing our best judgment at this point in time. More definitive answers must await further experimentation.

In thinking through the problem of visibility one aspect became abundantly clear; the appearance of speech sounds varies tremendously with who is making them and whether the speaker is attempting to provide maximum visual information. While this idea is not new, a description of the changes in appearance which speechreading movements undergo under less favorable viewing conditions has to the best of our knowledge not been reported heretofore. More will be said about this in later sections.

1.2. Speechreading Movements

In this chapter an attempt will be made to describe and to classify speechreading *movements, not speech sounds,* with respect to visibility. *A speechreading movement is defined as a recognizable visual motor pattern, usually common to two or more speech sounds.* And since these movements serve as clues to the identification of speech sounds, the sounds which can be associated with each movement will be indicated. This is a deliberate change from the usual organization of grouping speech sounds which "look alike" and then indicating the common visible movement pattern. The reverse approach to classification is considered to be important because it more clearly follows the actual task. The speechreader reads *visible motor movements, not speech sounds.* The movements which he sees are primarily of the lips and jaw, but occasionally of the teeth, tongue, and hyoid bone. They constitute only a fragment, a part of the total complex articulatory motor pattern which occurs when a given sound is formed. Moreover, the fragments which are seen are usually not characteristic of only one sound. From a series of such fragments he must mentally construct the complete speech pattern. The process involves a decision as to which speech sounds were actually seen as well as which ones belong together.

Hopefully, the organization which will be adhered to of describing speechreading movements and categorizing them with respect to visibility before pointing out their logical associations with speech sounds may serve to clarify some of the confusions inherent in the conventional approach.

1.3. Stability of Movements

It should be clearly understood that most of the possible or conventional speechreading movements are not stable and may not be present even though the sounds usually associated with them have been made. As a matter of fact, only three of them are probably made by most speakers regardless of speaking rate and, hence, can be considered stable. Their stability is due to the fact that they are essential parts of the motor movements involved in producing the sounds. All other speechreading movements are conventional or are helpful to the production, but not essential. They can be eliminated by the speaker; yet his speech will suffer little or no reduction in clarity. The three stable speechreading movements are (a) lower lip to upper teeth, (b) lips puckered, and (c) lips together. Unfortunately the third movement, lips together, while stable cannot be trusted as an indication that a speech sound has been produced. The speaker also brings his lips together as an oral punctuation mark to indicate the end of a thought unit or phrase.

Many of the "conventional"* but less stable movements will not be *made* if sounds are formed in an unconventional manner, if it is not expedient to do so because of a transition from or to a different movement, if considerable lip and jaw movement is not used, or if a rapid rate is used. And even when the movements are made, they will not be *seen* if the rate is too rapid for the eye to follow or when environmental conditions (light, distance from the speaker, etc.) are not favorable. Even under the best of conditions when all speaker and environmental variables are controlled (i.e. when the sounds are formed in the conventional manner, when considerable lip and jaw movement is used, when the viewing conditions are good, and when a moderate rate of talking is adhered to), the characteristic movements for many

---

* By conventional is meant the speechreading movements usually described; probably a better term is "possible speechreading movements." To our knowledge no count has been made of the relative frequency of their occurrence in the spoken language.

sounds will vary with and be altered by sounds which precede or follow. For this reason there can be no absolute description of speechreading movements.

1.4. Viewing Conditions—Relevance to Description of Visibility

Despite the limitations imposed by the variables listed above it is still possible to describe, if not precisely, at least usefully, the speechreading movements. But in order to do so *one must first state the viewing conditions.* Having stated them, one can then describe what can be seen under these conditions, classify the movements under a given condition as visible or obscure, and rank order them with respect to relative visibility.

In general there are two kinds of viewing conditions, ideal or highly favorable, and usual or relatively poor.* And, as a consequence, there are actually two sets of speechreading movements which can be described, those found under ideal viewing conditions and those present under usual viewing conditions, although the two sets are not completely dichotomous and, hence, have movements in common. If we assume satisfactory environmental conditions, the words *ideal* and *usual* have reference chiefly to the speaker, to the number and clarity of the visible and relevant motor movements that he produces when talking. *Under ideal viewing conditions* the viewer is receiving maximum visual information. The speaker provides it by using a relatively slow though normal rate of speech, by using ample though not exaggerated lip and jaw movement, by forming the sounds in the conventional manner, and by providing all possible visual clues. For example, when making an /s/ he will bring his teeth together; when producing a /θ/ or /ð/, he will protrude his tongue slightly between his teeth; when making a /ʃ/, /ʒ/, /tʃ/, or /dʒ/, his lips will move forward, etc. This is the kind of viewing condition which obtains when the speaker is aware that he is talking to a hearing handicapped person and has been trained to do so. It is also the kind that the teacher of speechreading must provide when giving instruction and the kind that *any*

---

* It has been the convention in speechreading texts to describe only those movements found under ideal conditions.[1,2,6]

speaker must provide if he wishes to communicate effectively with the hearing impaired.

The second viewing condition we have labeled *usual*. By this phrase is meant the speech visibility that is commonly found. While the label permits of considerable speaker variability, the condition can be described as one in which the speaker talks at from an average to a fairly rapid rate, rarely engages in lip, teeth, or tongue movements that are unnecessary to the production of speech sounds, and often uses little jaw movement. Under usual viewing conditions many of the speechreading movements that are present under ideal conditions are either altered in appearance, become less pronounced, or are entirely missing.*

In the succeeding sections a four-part organizational system will be adhered to. (a) The speechreading movements will first be organized under the general category of speech sounds with which they are associated, i.e. consonants or vowels. This will involve some overlap since some of the movements can be a clue to either a consonant or a vowel sound.

(b) They will next be classified and described with respect to viewing condition, ideal or highly favorable conditions, and usual or less favorable viewing conditions.

(c) For each viewing condition the various movements will be labeled as visible or obscure and the probable rank order of visibility indicated. *A speechreading movement classified as visible is defined as one that can readily be seen by anyone with normal vision under the stated viewing condition.* In contrast, *movements classified as obscure can only be detected under particularly propitious circumstances,* for example, when adjacent sounds do not blur the information, when the viewer is fairly close to the speaker, or when he is positioned in such a fashion that he is able to look into the speaker's mouth.

(d) Finally, the associated sounds for each movement will be indicated and enough information provided regarding their formation to make it clear to the reader the relationship between articulation and visibility. In addition, the importance of each

---

* Our grouping of the consonant sounds under Usual Viewing Conditions is analogous but somewhat less stringent than that found experimentally by Woodward and Barber. (10).

movement to understanding—the information load which it is expected to bear—will be given by indicating the relative occurrence of its associated speech sounds in telephone conversations.

1.5. Importance of Knowledge of Visibility to the Teacher

It is highly important for the teacher of speechreading to be thoroughly aware of how speechreading movements are altered by viewing conditions and to be thoroughly aware under each condition of which movements can usually be seen, which ones can sometimes be seen, and which ones can be observed only rarely, or not at all. He needs this analytic knowledge for a number of reasons. In the first place it enables him to modify his own speech habits so that when giving instruction he will without conscious thought provide maximum information to the viewer— our ideal viewing conditions.

In the second place, it enables him to diagnose difficulties which are due to lack of visual information. When a student fails to establish an important word or phrase, it should be *immediately* apparent to the teacher *why* he has failed. Was it because the pupil needs more training in the rapid perception and association of motor movements with speech sounds? Because the motor movements that were present were low in visibility? Because the same movements could logically result in multiple perceptual closures? If the latter were the case, pointing out to the pupil that his "speechreading" was excellent even though he missed the idea can give him a considerable psychological boost. When the teacher is armed with knowledge concerning the cause of pupil failure, he is in a position to improve his instruction. Speed of focusing can be improved; material can be restated to provide more visual clues, and additional contextual and associational clues can be provided through elaboration. But unless the instructor is thoroughly aware of what is and what is not visible, and is himself providing ideal viewing conditions, he will be unable to arrive at the proper diagnosis and to institute *immediately* the proper remedial action.

A third reason for the need for analytic knowledge with respect to the visibility of speechreading movements and their associated speech sounds is that it enables the teacher to evaluate commercially available materials. He will find that some of them, if presented properly, are highly visible, and if otherwise appropriate, usable. Still others must be reserved for advanced pupils, modified or discarded altogether. Since materials are consumed at a rapid rate in the course of instruction, skill in the evaluation of existing materials is of considerable help. It is the rare teacher who can find time to create all of the materials that he uses.

A fourth reason why the teacher should possess an overlearned and almost intuitive knowledge of the relative visibility of speechreading movements is that it enables him to prepare good materials of his own around current topics or topics of special interest to his class. A good teacher considers the conversational needs of his pupils and creates new materials which are relevant to them.

And finally, a fifth reason, and certainly a most important one, is that knowledge of visibility permits the teacher to use a graded approach in his teaching and to provide for individual differences within a group setting. The least skilled pupils are at first asked to speechread only the most visible and familiar materials and are gradually introduced to less visible material. The initially more advanced pupils, on the other hand, are started at different levels on the continuum, commensurate with their skills. Beginning pupils are notoriously variable with respect to speechreading aptitude. For this reason homogenous groupings are not usually practicable.

Analytic knowledge concerning the visibility of speech movements is essential to the teacher for the reasons discussed above. We earnestly hope, however, that the teacher will not feel impelled to communicate his extensive knowledge of the visibility of speechreading movements to his pupils. To communicate such knowledge to pupils is usually to do them a disservice. For the student, eye-to-mind is the aim, i.e. instant recognition with no intermediary verbal step. This is best achieved by teaching recognition through visual contrast. See the Chapter, "Methods," for the method and materials used to achieve this end.

1.6. Use of the International Phonetic Alphabet

The International Phonetic Alphabet symbols will be used throughout to identify the speech sounds. In this alphabet there is a separate symbol for each speech sound. It is necessary to use it because there are forty-one speech sounds commonly used in General American Speech (25 consonants, 10 vowels, and 6 diphthongs), while there are only twenty-six symbols or letters in the English alphabet. A key to the symbols with which the reader may not be acquainted is given in Table 2-I. The remaining symbols have been omitted because they correspond to those of the English alphabet.

TABLE 2-I

KEY TO THE IDENTIFICATION OF I.P.A. SYMBOLS
(International Phonetic Alphabet°)

Consonant Symbols

/hw/—*wh*ich, *wh*en, *wh*at	/tʃ/—*ch*ild
/θ/—*th*in, *th*imble	/dʒ/—*j*udge
/ð/—*th*en	/s/—*s*o, thi*s*
/ʃ/—*sh*oe, *s*ugar	/z/—*z*oo, the*s*e
/ʒ/—mea*s*ure	/g/—*g*oat, ba*g*

Vowel and Diphthong Symbols

/i/—b*ee*t	/u/—b*oo*t
/ɪ/—b*i*t	/ʊ/—b*oo*k
/eɪ/—b*ai*t, b*ay*	/oʊ/—g*o*, b*oa*t
/ɛ/—b*e*t	/ɔ/—b*ou*ght, l*aw*
/æ/—b*a*t	/ɔɪ/—b*oy*, l*oi*n
/ɝ/—b*ir*d	/aʊ/—c*ow*, l*ou*d
/ʌ/—b*u*d	/aɪ/—b*y*, h*igh*
/ɑ/—p*o*t	

° Only symbols different from those used in the English alphabet or symbols used in the English alphabet to represent more than one sound have been included.

2. CONSONANT SPEECHREADING MOVEMENTS— IDEAL VIEWING CONDITIONS

Given ideal viewing conditions, there are nine speechreading movements which serve as cues to the twenty-five consonant sounds. In other words less than ⅖ of the information regarding consonant sounds available through the ears is possible through the eyes.

The first six speechreading movements described in the succeeding paragraphs are considered to be *visible*, and the last three, *obscure*. They are presented in probable order of visibility, from most visible to most obscure.

2.1. *Lower Lip to Upper Teeth*—/f, v/

The lower lip moves upward and slightly backward and touches the upper teeth—"Squirrel Position." This is perhaps the most stable of all the speechreading movements. It is made by almost all speakers in producing /f/ and /v/ and, hence, can be seen under both the ideal and the usual viewing conditions. In fact, it is rarely missed under even the most adverse viewing conditions. It is not altered to any appreciable degree by transitional movements and can be seen even when the speech is very rapid. The stability of the movement is probably due to the fact that it constitutes almost the entire articulatory pattern of the two sounds with which it is associated.

The /f/ and /v/ sounds are described as labiodental fricatives. The fricative sound, which can be heard when either /f/ or /v/ is made, but is more pronounced when /f/ is formed, is due to the outgoing air hitting the obstruction formed by the upper teeth against the lower lip. The only difference in the production of the sounds, a nonvisible difference, is that one is voiceless and the other voiced.

The percent contribution to intelligibility of the lower lip to upper teeth movement can be gauged by noting the frequency of occurrence of the associated sounds in the spoken language. It has been found that the two sounds together account for 5.21 percent of the consonant elements found in the initial position and 5.60 percent of those found in the final position in the one hundred words used most frequently in telephone conversations.[5, p. 95] Of the two sounds, the /f/ occurs more frequently in the initial position in a word, and the /v/, more frequently in the final position. Because of this the speechreader can be expected to identify the movements as /f/ at the beginning of a word and as /v/ when it is recognized as belonging to the end of a word.

2.2. *Lips Puckered—Narrow Opening*—/w, hw, r/

In making this movement, the lips are contracted, from a position of rest, toward the midline of the body, resulting in a rounded or "kissing position." It is actually a vowel articulatory movement and is produced when a high back vowel, /u/ or /ʊ/ or the high mid vowel /ɝ/ is made. If we were to follow a strictly logical classification system, we would not include it under the consonant movements. We have done so, however, because the movement is never identified as a vowel sound, but always as

/w/, /hw/, or /r/ when it occurs in the initial position in a word. The consonants /w/ and /r/ are sometimes characterized as semivowels or glides because the identifying auditory events are not caused by static articulatory positions, but occur whenever there is a rapid transition from a high back vowel or high mid vowel *to any other vowel.* The word "we" is formed by saying the vowels /u/ and /i/ in rapid succession. And the word, "ray," is formed by saying the vowels /ɜ/ and /eɪ/ in rapid succession. As soon as one speeds up, the vowels /u/ and /ɜ/ lose their characteristic sounds, and the transitional sounds associated with the symbols /w/ and /r/ are heard. The lips puckered movement can also serve as a cue for /hw/ because the /h/ component has no movement. It is simply the sound of escaping air, unimpeded in its passage from the lungs to the outer air. "Witch" and "which" are homophenes, but it is unlikely that a woman would make the incorrect association if someone said to her, "You are a witch!"

The /r/ movement is not identical with that for /w/ and /hw/ because most speakers use less pucker in forming the /r/ than in forming the /w/ and /hw/.* Occasionally they can be distinguished. However, the movements are enough alike to be considered homophenous for all practical purposes.

The visibility of the lips puckered movement varies with the speaker, with the vowel which follows, and with the rate of speech. When the transition is to a low vowel, rather than to a high vowel, the movement is less pronounced. When speech is fairly rapid, the movement may actually be more pronounced than when it is slower. The reason for this is that the speaker is apt to use less jaw movement in forming his low vowels and so retain a more definite pucker in producing the /w/, /hw/, and /r/ sounds.

The sounds which are identified by the lips puckered movement account for 12.16 percent of the consonants found in the one hundred words used most frequently in telephone conversations.[5, p. 95] The /w/ and /hw/ sounds account for 9.30 per-

---

* Tentative experimental evidence that lip protrusion may be characteristic of /r/ was reported by Daniloff, R., and Moll, K.: Coarticulation of lip rounding, *J Speech Hearing Res, 11:*717, 1968.

cent, and the /r/, for 2.78 percent. These sounds are found only in the initial position in words.

2.3. *Lips Together*—/p, b, m/

The lips move to a completely closed position and are pressed firmly together This movement is highly stable and like the lip to teeth movement little affected by the speaker's habits and rate of speech or by transitional movements from or to another sound. It is ranked third in visibility because it serves as an "oral period," marking the end of a thought unit as well as being a cue to the identification of /p/, /b/, and /m/. It should also be noted that the lips are normally closed before one starts to speak. For these reasons the movement, as was noted earlier, although seen, may not be recognized as having occurred *because* a sound was made.

The stability of this movement, like that for /f/ and /v/, is probably also due to the fact that it constitutes almost the entire articulatory pattern for /p/ and /b/. Both sounds are classified as *bilabial plosives*. The lips must come together to permit the buildup of sound pressure which when released is the identifying auditory event. The only difference in the formation is that /p/ is voiceless, and /b/, voiced. The sound /m/, on the other hand, can be described as a nasal continuant. The velopalatal closure is relaxed, and the sound is permitted to escape through the nose.

The reader may wonder why /m/ is classified as looking like /p/ and /b/ when this is not so when the sounds are produced in isolation. The reason for this similarity in appearance is due to the transitional effect. Sounds are not spoken in isolation in forming words. The movements flow together. The release movement of /p/ and /b/ is not seen for it becomes part of the vowel which follows or the slight pause between adjacent consonants. "Pan," "ban," and "man" will all look alike and so will "Come to me," and "cup to me."

These three sounds with which the lips together movement is associated together account for approximately 13 percent and 7 percent, respectively, of the consonant sounds found in the initial and in the final positions of the one hundred words used most frequently in telephone conversations. The order of frequency of occurrence in the initial position is /m/, /b/, and /p/. In the final position it is /m/, /p/, and /b/.

Because of his knowledge of language, the speechreader can be expected to identify most frequently the lips together movement as /m/, despite the fact that from a strictly visual point of view it could as easily be /p/ or /b/.

2.4. *Tongue Between Teeth*—/ө, ð/

The tip of the tongue is momentarily seen between the teeth before it is quickly retracted—The "I don't like you" movement. The movement is visible when made, as under ideal viewing conditions, but is not noteworthy for its stability. It is not necessary to protrude the tongue when forming the /ө/ or /ð/, and many speakers do not habitually do so. Even when made, the movement can be obscured by the lower lip when the following vowel is from one of the high groups.

The two speech sounds for which the movement serves as a clue have identical articulatory patterns. The only difference is that /ө/ as in *thin* is not voiced, whereas /ð/, as *then*, is. They are generally classified as linguadental consonants.

Together they account for 8.74 percent of the consonants found in the initial position and 1.29 percent of those in the final position in the one hundred words used most frequently in telephone conversations.[5, p. 95] The voiced consonant /ð/ occurs more frequently, 6.72 percent as compared with 2.02 percent for /ө/ in the initial position. Neither sound occurs often in the final position in words: 1.25 percent for /ð/ and .04 percent for /ө/. Because of the relative frequency of occurrence of the sounds, the movement will most often be identified by th speechreader as representing the voiced sound.

2.5. *Lips Forward*—/ʃ, ʒ, tʃ, dʒ/

The lips move forward and assume a semirounded position reminiscent of the mouth movements made by fish when eating. We can describe it irreverently as the fish-mouth movement. Because the movement is not a basic part of the articulatory pattern and is not essential to the formation of the sounds which it is used to identify, it is highly unstable. Nevertheless, under ideal viewing conditions when the movement is made, it is of considerable help to the speechreader. It was identified correctly in sixty-one out of eighty-two nonsense syllable presentations, 74 percent of the time, in an informal experiment using two talkers and three viewers.

There are four sounds commonly associated with the movement, /ʃ,ʒ,tʃ,dʒ/. The first two, /ʃ/ and /ʒ/, result in the same speechreading movement because they are formed in the same fashion except that /ʃ/ is voiceless and /ʒ/ is voiced. They are both fricatives. The second two sounds are affricates. By an affricate is meant a sound that is formed by a combination of a plosive and a fricative. The only difference between them is that /tʃ/ is voiceless, and /dʒ/, voiced. They share the same speechreading movement with /ʃ/ and /ʒ/ because the plosive component cannot be seen by the viewer. The tongue moves to the alveolar ridge before the sound is started, but the movement occurs behind the teeth and is lost to view.

When examining speechreading materials for visibility, the teacher needs to keep in mind that the sounds are often spelled in various ways. For example, /ʃ/ is spelled as *sh* in *sh*oe, but as *s* in *s*ugar. The sound /ʒ/ is represented by the letter *s* in mea*s*ure, but by *g* in *g*arage. And the sound /dʒ/ is often spelled as *j*, but sometimes as *dge*, e.g., ju*dge*.

The sound indentified by the lips forward movement account for 3.14 percent of the consonant elements found in the initial position and for 1.00 percent of those found in the final position in the words most frequently used in telephone conversations.[5, p. 95] Some help is given to the speechreader in effecting a correct identification of the movement by the fact that /ʃ/ occurs more frequently than /tʃ/ in the initial position.

2.6. Teeth Together—/s, z/

The edges of the front teeth come together. Its appearance is usually not affected by the rate of speech or by transitional movements. However, it is a movement that is believed to occur only under ideal viewing conditions because most speakers probably do not put the edges of their teeth together in making the /s/ and /z/ sounds. In most mouths the upper front teeth overlap the lower to some extent and many people have overbites. Putting the teeth together is not an essential part of the articulatory movement pattern for the /s/ and /z/ sounds. All that is necessary is an approximation close enough to insure that the breath stream makes contact with the edges of the front teeth.

The sounds associated with this movement are used frequently in conversational speech. They accounted for approximately 6 percent of the consonant elements found in the initial position and 9 percent of those in the final position in the one hundred words used most frequently in telephone conversations.[5, p. 95] The /s/ occurs most frequently in the initial position, and the /z/, most frequently in the final position. This fact is of considerable help to the speechreader in associating the movement with the correct sound.

2.7. *Lips Back-Narrow Opening*—/j/

The lips move backward and the corners upward from their position at rest. The movement can be detected only under ideal viewing conditions, and even under these conditions it is considered to be obscure because the characteristic appearance can be altered by the transition movement to the following vowel. It is the movement which occurs when the mouth is positioned for a high front vowel. As such, it is a vowel rather than a consonant movement. Nevertheless, it can be used as a clue to the presence of the consonant /j/ *when the following vowel is a high back vowel or the high mid vowel, /ɝ/.* When the transition is to another vowel of the high front group, i.e. to /ɪ/ or /eɪ/ or to the mid vowel /ʌ/, the movement blends with that of the following vowel and cannot be distinguished from it except through context. If the movement is to a low vowel, some lip extension may still occur, but the characteristic "corners up" movement is usually not made. The sound may be recognized under these conditions through seeing the tongue move from the /i/ position to the low vowel, but can easily be confused with the other two obscure consonant movements—the tongue down movement, characteristic of /t,d,n,l/, or the tongue back movement, characteristic of /k,g,n/.

The /j/ sound with which the movement is associated is a semi-vowel or glide, and is the transitional sound which occurs when the speaker moves rapidly from the high front vowel /i/ to any other vowel. To satisfy yourself as to the nature of this sound, try the following experiment. First say the vowel /i/ as in meat, and then say any other vowel. Say the two vowels in rapid succession, and you will notice that you no longer hear the vowel /i/, but the consonant /j/.

Visibility will vary with the speaker, with the distance from the speaker, and with the vowel which follows.

Out of a series of 456 nonsense syllables beginning with /j/, the sound was identified correctly 59 percent of the time. Two talkers and three speechreaders were used; /j/ was followed by seven different vowels, /i,ʌ,ɑɪ,ɑ,ɝ,u,oU/ and was contrasted with the consonants /w/, /ʃ/, /l/, /s/, and /g/ followed by the same vowel sounds, e.g., /ji-si/, /gou-jou/, etc. When followed by the high back and high mid vowels, /u,ou, ɝ/, it was correctly identified 70 percent of the time. When followed by the mid vowels, /ʌ and ɑ/, correct identification fell to approximately 57 percent, and when followed by the high front vowel /i/ and the diphthong /ɑɪ/, correct identification was reduced to approximately 44 percent. The same order of ease of recognition with respect to the following vowel was noted for all three speechreaders, but the best speechreader made substantially better percent recognition scores. Higher scores for all three speechreaders were made with talker I than with talker II. The specific percent recognition figures obtained in this experiment could be expected to change if the experiment were repeated with more talkers and more speechreaders. Nonetheless, it is believed that the rank order with respect to following vowel groups would probably not be altered. Identification of /j/ would appear to be "good" under ideal viewing conditions if the following vowel is in the high back group, "fair to poor" if the vowel is from the low groups, and "poor" if the vowel is from the high front group.

The /j/ sound accounted for 6.48 percent of the phonetic elements found in the initial position of the one hundred words used most frequently in telephone conversations, presumably because of the frequency of the use of the word "you."[1, p. 95]

2.8. *Tongue Up or Down—Moderate Opening—*/t, d, n, l/

The tongue moves down from the alveolar ridge (upper gum ridge) into a vowel position if the sound is in the initial position in a word and up to the alveolar ridge from a vowel position if the sound occurs in the final position. The movement is usually blocked from view by the teeth and cannot be seen at all unless there is considerable jaw movement resulting in an open mouth position and unless the viewer is close to the speaker or viewing him from the side. It is often not seen unless the speechreader is seated below the speaker and can look up into his mouth. Certain anatomical features are also of considerable help. The movement is more easily seen if the speaker has wide lips and a large mouth—an undershot jaw is of special help! In general, as the speech rate is slowed, more jaw movement is used. But since it is not necessary to open the mouth very wide when talking, the upward and downward movements of the tongue as made by some speakers are never seen.

The visibility of the movement is markedly affected by which sounds precede or follow it. Let us consider for a moment the chances of seeing the movement when speechreading a speaker who habitually uses a fairly slow rate and considerable jaw movement and one who also has a normal dental bite. In this case the movement will probably be seen when the preceding or following vowels are low vowels, although it will be easily confused with the movements for /j/ and for /k, g, ŋ/. Transitions to or from the high vowels, on the other hand, will not be seen because the mouth is normally opened only slightly in making the high vowel sounds.

The speech sounds for which the tongue up or down movement serves as a cue, /t, d, n, l/, are all classified as lingua-alveolars, i.e. tongue to upper gum ridge. The first two sounds, /t/ and /d/, are plosives. They are formed alike except that /t/ is voiceless and /d/ is voiced. The /l/ sound is a voiced continuant, and the /n/, a nasal continuant. Despite these differences they all look alike in syllables or words. The tongue blade is slightly more narrow for /l/ than for the other sounds, but there is not enough difference to justify classifying it as a separate speechreading movement.

Unfortunately for the speechreader, the sounds which are identified by this obscure movement constitute over 23 percent of the consonant elements found in the initial position and almost 40 percent of those found in the final position in conversational speech.[1, p. 95] The order of frequency of occurrence of the sounds in the initial position is /t/, /d/, /n/, and /l/—7.86 percent, 6.21 percent, 4.99 percent, and 4.31 percent, respectively. For the final position the order is /t/, /n/, /l/, and /d/—14.3 percent, 12.52 percent, 8.40 percent, and 4.44 percent, respectively. These dramatic facts emphasize again the importance of using reduced voice in giving speechreading instruction. If given in this fashion, all but the profoundly deaf will hear enough of the voiced consonant energy to enable them to differentiate among the /d/, /n/, and /l/ sounds much of the time. The /t/, however, can be expected to be missed often, even when the combined approach—sight and sound—is used.

2.9. *Tongue Back—Moderate Opening*—/k, g, ŋ/

A slight backward movement of the tongue can *sometimes* be seen if the movement is to or from a low vowel—specifically to or from /ɛ, æ, ɑ, ɑɪ, ɔ, ɔɪ, ɑʊ,/. The anterior one third of the tongue is usually flat, but not invariably so. In order for the viewer to see the movement he must be close to the speaker and preferably seated or standing on a lower level. The light must be good. If the speaker does not open his mouth fairly wide when making the low vowel sounds, it cannot, of course, be seen at all. The movement is invisible if the transition is to or from a high vowel position. Some writers believe that the best identifying feature for this group of sounds is a slight upward movement of the hyoid bone.

Visibility will vary with the speaker, with the sound which precedes or follows, and with the environmental conditions. This is the least visible of all of the consonant speechreading movements. It is often missed, and when seen, it is easily confused with the movement for /t/, /d/, /n/, /l/, and the movement for /j/,

The sounds for which the tongue back movement may serve as a cue are classified as lingua velar (back of tongue to soft palate) consonants. The sounds /k/ and /g/ are plosives and are alike except that /k/ is voiceless, and /g/ is voiced. When making the nasal continuant /ŋ/, the articulatory pattern is the same, but the sound is directed through the nose.

These sounds accounted for approximately 10 percent of the phonetic elements found in the initial position and for approximately 7 percent of those found in the final position in the one hundred words used most frequently in telephone conversations. /k/ and /g/ occur more frequently in the initial position than in the final position—5.55 percent and 4.33 percent, respectively, as contrasted with 2.85 percent and .38 percent. /ŋ/ occurs only in the final position. Its relative frequency is 3.57 percent.

The consonant speechreading movements that can be seen under ideal viewing conditions are summarized in Table 2-II.

TABLE 2-II

CONSONANT SPEECHREADING MOVEMENTS

IDEAL VIEWING CONDITIONS

	Visible Movements	Obscure Movements	
Almost All Speakers	1. Lip to teeth /f,v/ 2. Lips puckered—narrow-opening /w,hw,r/ 3. Lips together /p,b,m,/	7. Lips back—narrow opening /j/ 8. Tongue up or down moderate-opening /t,d,n,l/	Occasionally Visible
Some Speakers	4. Tongue between teeth /θ,ð/ 5. Lips forward /ʃ,ʒ,tʃ,dʒ/ 6. Teeth together /s,z/	9. Tongue back—moderate-opening /k,g,ŋ/	Rarely Visible

There are seven speechreading movements that are cues to consonant sounds only; #2 and #7 are also characteristic of certain vowel sounds.

A speechreading movement is defined as *a recognizable visual motor pattern that is usually common to two or more speech sounds.*

3. CONSONANT SPEECHREADING MOVEMENTS (USUAL VIEWING CONDITIONS*)

Under less favorable viewing conditions, those that we feel may often represent the usual situation, a number of things transpire that result in a reduction in the amount of visual infor-

* Two research studies have provided evidence of the existence of usual

mation and the clarity of that which remains. Some of the movements become less pronounced and, hence, are now obscure; some are altered and, hence, take on a new appearance, and some are obliterated altogether. These changes result in a reduction from the eight or nine movements listed under ideal viewing conditions to four or at the most five movements which can be seen under usual viewing conditions.

3.1. Lower Lip to Upper Teeth; 3.2. Lips Puckered; 3.3. Lips Together

The first three speechreading movements described in preceding sections under ideal viewing conditions are listed again because they are also present under usual viewing conditions. While perhaps not quite as definite, they can still be considered to be visible, i.e. easily detected by the viewer. They are highly stable because, as stated before, they constitute basic parts of the articulatory movements which must be made in order to form the underlying sounds.

3.4. Tongue Between Teeth

The fourth movement, *tongue between teeth*, found under ideal viewing conditions, may or may not be present under usual viewing conditions depending on the habits of the speaker. The movement is not necessary to the production of the /θ/ and /ð/

---

viewing conditions—at least for the consonant speechreading movments. In both studies the talkers used normal articulation and made no special attempt to provide maximum visibility. Woodward and Barber[10] (1960) used one speaker and filmed a series of nonsense syllables with the consonants followed by either /ɑ/ or /ɔ/. They concluded that "four sets of English consonant initials can be classified as visually contrastive." They were unit 1, /p, b, m/, unit 2, /w, hw, r/, unit 3, /f, v/, and unit 4, /t, d, n, l, s, z, k, g, h, j, θ, ð, ʃ, ʒ, tʃ, dʒ/.

Fisher,[4] (1968) replicated their study, but used as stimulus materials sets of one, two, and three syllable words selected from the Multiple Choice Intelligibility Test by Black. He found five visual phonemes or "visemes" in the initial position. They were (a) /p, b/–/m, d/, (b) /f, v,/, (c) /k, g/, (d). /w, hw/– (r), (e) /ʃ, tʃ/–(n, l, s, z, dʒ, j, h). Parentheses indicate directional rather than reciprocal confusion. For example, /m/ was confused with /b/, but /b/ was not significantly confused with /m/. The visemes for the final position were (a) /p, b/, (b) /f, v/, (c) /k, g, m, ŋ/, (d) /ʃ, ʒ, dʒ/–(tʃ), (e) /t, d, n, z, s, r, l, θ, ð/.

sounds. The percentage of speakers who make this movement habitually is not known. Neither is the effect on production for a given speaker of adjacent sounds, e.g., "This is" as contrasted with "Is this?" It is also possible that many speakers who often make the movement may not do so when speaking more rapidly than usual. Certainly many speakers never protrude their tongue when making the sounds, but instead position it just behind the teeth where its rapid retraction is rarely seen.

3.5. Lips Forward

This fifth movement, *lips forward*, changes from a visible movement under highly favorable viewing conditions to an obscure movement under less favorable conditions. Under the latter condition the movement can occasionally be detected. There will normally be less lip movement and the movement may not be made at all whenever it is inexpedient to do so. As was noted before, the movement is not essential to the production of the associated sounds. Some of the factors tending to make this movement obscure under the usual viewing conditions are speakers' articulatory habits, and rate of speech and transition effects. Rate makes a pronounced difference. The amount of forward movement used by almost anyone will diminish with an increase in the speaking rate. And as important are the alterations in appearance due to the transitions or movement from one sound to another. For example, if one of the "lips forward consonants" is followed by a high front vowel, the speaker is set to move to a backward extension of the lips in making the vowel sound. Economy of effort dictates the use of little forward movement. This situation is repeated when the movement is either to or from a low vowel position. The speaker is set to lower or raise his jaw. It is not expedient for him to use much forward movement. For this reason "sawed" and "chawed" may look alike and also "sot" and "shot."

3.6. Teeth Approximated—/s,z: t,d,n,l: j: k,g,ŋ; θ,ð,)

This obscure and nondescript movement has not been mentioned or described before. It replaces the teeth together movement characteristic of the /s/ and /z/ sounds under ideal viewing conditions. Unfortunately the movement is the only identifying movement for /ǝ/ and /ð/, as well when the tongue is not protruded, and for /t, d, n, l/ when these sounds are either preceded by or followed by high front and high back vowels and/or when the speaker uses little jaw movement. It can also be interpreted to mean that a /k, g, ŋ/ or /j/ has been made. Because the movement is so indefinite and because so many sounds are associated with it, the movement is actually of little value to the speechreader. It is usually the only visual cue that the speechreader has to over 38 percent of all sound elements in everday connected speech. Probably the movement is most commonly identified by the speechreader as representing a /t/, /d/, /n/, or /l/ since these elements occur most frequently and by themselves constitute over 21 percent of the total consonantal auditory information.

3.7. Summary Consonant Speechreading Movements—Usual Viewing Conditions

The speechreading movements which can be seen under what we have termed the *usual* or *less than ideal viewing conditions*, when the speaker is talking naturally, but making no attempt to produce highly visible speech, are listed in Table 2-III. The viewer has only three to four visible movements and two obscure ones to aid him in the identification of the consonant sounds. Stated differently: Under usual viewing conditions vision will provide only approximately one-half the information available

TABLE 2-III

CONSONANT SPEECHREADING MOVEMENTS

USUAL VIEWING CONDITIONS

	Visible Movements	Obscure Movements
Almost All Speakers	1. Lower lip to upper teeth /f,v/	5. Lips forward /ʃ,ʒ,tʃ,dʒ/ (occasionally visible)
	2. Lips puckered, /w,hw,r/	6. Teeth approximated /s,z,θ,ð,t,d,n,l,j; k,g,ŋ/ (present but of little use.)
	3. Lips together, /p,b,m/	
Some Speakers	4. Tongue between teeth /θ,ð/	

visually under ideal conditions and only approximately one-fifth of the information that is available through hearing.

Our grouping of the consonant sounds with respect to homophenity for usual viewing conditions, though arrived at independently, follows the experimental groupings of Woodward and Barber[10] and Fisher[4] fairly closely. We differ from Woodward and Barber, but not from Fisher, in believing that under normal viewing conditions the /ʃ, ʒ, tʃ, dʒ/ sounds often form distinctive clusters. We depart from the experimental evidence of both studies in listing /θ, ð/ as a separate visual entity. A certain answer will have to await more experimental evidence. Only one speaker was used by Woodward and Barber and a limited number in the development of the M.C.I. Test used by Fisher.

4. VOWEL AND DIPHTHONG SPEECHREADING MOVEMENTS

Since no two vowel sounds are articulated in precisely the same fashion, there are no strictly homophenous vowel speechreading movements. But many movements look enough alike to be considered homophenous *for all practical purposes.* Thus it is possible to conclude that there are only two, or at the most three, speech movements that are sufficiently stable to be of any great help in identifying the vowels and diphthongs. The two basic movements are those characteristic of the high front vowels and the high back vowels, respectively. They can be briefly described as lips back-narrow opening and lips puckered. These movements have already been noted and described in considerable detail under the section on recognition of consonant sounds because they also serve as cues to the glide consonants /j/ and /w, hw, r/, respectively. Other vowel speechreading movements consist of alterations in these basic lip movements in combination with differences in the width or size of the mouth opening, itself. Unfortunately, it is not necessary, or even practical, to vary the width of the mouth opening to any great extent when speaking. But, if this is not done, changes in the lip and mouth positions may be minimal and not easily detected or differentiated. The visibility of many vowel sounds varies directly with the speaker, with his rate, and with the amount of lip and jaw movement which he uses. Individuals who habitually use more lip and jaw movement than the minimum necessary to be understood are usually those with special training in speech—actors, speech and hearing therapists, teachers of adult speechreading classes, and teachers of deaf children. No wonder that many a hearing handicapped person has complained that he can understand his teacher, but no one else! Vowel speechreading movements are, in general, less visible than those for the consonant sounds.

4.1. Relationship of Formation to Visibility

In order to understand the possibilities as well as the limitations for the visibility of these sounds, it is necessary to know something about the way in which they are formed. Vowels and diphthongs—which are a combination of two vowels—are often considered to be resonance phenomena. By this it is meant that for a given individual the formation of all of these sounds starts with the same laryngeal tone. Changes in the auditory pattern of the tone which we interpret as different speech sounds are due to changes in the size, shape, and texture of the throat and mouth resulting in the reinforcement of certain frequencies and the damping of others. These alterations are effected principally through tongue movement and the tensing or relaxing of the mouth, throat, and tongue. The lips are used to some degree to effect the changes, and the lower jaw is involved in the opening or closing of the mouth and hence in altering the size of the oral cavity. But as was noted earlier, the important element is apparently the change in the shape of the mouth cavity, rather than gross changes in its size. Since the tongue action takes place within the mouth, it cannot usually be seen. The speechreader gains information regarding which sound has been made from observing changes in the shape of the lips, and only very limited information from changes in the width of the mouth opening, or tongue movement.

In describing possible differences in the visible aspects of sound formation, it is helpful to make use of an organizational pattern know as the *vowel chart*. (See Table 2-IV.) In this chart,

TABLE 2-IV

VOWEL CHART—MODIFIED FOR SPEECHREADING°

Front Vowels	Mid Vowels	Back Vowels
/i/ beet		/u/ boot
High /ɪ/ bit	/ɝ/ bird	/ʊ/ book
/eɪ/ bait	/ʌ/ pun	/oʊ/ boat
/e/ cha-ot′-ic		/o/ o-bey′
/ɛ/ bet		
Low /æ/ bat		/ɔ/ ball
/a/ "dance"		/ɒ/ Bob
	/ɑ/—/ɑɪ/ pot, bite	

° 1. The mid level as in "high front," "mid front," and "low front" has been omitted because it is believed that this distinction is not important in speechreading.

2. The unstressed mid vowels /ɝ/ and /ə/ are not shown because they will have the same appearance as their visual counterparts.

3. The "slashed" sounds, /e/, /a/, /o/, and /ɒ/, have been included only to indicate visual distance. They occur infrequently, if at all, in general American speech.

4. The vowel /ɑ/ has been classified as a mid rather than a back vowel because of its visible characteristics.

5. Certain diphthongs have been included in the vowel chart: /eɪ/ and /oʊ/ because they commonly replace /e/ and /o/ in general American speech and have the appearance of a high front vowel; /ɑɪ/ because it does not usually appear as a separate entity, but has the appearance of a low front vowel.

6. Arrows have been used to indicate that: (a) The mid vowel /ɝ/ usually has the same appearance as the high back vowels and is at approximately the same level as /ʊ/, (b) The vowel /ʌ/ looks like a high front vowel and is at about the same level as /eɪ/, (c) The vowel /ɑ / has the appearance of a low front vowel.

the vowels are grouped with respect to differences in tongue and jaw movement. They are first broadly categorized as front, mid or back. These labels are descriptive of an important aspect of vowel production. If the front of the tongue is most active or most tensed in making a particular sound, it is called a front vowel; if the middle section of the tongue is most involved, a mid vowel, and if the back portion is most active, a back vowel. In order to appreciate these distinctions, say /i/ as in beat; /ʌ/ as in but, and then /u/ as in boot, but say them silently. Were you able to feel the change in tongue movement or site of tension? The sounds within each category are further designated as being high or low; high front, low front; high mid, low mid, and high back, low back. Some charts also include a mid position, but this finer classification has been omitted because it is not necessary for our purpose. The words "high" and "low" refer to the vertical width of the mouth opening, or more accurately to the jaw—whether it is in a high or low position. The terms high and low can be misleading. There are not just two positions, but a different position for each vowel. In order to *feel* the downward movement of the jaw and the successive changes in its position, rest your hand lightly under your chin and say the vowels in each category starting with the highest vowel. The order for the front vowels should be: /i/, /ɪ/, /eɪ/, /ɛ/, /æ/, as in beet, bit, bait, bet, and bat; the order for the mid vowels: /ɝ/, /ʌ/, /ɑ/, as in pert, pun, pot; and the order for the back vowels: /u/, /ʊ/, /oʊ/, /ɔ/, as in boot, book, boat, and bought. Did you feel your jaw moving from a nearly closed or high position to progressively lower positions? Did you also note that the movement from one vowel to the next was very slight, but that there was considerable movement from the highest to the lowest vowel in each category. The mouth is in its most open position when we say /ɑ/. No wonder the dentist asks us to say this sound. What a fix he would be in if we were to substitute /i/, /ɝ/, or /u/!

We are now ready to *see* the visible aspects of vowel production and the visual differences that can serve as clues to the identification of the various sounds. Say the vowels in the same order as you did before, but this time watch yourself in a mirror as you do so. Did you see a gradual widening or opening of the mouth as well as a gradual change in the *appearance of the lips*, i.e. in the amount of lip movement used? The amount of lip movement used in forming a given vowel is directly related to the height of the vowel. In general, the higher the vowel, the greater, or more pronounced, the lip movement.

Look in the mirror again, but this time say the *key words* in the order given above rather than the vowels in isolation. First say them slowly and then repeat using your normal or average speech rate. Did you use *less* jaw movement and *more* lip movement for the low vowels when you said the words rather than the sounds? If you did so, it was because you were getting set to move the jaw into a high position for the final consonant. It is not economical with respect to effort to use as much downward jaw movement under these circumstances. Because less jaw movement is used, the lip movement used is not reduced as much by the downward movement of the jaw and is therefore more pronounced for the low vowels. When you used your normal rate, did you use still less jaw movement and this time less lip movement in forming the high front vowels? If so, you were able to notice that all of the vowel sounds within one of the major categories, the front vowels, began to look alike. And if you were very observant you noted that the high mid vowel/ɚ/ looked like the back vowels and the mid vowels /ʌ/ and /ɑ/ like the front vowels.

4.2. General Visibility Rules

From the foregoing description of lip and jaw movements it is possible to arrive at certain general rules with respect to vowel and diphthong visibility.

1. The vowels /ʌ/ and /ɑ/ tend to have the same characteristic lip and jaw movements as front vowels and usually cannot be distinguished from them. When considerable jaw movement is used, /ʌ/ will look like a high front vowel, and /ɑ/, like a low front vowel.

2. The high mid vowel /ɚ/ has approximately the same lip movement as the high back vowels and usually cannot be distinguished from them.

3. Sounds which are adjacent on the vowel chart are for all practical purposes homophenous and usually cannot be distinguished from each other, regardless of the rate and the amount of lip and jaw movement used. For this reason the visual distinction between high and low vowels is obliterated if the two sounds in question are adjacent. For example, /e/ and /ɛ/ will look alike despite the fact that the former is a high front vowel and the latter, a low front vowel. Fortunately, the sound more commonly used, the diphthong /eɪ/ is not adjacent to /ɛ/ and can sometimes be distinguished from the low front vowels when careful speech—considerable lip and jaw movement—is used.

4. Under the "usual viewing conditions," when the speaker is using connected speech, is talking at an average rate, and is

making no special attempt to make his speech visible, only three vowel speechreading movements will normally be *made*. They are (a) lips puckered, (b) lips rounded, and (c) lips relaxed—narrow opening. The third movement—lips relaxed-narrow opening—is the only visual cue that the speechreader often has for identifying all front vowels, the mid vowels, /ʌ/ and /ɑ/, and the diphthongs /eɪ/ and /aɪ/ as in bay and bite—all told eight sounds. The upward movement and tensing of the corners of the lips which *can be* characteristic of the high front vowels, including the mid vowel /ʌ/, is not made.

5. Under "ideal viewing conditions" when the speaker is attempting to make his speech as visible as possible by using a slow rate, but normal rhythm and stress pattern, and considerable, but not exaggerated lip and jaw movement, four vowel speech movements will be made. The additional speech movement enables the speechreader to distinguish between the high and low front vowel sound groups. Under such conditions, the combination movements used in articulating the diphthongs /aʊ/, /ɔɪ/, and /aɪ/ can also usually be detected. This is the sort of speech that one must use in talking to the deaf, or to anyone who is hard of hearing, but without an hearing aid.

It should be noted too, that under these ideal conditions, two vowels from the same general movement category can be differentiated providing they are at opposite ends of the continuum, e.g., /ɛ/ and /ɑ/ as in "red" and "rob." Both are described as lips relaxed—moderate opening.

4.3. Vowel and Diphthong Movements—Ideal Viewing Conditions

Under ideal viewing conditions as many as four vowel speechreading movements and three combination movements or diphthong movements can be detected by the expert observer. They are described below in their probable order of visibility.

4.3.1 Lips Puckered-Narrow Opening, /u, ʊ, o, oʊ, ɝ/. This is the same movement that was described when discussing the visible appearance of the consonants /w/, /hw/, and /r/. The lips move forward into a puckered position, and the mouth is slightly open. The movement aids in the identification of the high back vowels, the mid vowel, /ɝ/, and the diphthong /oʊ/ as in "go." The latter diphthong is more commonly used in general American speech than the pure vowel /o/. The movement is relatively stable, but can be confused with that for the high front vowels when it is preceded by a consonant from the lips forward group.

The vowel sounds which are associated with this movement occur frequently in our conversational speech. They accounted for almost 28 percent (27.81%) of the vowel and diphthong elements found in the one hundred words most frequently used in telephone conversations. The sound /ɝ/ or /ɚ/ alone accounted for 13.85 percent of the elements, followed in rank order by /u/, 6.26 percent; /oʊ/, 4.74 percent; and /ʊ/, 2.96 percent.

4.3.2 LIPS BACK-NARROW OPENING, /i, ɪ, eɪ, e, ʌ/. The lips move backward and there is a slight upward movement of the corners. The narrow mouth opening is revealed through a slight parting of the lips. This movement aids in the identification of high front vowels, the mid vowel /ʌ/, and the diphthong (eɪ) which is more often used in general American speech than the pure vowel /e/. The movement will be obscured if the initial consonant sound is /w/, /hw/, or /r/. The lips must move backward following the initial puckering movement, *regardless* of whether the following vowel is a front, mid, or back vowel. "Wood," "word," and "weed" all look alike. This is the same movement that was described when discussing the recognition of the consonant /j/. Unfortunately for the person who must speechread the vowel sounds, the movement is most unstable. Unless great care is taken, the speaker will not normally differentiate between this movement and that for the low front vowels.

The sounds associated with it account for almost 45 percent (44.74%) of the vowel and diphthong elements used in conversational speech. The most common sound is /ʌ/ or /ə/ which accounts for 23.25 percent of the information followed in rank order by /ɪ/, /i/, and eɪ/ with relative frequencies of 10.27 percent, 6.44 percent, and 4.78 percent, respectively.

4.3.3 LIPS ROUNDED-MODERATE OPENING—/ɔ/. This movement is used in the identification of the low back vowel /ɔ/, as in "law." There is less lip movement, and the mouth is opened wider than it would be in forming the lips puckered movement characteristic of the high back vowels. There is a considerable distance between it and the closest high back vowel on the vowel chart. For this reason it is clearly seen provided the speaker uses careful articulation and considerable jaw movement. The /ɑ/ sound or the sound between—/ɒ/—is often substituted for /ɔ/.

The sound accounted for 4.15 percent of the vowel and diphthong elements found in the one hundred words used most frequently in telephone conversations[1] (p. 95).

4.3.4 LIPS RELAXED-MODERATE OPENING TO LIPS PUCKERED-NARROW OPENING—/ɑʊ/. When viewing the diphthong /ɑʊ/, as in "cow," the speechreader sees the speaker move from the lips relaxed mouth open position of the vowel /ɑ/ as in "top" to the relatively closed, lips puckered position for /ʊ/ as in "cook." When the sound is carefully articulated, it is possible to see the movement from the first to the second lip position.

This sound accounted for 1.69 percent of the dipthongs and vowels found in a count of the frequency of occurrence of elements in conversational speech.[5, p. 95]

4.3.5 LIPS RELAXED-MODERATE OPENING—/ɛ,æ-ɑ/. This movement is characteristic of the two low front vowels /ɛ/ and /æ/, found in such words as "bet" and "bat," and the low mid vowel /ɑ/, as in cot or father. While there is a vowel between /æ/ and /ɑ/, the /a/ as in dance when spoken with an "English" (southern England) accent, the difference in appearance is so slight as to make these three sounds appear to be the same under most circumstances. It differs from the movement for the high front vowels in that the upward movement of the corners of the lips has disappeared and the mouth is opened wider. It cannot be detected as a separate speech reading movement unless the speaker uses considerable jaw movement.

The three sounds identified through this movement constituted 18.7 percent of the vowel and diphthong elements found in the one hundred words most frequently used in telephone conversations. The most frequent sound is /æ/, followed in close order by /ɛ/, and /ɑ/.[5, p. 95]

4.3.6 LIPS ROUNDED-MODERATE OPENING TO LIPS BACK-NARROW OPENING—/ɔɪ/. When viewing the diphthong /ɔɪ/ as in "coy," the speechreader sees the speaker move from the lips rounded, mouth open position of the vowel /ɔ/ as in "law" to the lips extended, high jaw position for the vowel /ɪ/ as in bit. If the sound is slowly and carefully articulated, it is possible for the speech-reader to see the two movements and associate them with the sound.

This compound speechreading movement is probably of relatively little use because the sound /ɔɪ/ does not occur frequently in our language. It accounted for only 0.19 percent of the vowel and diphthong elements found in the one hundred words used most frequently in telephone conversations.[5,p.95]

4.3.7 Lips Relaxed-Moderate Opening to Lips Back-Narrow Opening—/ɑɪ/. This is the least visible of the three diphthong sounds, /ɑu/, /ɔɪ/, and ɑɪ/, as in "cow," "boy," and "tie." It is easily confused with the vowel /ɑ/ as in "top" or with the diphthong /eɪ/ as in "cake." The speechreader sees the mouth moving from an open, lips relaxed position to a closed, lips back position. The speaker, if he wishes to make the sound visible, needs to make a conscious effort to insure a backward movement of the lips as he completes the sound.

This sound is used frequently in our speech. It accounted for 7.58 percent of the vowel and diphthong elements found in the one hundred words used most frequently in telephone conversations.[5, p. 95]

4.4. Vowel and Diphthong Movements—Usual Viewing Conditions

The number of vowel and diphthong speechreading movements is reduced from seven to three or possibly four under less than ideal or usual viewing conditions. They are presented below in probable order of visibility. The change in appearance from a state of repose for the last movement listed (lips relaxed-narrow opening) is slight. Because of the lack of distinctiveness of the movement and the number of speech sounds for which it must serve as a cue, it is probably of relatively little help to the speechreader.

4.4.1 Lips Puckered-Narrow Opening—/u,ʊ,o,ɔ,ɝ/. Under usual viewing conditions when the speaker is not exerting conscious care to make his vowels visible, only one vowel speech-reading movement can be considered to have any substantial degree of visibility. This is the lips puckered movement. While less pronounced it still remains the most visible of the vowel movements.*

4.4.2 LIPS RELAXED-MODERATE OPENING TO LIPS PUCKERED-NARROW OPENING—/αʊ/. This diphthong, which was considered to be visible under ideal viewing conditions, is also visible under usual viewing conditions. While the movements are not as pronounced, they are, nonetheless, quite stable and easily detected.

4.4.3 LIPS ROUNDED-NARROW OPENING—/ɔ, ɔɪ/. Under usual viewing conditions this movement is missed often enough to be considered an obscure rather than a visible speechreading movement. The diphthong /ɔɪ/ cannot usually be differentiated from the pure vowel. There is less jaw movement than under ideal conditions, resulting in a somewhat narrower mouth opening. The rounding of the lips will also be less pronounced.

4.4.4 LIPS RELAXED-NARROW OPENING—/i,ɪ,eɪ,ʌ,ɛ,æ,ɑ,ɑɪ/. Under usual viewing conditions the lips back-narrow opening and the lips relaxed-moderate opening, i.e. the high front vowel and the low front vowel movements, respectively, combine into one movement, lips relaxed-narrow opening. It becomes impossible to differentiate between the high front and the low front vowel groups. Seven vowels and one diphthong /ɑɪ/, as in "pie," look alike as they are spoken. The slight backward movement characteristic of the high front vowels when carefully articulated is lost, and there is no longer an important difference between the high and low vowels in terms of width of jaw opening.

The low visibility of the lips relaxed-narrow opening movement, along with the large number of vowels associated with it, are two of the central reasons why so little information is gained through vowel speechreading. Another reason is the frequency of occurrence of the sounds subsumed under this category. When

---

* No significant protrusion was found in seventeen out of ninety, phonetic sequences, (approximately 19%): e.g., /tu/, /stu/, /stru/, and /instru/. Three speakers were used. Daniloff, R., and Moll, K.: Coarticulation of lip rounding. *J Speech Hearing Res*, 11:712, 1968.

the schwa, (unaccented ʌ), is included, an additional 21.76 percent, we find that the sounds comprising the group account for over 70 percent (73.67%) of the vowel and diphthong elements found in the one hundred words most frequently used in conversation, and close to 30 percent of all such phonemic elements (p. 95).[5]

The vowel and diphthong speechreading movements found under both ideal and usual viewing conditions are summarized in Table 2-V.

TABLE 2-V

VOWEL AND DIPHTHONG SPEECHREADING MOVEMENTS°

Visible Movements	*Obscure Movements*
A. Ideal Viewing Conditions	
1. Lips puckered—narrow opening /u,ʊ,oʊ,ɝ/	5. Lips relaxed—moderate opening /ɛ,æ,ɑ/
2. Lips back—narrow opening /i,ɪ,eɪ,ʌ/	6. Lips rounded—moderate opening to lips back—narrow opening /ɔɪ/
3. Lips rounded—moderate opening /ɔ/	7. Lips relaxed—moderate opening to lips back—narrow opening /aɪ/
4. Lips relaxed—moderate opening to lips puckered—narrow opening /aʊ/	
B. Usual Viewing Conditions	
1. Lips puckered—narrow opening /u,ʊ,oʊ,ɝ/	3. Lips rounded—moderate opening /ɔ,ɔɪ/
2. Lips relaxed—moderate opening to lips puckered—narrow opening /aʊ/	4. Lips relaxed—narrow opening /i,ɪ,eɪ,ʌ,ɛ,æ,ɑ,aɪ/

° Speechreading movements 2, 5, and 7 listed under "Ideal Viewing Conditions" combine to form movement 4 under "Usual Viewing Conditions." Probable rank order re visibility: Ideal Viewing Conditions: 4, 1, 2, 3, 6, 5, 7. Usual Viewing Conditions: 1, 2, 3, 4.

5. COMBINED SPEECHREADING MOVEMENTS—
ALL SPEECH SOUNDS

The speechreading movements for all speech sounds—consonants, vowels, and diphthongs—and for both viewing conditions have been combined in Tables 2-VI and 2-VII. There are, all told, eleven distinctive speech movements plus three combination movements which can be seen under ideal viewing conditions. They serve as cues to the identification of the forty-one speech

TABLE 2-VI

COMBINED CONSONANT AND VOWEL SPEECHREADING MOVEMENTS
IDEAL VIEWING CONDITIONS

Visible

1. Lower lip to upper teeth
/f,v/
2. Lips relaxed, moderate opening to lips puckered, narrow opening,
/aʊ/
3. Lips puckered, narrow opening,
/w,hw,r,u,ʊ,o,oʊ,ɝ/
4. Lips together,
/p,b,m/
5. Tongue between teeth
/θ,ð/
6. Lips forward,
/ʃ,ʒ,tʃ,dʒ/
7. Lips back, narrow opening
/i,ɪ,eɪ,e,ʌ,j/
8. Lips rounded, moderate opening,
/ɔ/
9. Teeth together,
/s,z/

Obscure

10. Lips rounded, moderate opening to lips back, narrow opening,
/ɔɪ/
11. Tongue up or down
/t,d,n,l/
12. Lips relaxed, moderate opening
/ɛ,æ,ɑ/
13. Lips relaxed, moderate opening to lips back narrow opening,
/aɪ/
14. Tongue back and up
/k,g,ŋ/

The movements are presented in an estimated order of relative visibility with #1 being most visible and #14 least visible.

TABLE 2-VII

COMBINED CONSONANT AND VOWEL SPEECHREADING MOVEMENTS
USUAL VIEWING CONDITIONS

Visible

1. Lower lip to upper teeth, /f,v/
2. Lips puckered, narrow opening,
/w,hw,r,u,ʊ,oʊ,o,ɝ/
3. Lips together, /p,b,m/
4. Lips relaxed, moderate opening to lips puckered, narrow opening, /aʊ/
5. Tongue between teeth, /θ,ð/*

Obscure

6. Lips forward /ʃ,ʒ,tʃ,dʒ/†
7. Lips rounded, moderate opening,
/ɔ,ɔɪ/
8. Teeth approximated, /s,z; t,d,n,l; θ,ð; k,g,ŋ; j/‡
9. Lips relaxed, narrow opening,
/i,ɪ,eɪ,e,ʌ,ɛ,æ,ɑ,aɪ/‡. .

---

* Many speakers do not habitually protrude the tongue when making these sounds; the cue becomes "teeth approximated."

† Not all speakers make a lips forward movement when articulating these sounds; others do so when convenient.

‡ Movements 8 and 9 are so imprecise and must serve as clues to so many speech sounds that their information-bearing content is limited.

Total: Four to nine speechreading movements are the only visual cues to approximately forty-one speech sounds under normal or usual viewing conditions.

The movements are presented in an estimated order of relative visibility with #1 being most visible and #9 least visible.

sounds most commonly used in General American Speech. This is less than one might expect from a simple total of the speechreading movements previously presented. In categorizing the basic movements as either *consonant* speechreading movements or *vowel* speechreading movements, two of them were presented twice. The lips puckered-narrow opening movement was considered a consonant movement when used to identify /w/, /hw/, and /r/, and as a vowel movement when used to identify the back vowels.

In like manner, the lips back-narrow opening movement was considered a consonant movement when used to identify /j/ as in "you," and as a vowel movement when used to identify the high back vowels and the mid vowel /ʌ/.

Under normal or usual viewing conditions, when the speaker is not attempting to convey maximum visual information, the number of speechreading movements available to the viewer varies from four to nine.

6. SUMMARY

From an examination of Tables 2-VI and 2-VII it can be seen that the odds are against the individual who is attempting to understand through vision alone. Out of fourteen speechreading movements, all of which can be detected at least occasionally under ideal viewing conditions, only four can be considered to be stable and visible under usual viewing conditions. They are (a) lower lip to upper teeth, (b) lips puckered-narrow opening, (c) lips together, and (d) lips relaxed-moderate opening to lips puckered-narrow opening. The visibility of the remaining movements will vary with the speaker, the rate of speech, and the transitional characteristics of the speech pattern. It is also unfortunately true that many of the sounds which occur most frequently in our language are among those that have many homophenes and are least visible, e.g., /ɪ/, /t/, etc. In addition, some of the most visible speechreading movements contribute minimally to total information because the sounds with which they are associated are not among the most frequent in our language. See Tables 2-VIII, 2-IX, and 2-X.

TABLE 2-VIII

Speechreading Movements	Sound	% Initial Position	% Final Position	% Medial Position	Total
1. Lip to Teeth	f	1.14	1.25		2.39
	v	.36	.40		.76
					3.15
2. Lips Puckered—Narrow Opening	w	2.70			
	r	.80			
	u			2.61	
	ʊ			1.23	
	oʊ			1.98	
	ɝ·ɚ			6.17	
					15.49
3. Lips Together	p	.73	.37		1.10
	b	1.34	.12		1.46
	m	1.70	1.62		3.32
					5.88
4. Tongue Between Teeth	θ	.58	.01		.59
	ð	1.94	.37		2.31
					2.90
5. Lips Forward	ʃ	.50	.09		.59
	ʒ	.01	.003		.013
	tʃ	.16	.16		.32
	dʒ	.24	.04		.28
					1.203
6. Lips Back—Narrow Opening	j	1.87			
	i			2.68	
	ɪ			4.28	
	eɪ			1.99	
	ʌ			1.73	
	ə			7.96	
					20.51
7. Teeth Together	s	1.57	.92		2.49
	z	.10	1.77		1.87
					4.36
8. Tongue Up and Down	t	2.26	4.22		6.48
	d	1.78	1.31		3.09
	n	1.44	3.69		5.13
	l	1.24	2.48		3.72
	l(le)		.40		.40
	nt		1.30		1.30
	nd		.76		.76
	ld		.22		.22
					21.10
9. Tongue Back	k	1.60	.84		2.44
	g	1.24	.11		1.35
	ŋ		1.05		1.05
					4.84
10. Lips Rounded—Moderate Opening	ɔ			1.73	
					1.73

11. Lips Relaxed—Moderate Opening   ɛ   2.75
                                         æ   2.87
                                         ɑ   2.17
                                                             7.79

12. Lips Relaxed—Moderate Opening to Lips Puckered—Narrow Opening   ɑʊ   .70
                                                             .70

13. Lips Rounded—Moderate to Lips Back—Narrow   ɔɪ   .08
                                                             .08

14. Lips Relaxed—Moderate to Lips Back—Narrow   ɑɪ   3.16
                                                             3.16

     Consonant Blends   1.84   5.27   7.11
                                                                100.00%

TABLE 2-IX

COMPARISON OF VISIBILITY AND FREQUENCY RANK ORDER OF
SPEECHREADING MOVEMENTS USED IN CONVERSATIONAL
SPEECH—IDEAL VIEWING CONDITIONS*

Speechreading Movements	Probable Rank Order Visibility	Rank Order Frequency of Occurrence	Percent Frequency of Occurrence	Number of Associated Sounds
Lower Lip to Upper Teeth	1	9	3.15%	2
Lips Puckered—Narrow Opening	2	3	15.49	7
Lips Together	3	5	5.88	3
Lips Relaxed—Moderate Opening to Lips Puckered—Narrow Opening	4	13	.70	1
Tongue Between Teeth	5	10	2.90	2
Lips Forward	6	12	1.20	4
Lips Rounded	7	11	1.73	1
Lips Back—Narrow Opening	8	2	20.51	4
Lips Rounded—Moderate Opening to Lips Back—Narrow	9	14	.08	1
Teeth Together	10	7	4.36	2
Tongue Up or Down†	11	1	21.10	4
Lips Relaxed—Moderate Opening	12	4	7.79	3
Lips Relaxed—Moderate Opening to Lips Back—Narrow	13	8	3.16	1
Tongue Back†	14	6	4.84	3

* Data with regard to percent frequency of phonetic elements from Fletcher.[1, p.95]
† Not visible unless mouth is opened fairly wide.

When the speaker is consciously trying to make his speech
visible, the speechreader is able to observe not much more than
approximately one third of the sensory information available
through hearing.° And under the usual viewing conditions he

° Fourteen speechreading movements.

TABLE 2-X
COMPARISON OF VISIBILITY AND FREQUENCY RANK ORDER OF
SPEECHREADING MOVEMENTS USED IN CONVERSATIONAL
SPEECH—USUAL VIEWING CONDITIONS*

Speechreading Movements	Probable Rank Order Visibility	Rank Order Frequency of Occurrence	Percent Frequency of Occurrence	Number of Associated Sounds
Lip to Teeth	1	7	3.15%	2
Lips Puckered	2	3	15.49	7
Lips Together	3	4	5.88	3
Lips Relaxed—Moderate Opening to Lips Puckered—Narrow	4	11	.70	1
Tongue Between Teeth	5	8	2.90	2
Lips Forward	6	10	1.20	4
Lips Rounded	7	9	1.81	2
Teeth Approximated	8	6	4.36	2
Lips Relaxed—Narrow Opening	9	1	31.46	8
Tongue Up or Down	10	2	21.10	4
Tongue Back	11	5	4.84	3

* Data with regard to percent frequency of phonetic elements from Fletcher.[1,p.95]
Under usual viewing conditions /ɔɪ/ cannot be differentiated from /ɔ/; many speakers do not make the tongue-between-teeth movement; the teeth-approximated movement is more commonly made than the teeth-together movement; the high-front and low-front vowels including the mid vowels /ʌ/ and /ɑ/ and the diphthong /aɪ/ cannot be differentiated, and they combine in the one movement—lips relaxed-narrow opening; the tongue movements (10 and 11) are not seen.

The last three movements are of little use to the speechreader. They constitute fifteen sounds and 57.4 percent of the phonetic elements.

will receive from about 10 percent to 25 percent of the available information.* The combined approach, sight and sound, would appear to be not only desirable, but mandatory. With it the speechreader can receive as much as 70 percent† of the total information, and since speech is patterned and redundant, it is then fairly easy for him mentally to fill in the remainder.

REFERENCES

1. Bunger, A.M.: *Speech Reading—Jena Method.* Danville, Illinois, The Interstate, 1961.
2. Bruhn, M.E.: *The Mueller-Walle Method of Lipreading.* Washington, D.C., The Volta Bureau, 1949.
3. Daniloff, R., and Moll, K.: Coarticulation of lip rounding. *J Speech Hearing Res,* 11:707–721, 1968.

* Four to nine speechreading movements.
† Fourteen vowels and diphthongs and from four to eight consonants.

4. Fisher, C.G.: Confusions among visually perceived consonants. *J Speech Hearing Res, 11:*796–804, 1968.
5. Fletcher, H.: *Speech and Hearing in Communication.* Princeton, Van Nostrand, 1953.
6. Nitchie, E.H.: *New Lessons in Lip Reading.* Philadelphia and New York, Lippincott, 1930.
7. O'Neill, J.J., and Oyer, H.J.: *Visual Communication for the Hard of Hearing.* New Jersey, Prentice-Hall, 1961.
8. *Webster's New International Dictionary,* Second Edition, Unabridged. Springfield, Massachusetts, Merriam, 1944, "Pronunciation," xxii–lxxxviii.
9. Woodward, M.F.: Linguistic methodology in lip reading. In Lowell, E.L. (Ed.): *John Tracy Clinic Research Papers.* Los Angeles, 1957, no. 4, pp. 1–32.
10. Woodward, M.F., and Barber, C.G.: Phoneme perception in lipreading. *J Speech Hearing Res,* 1960, pp. 212–222.

Chapter 3

HISTORY AND DEVELOPMENT OF SPEECHREADING IN THE UNITED STATES

COMPARISON OF METHODOLOGIES

1. OVERVIEW—INTERWEAVING OF SPEECHREADING WITH SPEECH TRAINING

Historical records indicate that hearing handicapped children have been taught to talk since at least as early as the sixteenth century. While there was often concern for the total education of such children, the one aspect of deafness that set them apart and that has always been the most disturbing to the normal population is the poor speech or lack of speech of those with severe hearing handicaps. For this reason major emphasis in training was usually placed on the development of speech. Expression was considered to be more important than reception. Speech, but not speechreading, was taught directly. Learning to understand through speechreading was believed to occur or was *acquired* as a by-product of the development of articulation skill. In the process of learning to talk, since the child had ample experience in observing his instructor, he often learned to speechread apparently sound by sound or word by word. And he did so, we might add, to the astonishment of his instructors who believed that too little sensory information was available through watching the lips to make such a feat possible. During the centuries methods of teaching speech, but not of speechreading, emerged and were recorded in the literature. The development of a philosophy and methodology of teaching speechreading as a receptive skill distinct from speech had to await the time when attention turned to helping the hard-of-hearing adult with established speech and language patterns. This did not occur until near the end of the nineteenth century. And by this time the teaching of speechreading was inextricably interwoven and confused with the teaching of articulation to deaf children.

In this chapter we shall attempt to trace the development of speechreading instruction in the United States. The history begins with the introduction of the oral method of teaching hearing handicapped children. In the oral method the child is taught to talk and to understand others through speechreading coupled with whatever residual hearing he may possess. This is in contradistinction to the manual method wherein both reception and expression are mediated largely or entirely through the use of signs and finger spelling. The first public school for the deaf in the United States was the Connecticut Asylum established in 1816. The manual method of instruction was used. Other states followed suit. By 1860 there were twenty-two schools for the deaf in the United States. In all of them the manual method was the sole method of instruction employed regardless of the amount of residual hearing that a child might have.

2. 1800–1900

2.1. Clarke School—The Beginning of the Oral Method in the United States

Despite the strength of the manual method, at least a few people were aware that it was possible to teach many hearing handicapped children to talk and to speechread, and they were working actively for the establishment of an "oral" school. In 1843 Horace Mann, then secretary of the Massachusetts Board of Education, and Samuel Gridley Howe, Director of the Perkins School for the Blind, visited Europe to study systems of education. On visiting schools in Germany they were surprised and delighted to discover that hearing handicapped children could be taught to speak and to understand through watching the lips. On his return Mann wrote a report strongly advising the adoption of this method of instruction in the United States. His report aroused considerable interest, but nothing came of it at the time. Over twenty years later the first publically supported oral school for the deaf was started in Northampton, Massachusetts. The school came about largely through the interest and efforts of these two men and the influential parents of three little girls with similar medical histories. All had been born with normal hearing; all had lost considerable hearing at around age three or four (two due to scarlet fever) after language and speech were well established. The girls were Jeanie Lippit, whose father later became the Governor of Rhode Island, Fanny Cushing, and Mabel Hubbard, who was to marry Alexander Graham Bell. Their parents were not willing to see their daughters lose their speech nor to wait for their education to start at age ten, the usual age for admission to a school for the deaf. Initially they hired private tutors for them and then banded their efforts together to seek the establishment of a State supported school.

This was not easy to accomplish inasmuch as the manual method was well entrenched as "the method" for teaching the hearing handicapped. They persevered, however, and were finally successful. The first oral school for the deaf, the Clarke School in Northampton, Massachusetts, was opened in October, 1867. It was named the Clarke School after John Clarke who contributed fifty thousand dollars towards its establishment and later left the school two hundred thousand dollars in his will. The first principal of the Clarke School was Harriet Rogers who had tutored Fanny Cushing for three years prior to the opening of the school. Two years later, in 1869, an oral day school was opened in Boston later to be named the Horace Mann School. Its first principal was Sarah Fuller who had worked with Miss Rogers. Her assistant was Mary True, the former tutor of Mabel Hubbard.

The first American teachers of the oral method were essentially self-taught. Joseph Watson of England had published a two-volume book on the Braidwood methods in 1809, and Friedrich Moritz Hill of Germany, who carried on and improved the methods, published a number of books in the nineteenth century. But evidently the beginning American instructors of the oral method did not discover these books. Miss Rogers was to describe herself as being "densely ignorant" when she first undertook the instruction of deaf children. Their chief guidance came from Dr. Howe's recollections and from a newspaper clipping dating from 1850. In 1869 Alexander Melville Bell gave a series of lectures in Boston on visible speech which were attended by Sarah Fuller. Bell's interest in a universal language had lead him to the development of a system of symbols which were descriptive of various portions of the organs of speech (tongue, lips, etc.). The symbols constituted essentially an organically based phonetic alphabet. From a description of a word written in these symbols it was possible to deduce its pronunciation. Miss Fuller felt that visible speech might be of considerable help in teaching deaf children to talk and, as a consequence, asked Bell to return and give a course for the teachers in the Boston School. Bell replied that he had other commitments which would prevent him from doing so, but suggested that his son, Alexander Graham Bell, who was then just twenty-three, might come in his stead.

2.2. Alexander Graham Bell

This was the start of Alexander Graham Bell's lifelong interest in the hearing handicapped. At first he did not believe it possible for the deaf to understand through speechreading. His mother, who had been severely hard of hearing since age four because of an attack of scarlet fever, had retained her ability to talk, but understood others only if they talked into her ear trumpet or used a manual alphabet. And since Bell was aware of how few speech sounds are visible, he at first doubted the value of speechreading. On one occasion, he said the following:[5, p. 37]

> Spoken language I would have used by the pupil from the commencement of his education to the end of it; but spoken language I would not have as a means of communication with the pupil in the earliest stages of education, because it is not clear to the eye, and requires a knowledge of language to unravel the ambiguities. In that case, I would have the teacher use written language and I do not think that the manual language (finger spelling) differs from written language except in this, that it is better and more expeditious.

But after observing the pupils at the Boston School, he changed his mind and said:[4, p. 117]

The children really did seem to understand to a very useful extent, the utterance of their friends and their teachers; they were not deaf at home; they were not deaf with their teachers; my curiosity was so much aroused to ascertain the cause of what seemed from my point of view impossible as to lead me to make the instruction of the deaf my life work.

And later on in 1874 he made this sanguine comment:[4, p. 119]

I have lately made an examination of the visibility of all the words in our language contained in a pocket dictionary and the result has assured me that there are glorious possibilities in the way of teaching speechreading to the deaf, if teachers will give special attention to the subject. One of the results of my investigation has been that the ambiguities of speech are confined to the little words, chiefly to monosyllables. The longer words are nearly all clearly intelligible.

When Bell opened his School of Vocal Physiology, he advertised that he was prepared to give instruction in "Lip-Reading or the art of understanding speech by watching the mouth, including practical methods of teaching the art to those who are deaf."

One of the pupils who came to Bell's school for further improvement of her speech was Mabel Hubbard who had now grown to young womanhood. Bell fell in love with her and asked for her hand in marriage. At first the family was opposed because of Bell's shaky financial situation, but after he got a patent on his telephone, they withdrew their objection. They were married on his twenty-ninth birthday, July 11, 1877. Bell considered himself to be primarily a teacher of the deaf, and almost everything that he did was motivated by this interest. For example, the invention of the telephone grew out of his experiments in developing sound amplification for the hearing handicapped. When the French government in 1880 awarded him the Volta Prize of fifty thousand francs (established in honor of an Italian, Alessandro Volta, who developed the first battery) for his invention of the telephone, he used the money to help establish in Washington, D.C. the Volta Laboratory. There, he and his associates developed the basic method of making phonograph records on wax discs. The patents were sold, and Bell used his share of the proceeds to establish the Volta Bureau in 1877 which continues to this day as an information center on deafness. The

American Association for Teaching Speech to the Deaf was also started by Bell. In recent years it has been renamed in his honor, the Alexander Graham Bell Association for the Deaf.

2.3. First Teachers—Speechreading for Adults

It was not until the 1870's that speechreading was considered to be a separate skill to be taught apart from the teaching of articulation to deaf children. Before the 1870's this distinction had not appeared to be important. As was stated before, in the process of teaching deaf children to produce consonant and vowel sounds, they somehow learned to speechread. It apparently did not occur to anyone to consider how this learning might have taken place or how the approach to instruction might be different if one were dealing with individuals with established speech and language patterns. But during the 1870's with the publicity attendant upon the opening of oral schools for the deaf in the United States, many hard-of-hearing adults became aware of speechreading and asked that classes be started for them. Both Sarah Fuller and Mary True taught adult classes. It was natural for them to use the only materials and approach with which they were familiar. They taught speechreading just as though they were teaching articulation, and they used the same time-honored approach—working from the part to the whole, i.e. from the "element" to the syllable to the word to the phrase. Both used the Melville Bell Visible Speech Symbols to teach the positions of speech and proceeded to teach their adult students how the various speech sounds were formed.

Miss Fuller wrote a pamphlet entitled, *Speech Reading: A Guide for Self-Instruction Where Trained Teachers are not Available,* that was to have considerable influence on the development of speechreading. Each speech sound was analyzed and described in detail. The student was to use a mirror and observe the way in which he formed the sound. An excerpt from the pamphlet follows:[4, p. 127]

k in the word *key*
c in the word *cat*
g in the word *gun*
ng in the word *ring*

These consonant elements require a close study of the back of the tongue. The appearance of the lips, the teeth, and the mouth aperture is the same for all. With a mirror and with the head thrown back, the learner should give, successively, the sound of *k* and *g* and notice the movement of the back of the tongue . . .

Lists of sentences were given for each "element" and the sentences often unnaturally loaded with the sound that was being stressed, e.g., "Who knew about the gnu?" and "The man will tie the bough to the bow of the boat."

Following the description of the "element," a list of words was given, each word containing the sound in question, and then a number of sentences using the words. An example follows.[4, p. 128]

Far

Are you far from home?

Have you far to walk?

Do you live far from the station?

Mary True did not confine her methodology to a description of the elements, but expected her pupils to follow connected speech. Her selections for speechreading practice might however leave something to be desired. It is reported that "she managed to drag her beginners bodily through whole volumes of Phillip Brooks' Sermons and Mathew Arnold's Poems," and also expected them to speechread Sohrab and Rustum.[4, p. 129]

When Miss Fuller became too busy to continue her speechreading classes for adults, she trained a Miss Eleanor L. Hough, "a lady who had had much experience in visiting and reading to invalids, to whom her refined gentle manners and her delicate attentions brought pleasure and needed cheer." After Miss Hough's death in 1893 the classes were continued by Mrs. Alice Mary Porter. Mrs. Porter had studied under Bell and had been trained in the visible speech symbols. She also made use of a book which she had requested that Alexander Melville Bell write entitled, *Speech-Reading and Articulation Teaching*, and Alexander Graham Bell's book, *Principles of Speech and Dictionary of Sounds*.

A few months prior to the establishment of the Clarke School in Massachusetts, a private oral school was opened in New York City, The New York Institution for the Improved Instruc-

tion of Deaf Mutes. Later the school moved from its original
Times Square location to Lexington Avenue, received partial
public support, and has been known ever since as the Lexington
Avenue School for the Deaf. David Greenberger, one of the
first principals of the school offered speechreading classes for
adults there in the early seventies. His work was followed by
that of Sarah Warren Keeler, a teacher of the same school,
who started giving speechreading lessons to adults in 1882.
Speechreading for adults was also pioneered at the Western New
York Institution for the Deaf in Rochester, New York. Adults
applied for instruction there as early as 1884 and were at first
included in the classes along with the deaf children.

2.4. *Lillie Eginton Warren*

Perhaps the best known and most influential of the early
teachers of speechreading was Lillie Eginton Warren of New
York City. Miss Warren gave frequent talks before professional
groups on speechreading and had a number of publications to
her credit.

She was highly analytic in her methods and helped to continue the confusion between the teaching of speech and speechreading. Before deciding to specialize in adult speechreading
classes, Miss Warren had been a teacher of speech correction
and had made considerable use of the Bell Visible Speech Symbols. From 1890 to 1903 she specialized in the teaching of speechreading to adults and named her school "The Warren School
of Expression Reading." One of her advertisements read in part,
"Adults growing deaf taught to read speech in the expression
of the face." In 1903 she was granted a patent for the invention
of a "means for teaching reading of the facial expressions which
occur in speaking." Her school offered personal instruction, instruction by correspondence, and normal school instruction. Her
school attracted pupils from all over the United States, and
branches of it were started in other cities. She described her
method in this fashion:[4, p. 135]

> The object of my system is to teach the learner to associate the
> elementary . . . sounds with the special expression of the human
> face which invariably accompanies the utterance of such sounds. It

includes a series of pictures of the human face in which . . . every expression is shown which the face assumes in uttering the elementary sounds used in speaking the language, and it also includes with this series of pictures a series . . . of . . . marks, . . . one for each . . . expression, each arbitrary character referring to its appropriate picture.

Her pupils were told that the "forty-odd" sounds were revealed in "sixteen outward manifestations or facial expressions." Speechreading was reduced to "a knowledge of these expressions, and ability to follow them as they appear rapidly in the face." Each student received sixteen photographs of Miss Warren. Each photograph had a number which represented a particular expression. For example the first photograph was of "the mouth more or less rounded when giving the sounds which are represented by the letters *w, wh,* long *oo* and short *oo.*" Photograph and expression number two was described in this fashion: "The mouth is elongated when giving the sounds which are represented by the letters *y,* long *e,* and short *i.*" Expressions number one and two could be combined to form words. One followed by two was the facial expression seen when someone said "we," and two followed by one, the expression when the word "you" was said.[4, p. 136]

we 1.2   you 2.1

According to Miss Warren every word could be described in this fashion. Pupils were required to practice before the mirror until they learned all of the sixteen expressions and the numbers associated with them. They were then to practice translating words into numbers and numbers into words.

Edward B. Nitchie, who was later to become the most famous and influential of all the teachers of speechreading, was originally a pupil of Miss Warren. After finishing his course of instruction, he continued on at her school as her secretary and assistant. While with her he wrote a text, *Self-Instruction in Lip-Reading.* Miss Warren was extremely angry for she felt that she must guard her methods, and she claimed that he had plagiarized them. She filed suit against him, but dropped it, discontinued her school in 1903, and went to Italy where she stayed for the remainder of her life.

2.5. *Confusions in Thinking*

The confusion between expression and reception, between speech and speechreading, was to continue for many years and never to be completely eradicated in methodology. In retrospect it appears that there were three major errors in thinking. The first was the assumption that the student must know *how* the sounds are formed. While such knowledge may be of use to the person who is learning to talk, it has scant relevance with respect to understanding what someone else is saying. The second and perhaps major error was the implicit assumption that skill in speechreading could be developed sound by sound, i.e. through a cumulative knowledge of the lip movements or articulatory positions. It was assumed that all speech sounds were visible, at least to some degree. Sounds that were not normally visible were made visible. Factors that were scarcely noted were that little sensory information is available to the speechreader, that under normal circumstances speechreading is largely a guessing game, that training in association is as important as or more important than training in visual recognition, and that there are limits to the usefulness of visual training.

The third confusion had to do with the importance of mirror practice. This idea also stemmed from the teaching of articulation. It is possible for the deaf person to monitor his speech to some extent through vision in lieu of the normal monitoring by means of hearing. But to attempt to learn to speechread others by watching oneself is comparable to trying to learn to read through reading what one has just written. Since the student knows what he is saying, the practice can scarcely be considered speechreading. But more important, to verbalize and to identify consciously certain movement patterns is to slow down the receptive process which when most efficient is eye to mind with no intervening "talking" or descriptive stage.

3. 1900–PRESENT

3.1. *Edward B. Nitchie*

The first teacher of speechreading to realize that something was wrong with the part to the whole method of teaching was

Edward B. Nitchie. It took, however, a number of years for this insight to develop.

Nitchie was born in Brooklyn, New York in 1876 and died in 1916, when he was only forty years old. He had plans to be a minister, but when he was fourteen years old he suffered a rapid loss of hearing. At first he was very despondent and, it is said, spent hours praying for death. But he managed to rally his courage. With the help of an ear trumpet he finished high school and went on to graduate from Amherst College with honors and a Phi Beta Kappa key. After college he knew the discouragement of the hearing handicapped of those years. No one wanted to employ him. Finally after months of searching for work, he was given an editorial position by the Ecumenical Council. It was while he was employed there that he heard of Miss Warren's school and became a pupil of hers.

After quarreling with Miss Warren over his first book, Nitchie left her employ and opened a school of his own. Remembering his own experience, Nitchie's idea in starting his school was to help hard-of-hearing children by tutoring them in school subjects. He had few applicants. He was finally forced to abandon this idea and focus his attention on the hard-of-hearing adult whose chief need was speechreading. He was then twenty-three, and the year was 1903.

From the beginning Nitchie was concerned with the total well-being of the hard-of-hearing—with their emotional health and their opportunities for employment as well as their speechreading skill. In 1907, he started a small magazine for them entitled *Courage,* and in 1910, the first league for the hard-of-hearing, which is still in existence and has retained its original name, The New York League for the Hard of Hearing. The original league provided lip reading scholarships, a handicraft shop, and an employment bureau. Before long additional leagues were started in almost every major city in the United States. In time they changed their names to Hearing Societies, and all became affiliates of a national organization known as The American Hearing Society. Rather recently there has occurred a reorganization and another change in name. The American Hearing Society is now called the National Association of Hearing and Speech Agencies.

From an examination of Nitchie's first text, *Self-Instruction in Lip Reading,* which caused the rift with Miss Warren, it would appear that he had indeed plagiarized her method. But in truth, *her method,* even though patented, could not be said to differ markedly from the way in which the first teachers of adult speechreading taught. The legacy of teaching speechreading in the same fashion as was then used to teach deaf children to talk was handed down from generation to generation. In any event, the changes from the Warren System were minimal. A system of using letters rather than numbers to represent the various speech sounds was instituted. The letters represent a shorthand description of either the articulatory movement or the appearance of the mouth as the sound was being said. Long *e* "revealed" as a narrow opening of the lips was symbolized as *na.* The letter *na* stood for narrow aperture; f, v were described as "lip to teeth" and designated *lt;* p, b, m as *ls* for "lip shut," etc. This was the only change made. Pupils were still expected to spend long hours before the mirror observing their own articulatory movements. They were also, as in the Warren method, expected to translate words into symbols and symbols into words. For example, assignments were given to translate excerpts from the Rubaiyat. The sentence, "Will you dine with me?" would be translated in this fashion.[4, p. 166]

Will	you	dine	with	me
so-rn-ag	rn-up	tg-wi-rn-tg	so-rn-tf	ls-na.

Additional evidence that Nitchie was not yet aware of the visual limitations of speechreading can be seen in the following exercise.[4, p. 167] Nonsensical sentences were used to illustrate differences that do not normally exist.

The bell is loud.
The bear is loud.
The pen is loud.
The Bess is loud.
The peck is loud.

This was the start, but as the years went by Nitchie gradually evolved a philosophy of teaching which was to be the reverse of his original part to whole approach. His second text, *Lessons in Lip Reading,* published in 1905, differed very little from his original text. But in its 1909 revision, beginning changes were apparent. Mirror practice was recommended, but he no longer asked pupils to "resolve words into their positions." Photographs of the various mouth positions for the vowels were retained, but those for consonants were eliminated. Nitchie noted that,[9, pp. 56, 57]

> No *movement* can be shown by a picture, hence pictures have no value as a means of practice, However, . . . vowels partake more of the nature of shapes than consonants, and those shapes can be shown by pictures. But the value of pictures is as an aid to a clearer exposition of the vowel characteristics and not at all as a means of practice.

Nitchie's writings show a steady progression in philosophy over the years from the element to the holistic approach. In 1907, in the first issue of *Courage,* he said,[4, p.169]

> The modern method of teaching a child to read is to begin with words and sentences: i.e., with ideas and not with the alphabet. So the most approved method of teaching lip-reading to adults begins with a training of the mind to grasp ideas.

Nitchie's inspiration was derived from Mrs. Alexander Graham Bell (Mabel Hubbard) for it was she, a skilled speechreader, who first made it abundantly clear *how* it was possible to speechread. In an address before the American Association to Promote the Teaching of Speech to the Deaf held in 1894 she had said,[4, pp. 147, 148]

> Speechreading is the systematized result of practice:
>
> I. In selecting the right word from a large assortment of possible words presented to the eye.
>
> II. In the power of grasping the meaning of what is said as a whole, from possibly a few words, or from parts of those words recognized here and there.
>
> Speechreading is essentially an intellectual exercise; the mechanical part performed by the eye . . . is entirely subsidiary.
>
> The aim of the speech-reader should be to grasp a speaker's meaning as a complete whole, and not attempt to decipher it word by word or even sentence by sentence.

Nitchie acknowledged his debt to her in these words,[4, p. 148]

> Mrs. Alexander Graham Bell, in her address before the Fourth
> Summer Meeting, emphasized the value to a speech-reader of
> the power of grasping the meaning of what is said as a whole . . .

> Mrs. Bell was one of the first, if not the first, to recognize the
> need of synthetic and intensive training in lip-reading, and I
> owe her a real debt of gratitude for the clues she gave me in
> working out my methods, and this I have acknowledged by
> dedicating one of my books to her.

By 1912 in his last text, *Lip-Reading Principles and Practices*,
he was ready to set forth the basis of his improved method and
said,[4, p. 168]

> Thought is quicker than speech . . . Thought looks ahead and
> anticipates . . . The method of mind training should aim to
> develop the power of grasping thoughts as wholes.

In this same text he made clear the difficulties and limitations
inherent in speechreading and stressed the importance of "mind
training." Nitchie trained over one hundred teachers as well as
countless hard-of-hearing pupils. After his death his school was
carried on by his wife, Elizabeth Helm Nitchie.

She is also responsible for the 1919 and 1930 revisions of the
1912 text. Finally in 1930 she wrote a new text following the
general plan and principles made explicit in her husband's book
but making all sentences conversational. (Nitchie, E.H.: *New
Lessons in Lip Reading*. Philadelphia and New York, Lippincott.)

The hard-of-hearing owe a great debt of gratitude to Nitchie
for his clear perception of the importance of training in association and his recognition that speechreading requires more of the
individual than the identification of a series of lip and tongue
movements. He established the philosophical foundation and
premises on which modern speechreading instruction is based.

Nitchie was aware of the sensory limitations and pointed out
that "the difficulties for the eyes to overcome are two: First, the
obscurity of many of the movements, and second, the rapidity
of their formation."[10, p. 26] He knew that one speech sound movement often alters the appearance of a preceding or following

movement and said that, "With such difficulties as these, the wonder is that anyone can read the lips at all."[10, p.27] He believed that both the eyes and mind must be trained, but in view of the visual limitations imposed on the speechreader that mind training was the more important factor. By "mind-training," he meant training and practice in "grasping the thought as a whole," whereby the mind fills in much of the information that cannot be seen, and training in being "set for" and anticipating what may follow on the basis of the situation, subject of the conversation, etc. He pointed out that, while it is not possible for the eye to see each movement, that it is possible for the mind to grasp a complete impression, without being conscious that it has "supplied" so many of the movements and sounds, and indeed that the speechreader need not even be aware of all of the words. He felt that the ". . . type of mind which is uniformly most successful (in learning to speechread) . . . is a mind which is quick to respond to impressions, or quick in its reaction time, and a mind in which the synthetic qualities are dominant."[10, p. 28] Poor speechreaders, he believed, are apt to demand verbal accuracy and to have a type of mind that is literal, analytical, and unimaginative. Nitchie listed three requisites for a method of teaching speechreading.[10, p. 27]

> The method should aim first always to study or see the movements in words or sentences, not formed singly by themselves. Sounds pronounced singly all tend to be exaggerated, and many of them even to be grossly mispronounced . . . In the second place the method should aim always to study or see the movements as the words are pronounced quickly. It is true that it would be easier to see them when spoken slowly, but it is also true that to produce the best results the eye should be trained from the first to see things as they must always be seen in ordinary speech, and that is rapidly. And, in the third place, the method should aim to inculcate a nearly infallible accuracy and quickness of perception of the easier movements, leaving to the mind in large measure the task of supplying the harder movements.

Nitchie felt that, "most of us, however analytical, have some synthetic powers, some ability of putting things together, of constructing the whole from the parts, of quick intuition," and that ". . . by developing these powers . . . real success in lip read-

ing can be attained."[10, p. 29] The Nitchie Method makes use of
stories, i.e. humorous anecdotes, as well as sentences, to effect
"mind training," but sentences are the primary tool. Pupils are
not permitted to interrupt the instructor when they fail to catch
a word or a phrase and are encouraged not to give up but to
continue watching.[10, p. 39]

> . . . the student should be trained from the first to grasp the
> thought as a whole. Sentence and story work will develop this power
> if given in the right way. The student should not be permitted to
> interrupt until a sentence, or a complete thought, is finished, thus
> training the mind to continue working instead of stopping as soon
> as something is not understood, for often the sentence, or the idea,
> will come "in a flash" before the sentence is finished. In conver-
> sation there is not time to stop and either think back or ask what
> has been said, and so the *mind must be trained to continue to
> follow the speaker.*

Sentences that are unrelated in thought content are considered
to be particularly valuable because they give practice in one
of the things most difficult for a speechreader, the following
of a conversation when the subject changes without warning.
Elizabeth Helm Nitchie stressed the importance of using voice
in giving instruction and warned the speaker against mouthing,
breaking rhythm, and repeating single words in talking to the
hard-of-hearing.

3.1.1 DESCRIPTION AND CRITICISM OF NITCHIE METHOD. While
we are profoundly grateful to Edward B. Nitchie for his many
insights into the problems of the hearing handicapped and his
clear perception of the importance of associational training, we
are bound to be disappointed when we examine the actual teaching materials. There appears to be a wide disparity between
philosophy and implementation. Or perhaps a fairer statement
would be to the effect that his insights were implemented with
respect to materials to a very limited extent.

Chiefly they resulted in the elimination of mirror work designed
to teach recognition of sounds in isolation. The appearance of
the sounds was still to be studied but in words rather than in
isolation. Practice was to consist of watching oneself in the mirror
saying a particular movement as it occurred in a series of words.

This shift from the sound in isolation to the sound in words, or from "position" to "movement" as it was called, was considered to be a fundamental change. It was recognized that appearances were not static but fluid and that sounds might look different in words than in isolation. It is possible that Nitchie was influenced by the Mueller-Walle System which lays much stress on the change in appearance of the various sounds because of transition. Miss Bruhn had opened a school to teach the Mueller-Walle System a year before Nitchie opened his own school. Other improvements in methodology consisted of the elimination of artificial sentences that had been created through loading with a particular sound movement and of sentences requiring impossibly fine visual discrimination.

Nitchie clearly perceived that "mind-training" could not be developed from "eye-training," but was a separate sort of skill, and had said,[9, p. 81]

> Lip-reading as an art comprises fundamentally two different kinds of skill: (1) the ability to recognize quickly the sound and word formations as shown by the visible organs of speech, and (2) the ability to grasp the thought of the speaker.

But in examining the actual practice materials we find that this distinction became obscured. In the 1912 exposition of his method we find that mind-training was in part separated from and preceded eye-training. The lesson was to start with a *story* which was followed by a *conversation*. In later revisions, however, the conversations were eliminated and finally the stories were used as a supplementary rather than a basic part of the lesson unit. Because the stories were not rewritten for easy association of ideas, they proved to be too difficult. To obviate this difficulty pupils were instructed to read the story in advance of the speechreading lesson in which it was to be presented. The chief difficulties with the material, however, lie not with the order of presentation or whether stories are considered to be fundmental or a supplementary part of the lesson. They would appear to be twofold and consist of (a) the failure to develop good associational materials and (b) the attempt to stress one sound movement at a time and to base a lesson or a unit around each movement.

In doing the latter, sentence work which is considered to be primarily "mind training" material is not separated from but evolves out of the materials designed for "eye training." Each sentence contains one of the *practice words* for the movement being studied that day. As a consequence two things occur: (a) the sentences are often studied rather than conversational, and (b) the practice words often do not give useful clues to the meaning of the sentences. No provision is made for association of ideas, either through the use of words that are truly clues to the meaning of the sentences or through the use of related sentences. The lesson format consists of a description of each movement followed by practice words which are in turn the clue words for the unrelated sentences to follow. This lesson format, it should be noted, is not very different from that used by Sarah Fuller, one of the first teachers of adult speechreading classes, which was described earlier in this chapter. Additional sentences for each clue word are provided in the revised texts, but they do not expand or restate the idea expressed in the original sentence. Apparently they were designed with the severely hard-of-hearing or deaf child in mind, and if used with these groups, may serve to enlarge word connotations. Each sentence of a group contains the practice word, but in each it is used in a different connotation. In addition, practice is given in the recognition of homophenous words through context and of idiomatic expressions or adages. *The assumption that one can build speechreading skill from part to whole is implicit in the materials though denied in the text.* Perhaps if Nitchie had lived longer we would have seen a closer merging of philosophy and materials, rather than the sharp discrepancy which is evident today. Excerpts from a typical lesson are as follows:[10, pp. 69-72]

Short e—Extended—Medium

For the sound of short *e*, as in "get," the lips are slightly extended at the corners, and the opening between the lips is neither narrow nor wide, but medium.

Movement Words
peat-pet-heap-hep
beet-bet-eeb-eb
meet-met-team-hem

Practice Words

mend	led
bell	melt
fell	tell
well	
rest	etc.

Sentences

(Four for each practice word, e.g., those for "melt.")
1. The story you told would melt a heart of stone.
2. It was so hot in the sun I though I would melt.
3. You should melt the butter before making the sauce.
4. The ice in the river will melt rapidly in this weather.

Homophenous Words

Elm, helm, help
There is a large elm tree in front of the house.
You may take the helm of the boat for awhile.
How much help will you need to finish the work?

Idiomatic Expressions and Adages

Penny: The tramp hasn't a penny to bless his name.
Men: You'll have to wait for dead men's shoes in that company.
End: Both countries will fight to the bitter end.

With respect to "eye-training" the materials can actually be said to be in *advance* of the philosophy. It is assumed that it is necessary for the speechreader to understand *how* he recognizes the various speech sounds, and a description of each movement is presented. Association of the appearance of speech sounds with the sounds is first made conscious though the aim is to make such associations unconscious through much practice. But as additional movements are introduced, the movement words become, in fact, contrast words, e.g., *pack, fag, whack*, which are alike except for one sound movement. Because of these movement words the Nitchie materials permit the establishment of unconscious recognition from the first. It becomes possible to fix the appearance of the movements from "eye to mind" through visual contrast rather than verbal analysis and identification.

In the Nitchie system the speech movements are classified

with respect to their visible appearance. The consonants are divided into four groups (pp. 46–48, "New Lessons") as follows:

 I. Those formed and revealed by the lips.
   (a) P, b, m—Lips Shut.
   (b) F, v—Lips to Teeth.
   (c) Wh and w—Puckered—Variable.
 II. Those formed by the tongue and revealed by the lips.
   (a) R—Puckered Corners.
   (b) S, z—Extended—Narrow.
   (c) Sh, zh, ch, j—Lips Projected.
 III. Those formed and revealed by the tongue.
   (a) Th—Tongue to Teeth.
   (b) L—Pointed Tongue to Gum.
   (c) T, d, n—Flat Tongue to Gum.
 IV. Those revealed by the context.
   (a) Y—Relaxed—Narrow.
   (b) K, g—Throat Movement
   (c) H—No Movement (Aspirate).

The vowels were classified with respect to the appearance of the lips, "puckered," "relaxed," or "extended," and the width of the mouth opening, whether "narrow," "medium," or "wide."

Width of Opening	Shape of Lips		
	Puckered	Relaxed	Extended
Narrow	Long $\overline{oo}$ (coon)	Short ĭ (kid)	Long ē (keen)
Medium	Short ŏŏ (good)	Short ŭ (cut)	Short ĕ (get)
Wide	Aw (caw)	Ah (cart)	Short ă (cat)

Diphthongs were categorized with respect to the final movement.[10, pp. 46-48]

 1. Those with a puckered final movement.
   (a) Ow as in "how." Relaxed-Wide, followed by a puckered movement.
   (b) Long ō as in "go." Contracting puckered movement.
   (c) Long ū as in "mute." Relaxed-Narrow and Puckered-Narrow.
 2. Those with relaxed and narrow final movement.
   (a) Long ī, as in "pipe." Relaxed-Wide and Relaxed-Narrow.
   (b) Long ā, as in "late." Extended-Medium and Relaxed-Narrow.
   (c) Oy, as in "boy." Puckered-Wide and Relaxed-Narrow.

3.1.2 SUMMARY—NITCHIE METHOD. As was stated earlier, Nitchie established the philosophical foundations and premises on which modern speechreading instruction is based. His philosophy stressed the separation of associational materials from those designed for eye-training and more emphasis being placed on training in association than on training for visibility. But unfortunately his materials do not follow his philosophy. The associational materials consist only of series of *unrelated* sentences and of short stories that are written for reading rather than for conversation. The sentence materials are based on the various movements and evolve from the eye-training materials rather than being separated from them.

3.2. Martha E. Bruhn—The Mueller-Walle Method of Lipreading

One of the important teachers of speechreading of the early years of the twentieth century was Martha E. Bruhn. Miss Bruhn was a foreign language teacher in a Boston high school when she became aware of having increasing difficulty with her hearing. At first she attended the speechreading classes taught by Mary Alice Porter and later took lessons at the Boston branch of the Warren School. Her progress was, however, far from encouraging. When she read in a German newspaper that a man named Julius Mueller-Walle was offering adult lip-reading classes in Hamburg, Germany, she decided to go to Europe to take his course. Mueller-Walle had originally been a teacher of deaf children, but had given it up in order to concentrate on the teaching of speechreading to hard-of-hearing adults. Miss Bruhn first studied with him for six weeks, and then, since he encouraged her to open up a school of her own in the United States, returned to Germany again for his "normal course." Finally in September, 1902, a year ahead of Nitchie, she opened her first school in Boston, but did not publish a text until 1915. The school was to continue in operation for over twenty-five years. It was called the Mueller-Walle School of Lip-Reading and the Mueller-Walle Training School for Teachers. Miss Bruhn wrote three texts on speechreading. They were *The Mueller-Walle Method of Lip-Reading for the Deaf*, Lynn, Massachusetts, The Nichols Press, 1924 (originally published in 1915); *Elementary Lessons in Lip-Reading, The Mueller-Walle Method,* Lynn, Massachusetts, The Nichols Press, 1927, and the most recent, *The Mueller-Walle Method of Lip Reading for the Hard of Hearing,* Boston, Leavis, 1947.

The second text, listed above, *Elementary Lessons in Lip-Reading,* is the first text to be published for use with the hard-of-hearing child enrolled in a regular classroom.

3.2.1 DESCRIPTION AND CRITICISM OF MUELLER-WALLE METHOD. In the Mueller-Walle System speech sounds are categorized with respect to their visible characteristics, and lessons are based upon a sound movement or a group of sound movements. Consonants are divided into two classes. Class I includes those consonants with the *cavity of the mouth closed.* Class II includes those consonants with the *cavity of the mouth open.* Within each category the sounds are described with respect to their appearance, e.g., /f/ and /v/ "the lower lip is placed against the upper teeth;" and for /m/, /b/, and /p/, "the lips are closed.[2, p. 20] Vowels are considered to have four principal movements. "The lower jaw moves downward and upward. The lips move forward and backward."[2, p. 19] All of the Class I consonants are introduced in the first lesson. They are f, v; s, z; p, b, m; w, wh; sh; and th. These sounds constitute *all of the visible consonant movements.* Five vowels are also introduced in the first lesson. They are ah, ō, o͞o, ā, ē (IPA: a, oʊ, u, eɪ, i). Vowels are considered, in general, to be more visible than consonants and hence . . . "the most important part of the word."[2, p. 20] Syllables are made by combining the consonant and vowel sounds. Only such syllables as can be found in words in the English language are included. As additional sounds or groups of sounds are introduced in succeeding lessons, they are combined with sounds previously introduced. Eye training is effected through the use of syllable drill. Each consonant is first practiced in combination with each vowels sound, e.g., fä, fō, fo͞o, fā, fē, and sä, sō, so͞o, sä, sē. Finally the syllables are put together providing consonant as well as vowel contrast and are given in groups of two or three, e.g., fä-mä; sō-fa; sē-mē-sō; mä-sē-mē; etc.[2, p. 21] Originally mirror-practice was recommended, but this was deleted in later editions. Rapid, rhythmic syllable drills form the basis of the method and are the framework upon which sentences are built.

An example of a syllable drill used for eye training and leading to a meaningful sentence is given below[*][2, p. 22]

mā mō	Sho me
mā sō	Show me the way.
mā sē	Show me the way to the shop.
mā thā	Show me the way to the sea.
thā shō	

Note that syllables that are not truly "nonsense" syllables are written as though they were, until put into sentence form. Additional simple sentences are, for the most part, based upon words that can be formed from the sounds introduced in the lesson and in previous lessons. To illustrate some additional sentences from Lesson I are as follows:[2, p. 24]

Show me the way to the sea.
Show me the path to the beach.
May we bathe in the sea?
May we see the fish in the sea?
You may pass the beef to Sue.
You may pass the beef soup to May.
You may pass the fish to me.

Note the use of the "add a word" or "add a phrase" technique illustrated above. The stem of the sentence is repeated, and a new phrase or ending is added on in each instance. Bruhn appears to be the first instructor to use this technique. Later we see liberal use made of it in the materials of the Kinzie sisters and of Morkovin and Moore.

As in the Nitchie system, the pupil is first told *how* he speech-

---

* Dr. Donald Moores of the University of Minnesota has pointed out that the syllabic structure of the English language is very complicated and does not consist solely of CV (consonant-vowel) units. English syllables can consist of such combinations as CVC, *make*; CCV, *dry*; CCVCC, *drink*, etc. For this reason an attempt to develop speechreading skill by building from the syllable to the word to the phrase would appear to be unrealistic. (Personal correspondence with the authors.)

reads, i.e. the visible appearance of each movement. He then is given sufficient practice in actual speechreading to enable him to forget this conscious analysis and recognize sound movements without thinking about what he is doing.

By trying to base the lessons around a limited number of sound movements, the Mueller-Walle Method ends up with lesson material that is usually highly visible, but despite this, often difficult to speechread. The difficulty stems from the fact that sentences that are artificially constructed to meet the criteria are often not functional. Especially is this true of the sentence material of the first few lessons. One just does not often have the opportunity to say, or to speechread such sentences as the ones given above, or from Lesson II:[2, p. 26]

> They may bow to you.
> Sue may bow to them.
> I may buy the vase for my wife.
> The mouse found the pie.

One of the most useful Mueller-Walle techniques is the exercise story given perfunctory treatment in the latest text. The "exercise" portion consists of a series of sentences presented prior to the story which serve to introduce the story and establish a mental set which will enable the speechreader to anticipate the vocabulary. The instructions are as follows:[2, p. 11]

> Lead up to the story by short colloquial sentences. These sentences should contain prominent words in the story and should give the clue to the subject. Then tell the story without interruption and finally ask questions to be sure the thought of the story is understood.

The Mueller-Walle Method recognizes the importance of the use of voice in teaching speechreading and the help that accrues to the speechreader through rhythmic and kinesthetic clues. In the early stages of learning to lip-read it is recommended that the student be held to word for word repetition in order to train the eyes for accuracy. It is recognized that at a later stage this practice would not be desirable or necessary.

3.2.2 SUMMARY MUELLER-WALLE SYSTEM. As in the Nitchie

System, the order of teaching is analytical and from the part to the whole. Eye training is effected through contrasting syllables, but the syllables are restricted to the sound combinations found in the English language. Training in association is not separated from eye training. Sentences evolve out of the syllables designed for eye training. Because of this limitation and because of the further restriction that sounds not yet introduced in the course of study may not be used to form new words, the sentences of the first few lessons are stilted, unnatural, and for the most part, nonfunctional.

There is no clear cut separation of eye training and mind training. Nonetheless, training in association is provided for. Numerous techniques designed to build association are exemplified. Such techniques include the use of "add a phrase" groups of sentences that are related in thought content and the use of an exercise, i.e. a group of sentences to introduce a story.

3.3. Cora Elsie and Rose Kinzie—The Kinzie Method

Cora Kinzie was a student at the Women's Medical College of Pennsylvania and had planned to become a medical missionary when she became aware of a gradually increasing hearing loss. At first she studied lipreading under Martha Bruhn with the hope of becoming adept enough to permit the finishing of her course of study. However, when it became apparent that she was losing hearing in her "good ear" as well, she gave up the idea of becoming a medical missionary and decided to teach speechreading. After studying a year with Miss Bruhn, she opened a branch school in Philadelphia in 1914. She was also curious about the possibilities of the Nitchie System and so took one day a week off from her work to commute to New York and study under Nitchie. In time, her sister Rose joined her in her work. After studying under Nitchie, Miss Kinzie became convinced that the best way to teach speechreading was to combine what she considered to be the best features of the two systems. From Nitchie she took the philosophical and psychological premises, and from Bruhn, the Mueller-Walle classification of sounds and their order of introduction. In 1917 the Kinzie sisters changed the name of their school to the Kinzie School of Speech-Reading. They also started a Speech-Reading Club whose membership at its peak was close to nine hundred. In 1924 they were to sell their school and spend their time from then until 1929 in developing a graded system of speechreading. The first two grades are for children. Grade III is intended for juniors and grade V for the deafened adult.

3.3.1 DESCRIPTION OF THE KINZIE METHOD. The Kinzie sisters were the first to develop materials specifically for the preschool and primary school age hard-of-hearing child. In Grade I materials, no attempt is made to teach formal and analytic knowledge of speech sounds or speechreading movements. The material is clued by means of visual aids, such as objects, pictures, charts, and dramatization. Typical beginning exercises are illustrated below. The child indicates understanding through a simple motor response.[4, p. 182]

Show me the baby
Show me the mother.
Show me the baby's mouth.
Show me the mother's shoe.
Show me the mother's watch.

Show me how the birds fly.
Show me how the baby birds open their mouths.
Show me how mother holds the baby.
Show me how the baby waves his hand.
Show me how mother washes your face.
Show me how mother puts the baby to sleep.

In Grade II there is still no formal explanation of speechreading movements, but the teacher directs the childrens' attention to the formation of the particular sound or sounds under consideration in each lesson. Much variety is provided. Each lesson consists of six parts: movement words, conversational exercise, rhyme, motor exercise, sentence drill, and story exercise. Excerpts from Lesson I, Grade II are presented below.[6]

Lesson I

Long Vowel Sounds
Visible Consonants

Movement Words

baby	father	sheep	sofa
bee	face	show	save
mother	farm	shoe	soup

Conversational Exercise

Have you a baby at home?

What is your baby's name?

Can your baby walk? etc.

Rhyme

Bee, bee

Fly away

Little boys

Want to play

Motor Exercise

Once I was a baby.

A baby was I.

It was this way and that way, etc.

Story Exercise

(The sentences are read one at a time.)

The baby was in the high chair.

Mother was on the porch, etc.

With Grade III, intended for juniors, the pupil enters upon what is described as "formal, conscious speechreading instruction." The "lesson proper" is considered to consist of the speechreading movement or movements under consideration, vocabulary and sentence drills. Supplementary material consists of stories and materials for general practice—riddles, guessing games, etc.

Excerpts from Lesson I, Grade II are given below.[6]

Lesson I

Long Vowel Sounds ä ō ōō ã ē

For *ä* there is a downward movement of the jaw with wide opening.

For *ō* there is a forward movement of the lips with medium opening.

Etc.

Drill on Vowels

ä ē o͞o ā ō

ō-ē ē-o͞o ä-ō ō-ä o͞o-ä

ō-ä-ē ā-ē-o͞o ē-ō-ä o͞o-ä-ä

Visible Consonants f, v; s, soft c, z; m, p, b

For *f* and *v* the lower lip is placed against the upper teeth as in fay.

For *s*, soft *c* and *z* the teeth are brought together as in say. Etc.

Vocabulary

farm	move
face	beef
foam	palm
save	peep
same	piece

Sentence Drill

1. Have you ever been on a *farm* in the summer?
   Mother is at the farm with the baby.
2. Mother has a very happy face.
   The baby's face is as beautiful as a flower.
10. Will you have a *piece* of my orange?
    The *piece* of soap is on the shelf.

For very advanced pupils such clue words and sentences as the following were used:[4, p. 115]

Clue word.

wave

When Abraham Lincoln rose to speak at a political meeting early in his first presidential campaign, a wave of amusement swept over the audience because of his awkward appearance, but it soon became evident to many who were present that he was to be the next president of the United States.

In a formal lesson the teacher was to write the description of the speechreading movement on the board as in the Nitchie Method. The pupils were directed to read it silently, and then the teacher read it aloud to the class. Following this there was to be drill on the vocabulary words and sentences. The words were to be first given in order and then in scrambled order until their recognition had been mastered. In practicing the sentences, students were given additional clue words if one did not suffice.

Voice was used in giving instructions, but not used when presenting the actual speechreading material. Kinzie teachers were required to memorize all of their lesson material!

The Kinzies' believed that speechreading material should have intrinsic appeal, should be educational and cultural. In creating material for children one should be aware that children have strong rhythmic sense, vivid imaginations, and love for animals and for stories about other children. Excellent advice was also given with respect to story type material. Because of the limitations of speechreading, in improvising or making selections for adaptation, one must keep in mind the importance of visibility, and simplicity of ideas and sequence.

3.3.2. SUMMARY AND CRITICISM OF THE KINZIE METHOD. From the Mueller-Walle Method the Kinzies' abstracted and incorporated in their own method the "add a phrase" and exercise-story techniques and the introduction of a group of visible speechreading movements simultaneously. From Nitchie they borrowed the movement words and clue word techniques and his philosophy regarding the greater importance of "mind-training," i.e. training in the association of ideas and the grasping of thoughts as a whole, over eye training.

The Kinzie sisters are to be credited with producing much excellent associational type material for use with pre-school and school-age children. They used a variety of techniques, designed their materials for ease in viewing, and incorporated in them much that holds interest and appeal for the child. They made good use of the Mueller-Walle "add a phrase" and exercise-story techniques. In addition they introduced valuable new techniques of their own, such as the conversational exercise, the rewriting of stories and riddles for easy association, and the use of dramatization and simple rhythmic poems. It is only when they introduce "formal, conscious, speechreading instruction" at the junior and adult levels that their materials tend to become stilted. As with

Nitchie, because their clue words are illustrative of a particular sound or speechreading movement, they are often just one of the words in the sentence to follow and hence are often an insufficient or inappropriate clue to the content. Apparently they too believed that it was necessary for the pupil to know "how" he recognized the various sounds and that it was possible to combine eye-training practice with practice in association. Evidently it did not occur to them that most adults without prior training and most children trained in their holistic approach would have unconsciously learned to associate speech sounds with movement.

Another criticism of the Kinzie Method is their failure to coordinate vision and hearing in their teaching. They stipulate that no voice should be used in giving speechreading instruction.

3.4. Anna M. Bunger—The Jena Method

Miss Bunger was for many years an instructor in the Department of Special Education, Michigan State Normal College, at Ypsilanti, Michigan. In 1926 when she and Bessie L. Whitaker were in charge of the classes in speechreading for adults, they were first made aware of the Jena Method. Professor Jacob Reighard, of the University of Michigan, himself a skilled speechreader, had translated two booklets by Karl Brauckmann and presented the translations to them for consideration. Brauckmann, who headed a private school in Jena, Germany, had been in the process of developing his method since around 1900 and had published the booklets in 1925. Miss Whitaker and Miss Bunger started using the Brauckmann Method in their classes in 1927. The method is known as the Jena Method in the United States because of the fact that Miss Bunger labeled her first text, published in 1932, and subsequent revisions of it as *Speech Reading—Jena Method.*

3.4.1 Description of the Jena Method. The Jena Method differs from the Nitchie and Mueller-Walle methods in a number of important respects. In the first place, the description and classification of consonant sounds is based not on their visible appearance, but on their formation.

They are classified with respect to whether the primary movement is of the lips, tongue, or tongue-soft palate. The classification is present in table form as follows:[3, p. 19]

Lips	Tongue	Tongue-Soft Palate
b	d	g
p	t	k
v	z, zh, j	y-
f	s, sh, ch	
m	n	-ng, -nk
w-	r	
wh-	th (thin)	h-
	th (father)	

The vowels are not described, but a basic vowel order is *memorized*.[3, p. 12] It is the following: IPA: eɪ, i, oʊ, ɑ, ɔ, ɛ, ʊ, æ, ju, ɑʊ, ɑɪ, ɔɪ, ʊ, ɪ, ʌ, ɝ.

Like Nitchie and Mueller-Walle, eyetraining is accomplished through syllable drill. Unlike them, the pupil is expected to speak in unison with the instructor and to imitate his lip and jaw movements. At the same time he is imitating, he is to concentrate on the kinesthetic sensations which he experiences. The vowel sounds are combined with the various consonant sounds, presented and imitated in one of the four basic rhythms of speech. The four rhythms are (1) first syllable accented, second unaccented; (2) first syllable unaccented; second accented; (3) first three syllables unaccented, fourth syllable accented; (4) first two syllables unaccented, third syllable accented. Examples of the four rhythms in order would be:[3, pp. 60, 61]

(1) Péter, Péter, púmpkin eáter.
(2) The mousé ran uṕ the clock.
(3) Baking a pié.
(4) If I gó it will bé in the fall.

According to Brauckman, speech has five forms.[3, p. 10]

1. The movement form,—the total of all movements made by the speech organs, or the complete physiological process.

2. The audible form,—the sound effect which corresponds in every detail to the complete movement form.
3. The visible form,—the movements of the speech organs which are visible to the watcher.
4. The mimetic form,—facial expression, the glance of the eye, the smile, the frown, the nod or shake of the head, posture attitudes; any bodily movement timed with the words in order to give a clue or to clarify meaning; a visible phenomenon.
5. Gesture,—primarily arm and hand movements used for emphasis; a visible accompaniment of speech closely bound up with meaning and rhythm.

It is pointed out that the "movement form" is the only form of speech, other than the audible form which is complete. And it is hypothesized that if a man without hearing could in some way become aware of all the movements of speech, he could understand as well as though he heard. The way to effect this knowledge is through imitation. Once the speechreader has had ample practice in talking along with the speaker while focusing his attention on his kinesthetic and tactile sensations, it is assumed that when he watches without talking that he will make subliminal movements and that the accompanying sensations will aid him in understanding what the speaker is saying.

In earlier editions of the Jena Method, the student was led directly from syllable practice to speechreading of conversation built around a simple topic or a simple story. In the most recent edition, practice is given in the imitation of numbers, words, common phrases, etc., before or along with the introduction of context material.

3.4.2 CRITICISM OF JENA METHOD. The Jena Method might be categorized as "The Talking Way to Speechreading." Close observation of the speaker's lip and jaw movements is assured by the requirement that the pupil talk along with the speaker. The importance of kinesthetic sensations to the comprehension of speech has not been established. It is obviously true that the speechreader can imitate only that portion of the message that he *can see or hear*, the same information that he gets without imitation. Moreover, he is just as apt to make errors as the non-imitator, if he imitates a message incorrectly. And he has the same job of mentally filling in information which he can neither see or hear. Probably the best that can be said in defense of this procedure is that it is good speech training and may be a useful tool in a combined approach if one is attempting to teach speech conservation or speech correction along with speechreading. There is also no evidence to support the analytic approach to teaching the rhythm of speech as an aid to speechreading. There is no question but what the speechreader is to a considerable degree dependent upon the rhythm and stress pattern of the language and has real difficulty in understanding if the speaker breaks this normal pattern. He expects the pattern because he knows the language; he does not have to be taught what it is. The analytic approach to rhythm may be helpful in teaching profoundly deaf children to *speak,* but perhaps is of little value in teaching them to speechread.

3.5. *Morkovin-Moore—Life Situation Speech Reading*

3.5.1 DESCRIPTION OF METHOD. This method of teaching speechreading, first developed in 1938, was the joint effort of Boris V. Morkovin of the University of Southern California and Lucelia M. Moore who was herself severely hard of hearing. The units for instruction are filmed conversations such as might emerge from *life situations.* A hearing handicapped person, in their view, if he is to learn to follow conversation, must make use of a number of senses and must make simultaneous progress in a number of directions.[8, p. iv] He needs to develop situational insight, language proficiency, ability to piece together fragments of words, ability to substitute visual for auditory cues, and ability to gain information from kinesthetic and rhythmic cues. This "cooperation of the senses," essential to skill in speechreading, can be expressed by the letters AVKR, which stand for auditory, visual, kinesthetic, rhythmic sensory integration. Titles of some of the earlier life situation films are "The Family Dinner," "At the Bank, "At the Grocery Store, "At the Service Station," etc. The more recent films are based more closely on the interests of children. Some of these titles are "Bow Belinda" (teaching of a folk dance), "Barbara's New Shoes," "The Cowboy," "Magic," "Tommy's Table Manners," etc. The movies are usually shown at least three times. The student is asked to focus his attention on the whole situation the first time, on the "detailed parts of incidents" the second time, and "on the lip movements" the third time.[8, p. vii]

Following the showing of the movies, questions are asked about motivation, situation, setting, etc., but not about script, e.g., from "The Family Dinner," "What did they have for dessert?" After the second showing, questions are asked to discover if the pupils followed the dialogue, e.g., "Name the three things Martha wanted her Dad to give her." After viewing the film for the third time, pupils are asked questions to bring out knowledge of exact vocabulary, e.g., "Which did Mother say: (a) 'Robert, forget your airplane' *or* (b) 'Robert, put away your airplane.' "[8, pp. 3-5]

Each script is intended to emphasize certain speech sounds. Following the script for the movie and questions related to it are additional exercises designed for auditory training, visual or eye training, and kinesthetic-rhythmic training, and vocabulary expansion. The Morkovin-Moore System proceeds from the whole to the part, but does not neglect the "part."

3.5.2 CRITICISM OF MORKOVIN-MOORE SYSTEM. The Morkovin-Moore System would appear to be the logical way to train for skill in speechreading. Since the mind must fill in much missing information, the topic or situational approach should be used from the beginning lesson. The speechreader speechreads conversation; hence, conversations deriving from common every day situations would appear to be most appropriate. It is doubtful, if this approach were used, that there would be much need for specific training in recognizing individual speech movements. Nonetheless, such materials are provided and can be used by the teacher if he deems it desirable. The major adverse criticism of the Morkovin-Moore System has to do not with the philosophy, but with the *materials*. The scripts for the older movies cannot for the most part be used independently of the movies. One is dependent upon the movies to understand the action and the conversation evolving from it. The materials do not provide a graded approach from easy to more difficult associations. One of the problems would appear to be that the topics or life-situations that are portrayed are too general to permit one to anticipate the dialogue. The movies themselves are old, technically poor, and the scenes often contrived rather than natural. The newer films suffer from many of the defects of the original ones. While they are technically excellent and available in color, the articulatory movements are often so minimal or so rapid as to make speechreading almost impossible. As with the original the situational clues are of very little help in anticipating the conversation of the characters involved. No manual has been published to accompany the newer films and only one lesson has been developed in detail.

REFERENCES

1. Bender, R.E.: *The Conquest of Deafness*. Cleveland, Ohio, The Press of the Western Reserve University, 1960.
2. Bruhn, M.E.: *The Mueller-Walle Method of Lip-Reading for the Hard of Hearing, Seventh Edition*. Washington, D.C., The Volta Bureau, 1955.
3. Bunger, A.M.: *Speechreading—Jena Method*. Danville, Illinois, The Interstate Press, 1961.
4. DeLand, F.: *The Story of Lip-Reading, Its Genesis and Development*. Washington, D.C., The Volta Bureau, 1931. (Revised and completed by Montague, H.A.)
5. DeLand, F.: An ever continuing memorial. *Volta Review*, 1923.
6. Kinzie, C.E., and Kinzie, R.: *Lipreading for Children*. Seattle, 1929.
7. Kinzie, C.E.: The Kinzie method of speech reading. *Volta Review, 22*: 609–19, 1920.
8. Morkovin, B.V., and Moore, L.M.: *Life Situation Speech-Reading Through the Cooperation of the Senses, A.V.K.R. Method*. University of Southern California, Los Angeles, 1948.
9. Nitchie, E.B.: *Lip-Reading Principles and Practise*. New York, Frederick A. Stokes Co., 1912.
10. Nitchie, E.H.: *New Lessons in Lip Reading*. Philadelphia and New York, Lippincott, 1950.

Chapter 4

THE PROCESS OF SPEECHREADING ORGANIZATION AND EVALUATION OF RESEARCH FINDINGS WITH RESPECT TO A THEORETICAL MODEL

1. INTRODUCTION

Speechreading has been taught for many years—for over one hundred years in the United States alone and for three or more centuries in Europe. Despite all of this experience in teaching and in learning, there has been relatively little interest in research in the area. Undoubtedly a number of reasons account for the paucity of the research literature. For one, teachers are more concerned with teaching than with research and with results than with theory. They are not usually willing to work with control groups and to subject students to an "inferior" approach to determine if in fact it really is inferior. A second and perhaps principal reason for the shortage of research literature may be the complexity of the subject matter. Many factors are believed to affect the acquisition of speechreading skill: visual acuity, memory, synthetic ability, language proficiency, motivation, to name only a few. It is extremely difficult, if not impossible, to study one variable while controlling all others. Research has not been as productive as one might wish it could have been. Consequently, a general air of discouragement pervades the literature. As Reid[37, p. 82] has said, "Knowledge of the phenomenon of lip reading appears to be a sort of will-o-the-wisp that eludes objective study."

Much of the early research was an outgrowth of attempts to develop tests of speechreading for deaf children (Pintner, 1929,[35] Heiders', 1940,[22] Utley, 1945,[43] and Reid, 1947[37]) and

114

was done in a search for criteria to be used in establishing norms (i.e. average performance for age, intelligence, grade level, reading, achievement, etc.) that would permit standardization of the tests. In order to standardize a test it is necessary to find some other measure (such as one of those indicated above) that is so closely associated with the skill one is attempting to measure that it is possible to predict performance on the test in question from the extraneous measure. One measure must vary or change with a change in the second measure.

One would expect to find a high correlation between silent reading and educational achievement in either a normal or deaf population. Utley,[43] for example, found a correlation of .912, P.E. .007 between reading and total achievement for a group of 207 deaf children. This is high enough to permit the prediction of reading skill from achievement and vice versa. And if one *ignores* the visual limitations of speechreading and *assumes* that it is as good an avenue for the acquisition of knowledge as silent reading, one would expect to find high correlations between speechreading and such indirect indices of language attainment as reading level, educational achievement, and grade placement, and respectable, though not necessarily high, correlations with factors that are bound to affect learning, such as age, intelligence, extent of loss, age at which loss was incurred, years in school, and emotional adjustment.

Since speechreading is the main vehicle used in instructing the deaf child (trained orally) and in establishing a knowledge of language, it was mistakenly assumed that a strong relationship should exist between it and indirect measures of either language comprehension or training. There was, however, a major fallacy in this kind of thinking which was not immediately apparent. *Because of its visual limitations, speechreading is not a good avenue for the acquisition of language, and a high degree of skill is not available to everyone.*

The hypothesis that it should be possible to predict speechreading skill from measurements of learning or training was repostulated by both Utley[43] and Reid,[37] notwithstanding the fact that prior research by Pintner[35] and Heider and Heider[22] had indicated that a predictive relationship did not exist. The idea that a high degree of association should exist has died hard because of its *apparent* reasonableness and the desirability of having a standardized test. It was thought that strong relationships had not emerged because of deficiencies in test design, such as inadequate measures of speechreading skill (Pintner's view) or too few subjects used in the experimental studies. When "facts" defy "logic," the facts are often disregarded and new facts sought to establish the logic of the situation. Yet there were other "facts," the "facts" of experience that clearly showed that expert speechreaders were "born, not made." Teachers of speechreading have always been aware of the marked individual differences in their pupils' ability to master the skill, differences that could not be explained away by such factors as motivation, length of training, type of training, intelligence, mastery of language, or other variables that often account for differences in learning in subject matter areas.

Both Kitson, 1915[27] and Nitchie, 1917[31] believed that there was some "mental ability or combination of mental abilities" at the basis of speechreading and that the ultimate analysis of the abilities involved was a task for psychological experimentation. They suggested the possible importance of concentration, visual memory, and intuitive reasoning.

But it was not until 1951 and thereafter that many research workers heeded these words. The turning point with respect to thinking about factors that influence speechreading ability appears to have occurred following the research of Utley and Reid in 1945 and 1947. Utley's monumental work is probably especially important in this respect. Her speechreading test had a high degree of internal reliability and was given to a very large number (761) of deaf and hard-of-hearing individuals. Correlations *high enough to permit prediction* were not found between her test and reading level, school achievement, chronological age, age of onset, or grade placement. It had finally been established to almost everyone's satisfaction that speechreading was not highly correlated with indices of language comprehension or training and that skill could not be predicted from such measures. Since then research workers have turned their attention more and more in the direction that Nitchie originally suggested, toward an investigation of the relationship between speechreading and specific visual and mental aptitudes that might reasonably account for the wide differences that are found with respect to speechreading proficiency.

Despite this trend, the total picture is still one of confusion. The same factor has often been found to be associated with speechreading in some research studies, but not in others. Because there have been so many conflicting reports with respect to the various factors studied, the reader has difficulty sorting what is known from what is not known and arriving at a coherent picture. But in reviewing the literature, there was a growing awareness on the part of the writer that more was actually known about the acquisition of speechreading skill than had been emphasized in the summaries of research or in the experimental literature, itself. It was noted that, *because predictive relationships had not been established, significant relationships were often ignored or minimized by the very research workers themselves.*

2. DEVELOPMENT OF A THEORETICAL CONSTRUCT

It occurred to us that much of the confusion was due to the failure of theorists to relate the many factors or subskills believed important in the development of speechreading skill and to develop a hypothetical construct with respect to the relative importance and interaction of the subskills. It also occurred to us that, if the research findings were organized in relationship to a logical construct, a fairly clear picture might emerge of what is already known and what could be postulated from our present knowledge but would still need to be experimentally verified or refuted. Accordingly, an outline which appeared to us to be related logically to the acquisition of speechreading was developed. (See Table 1-I.) It was discussed in detail in Chapter 1. The theoretical construct is in part based on our own thinking and experience and in part on relationships which emerged or were clarified by the literature. It is not necessarily the best or final one. We present the construct as our present view and offer it for consideration and dispute. We hope that it may serve as a hypothetical model, one to be proved, disproved, and certainly to be modified by carefully controlled research. It is our view that only through the use of such a construct can the relative importance of the factors contributing to a composite skill be apprehended. Without such a construct to serve as a guide, "truths" may be revealed, but not appreciated or disregarded as being of very little import.

At this point we should like to make it clear to the reader that the theoretical construct and the research findings reported in this chapter are concerned only with the viewer—with the factors which affect his acquisition of speechreading skill and which differentiate among speechreaders. There are other factors (discussed in Chapters 1, 2, and 5) which affect the quality of the speechreader's performance at any given point in time. These are such things as the readibility of the speaker, the effect of environmental conditions (light, distance, nonverbal cues), and the language he is attempting to speechread—its visibility, familiarity, and structural pattern. Research with respect to these factors is reported along with the discussion concerning them in the chapters cited above.

Also, this review of the literature is not intended to be a treatise on the psychology of the deaf, except as such psychology relates to the speechreading process. A great many references to the deaf are included because they have been the chief populations studied.

3. INTERPRETATION OF STATISTICAL TERMINOLOGY

3.1. *Coefficient of Correlation*

Most of the studies on speechreading have made use of the coefficient of correlation in comparing their test results. Because some of the readers of this text may not have had a course in statistics, we are including this section in the hope that it may make the reporting of some of the findings more understandable for them.

The coefficient of correlation is a statistical index or measure of the extent to which two variables or measurements are associated. If the measures are positively related or "correlated," then as one measure increases from small to large, the second measurement will also increase in the same direction. If the measurements are negatively correlated, the reverse is true. To refer to the example cited in Section 1, if one were to study a group of children and find that the children who made the best scores on a reading test were also those that made the highest scores on an achievement test, one might conclude that reading and scholastic achievement either have a causal relationship or are both dependent on some other variable. If the reverse were true, the two measurements would be considered to be correlated negatively. To cite another example, if reading scores improve with age, then reading and age are positively correlated. The coefficient of correlation does not indicate that improvement in one measure is the cause of the improvement in the second measure. In the first example cited, one might well be justified in concluding that educational achievement is predicated in good part on the ability to read. But in the second example, it would not be logical to assume that as one grows older one necessarily learns to read better. This, to be sure, would be true in general of a group of children who are receiving training and whose mental capacity is increasing with age; but age, in itself, does not "cause" reading skill. It is only associated with it.

The product moment correlation coefficient is symbolized by the letter "r." A correlation coefficient of $+1.00$ indicates a perfect positive relationship; a zero coefficient, no relationship, and a coefficient of -1.00, a perfect negative correlation. The practical problem becomes one of evaluating or interpreting coefficients between .00 and 1.00. If the correlation coefficient is high enough, it is possible to predict a score or a level of achievement on one measure from a score on a second measure. It is then possible to establish norms or standards of development or achievement. A *norm* is usually the average or median achievement of a large group of a particular age or characteristic. For example, when norms are established for a given test (reading, arithmetic, spelling, etc.), it is then possible to view the individual and to determine if he is doing as well as the average student of his age, or better or worse than the average.[*]

How high must a coefficient of correlation be between two measures in order to establish such norms? There is probably no pat answer to this question because it depends partly on the judgment of the person who is establishing the norms and partly on the nature of the concept being studied. In general, however, a coefficient of correlation from .00 to .45 is considered to be very low; from .46 to .63, low; from .64 to .77, moderate; from .78 to .89, high, and from .90 to 1.00, very high.[†]

The problem is complicated further by the fact that the coefficient of correlation is not a linear measurement of the degree of association. An "r" of .60 does not indicate twice the relationship of an "r" of .30. In order to determine the variability on one measure that can be associated with the variability in a second measure, it is necessary to employ still another statistic called the "coefficient of determination," or the "index of forecasting efficiency—E." This statistic is arrived at by multiplying the square of "r" by 100. "E" then becomes an indication of the importance of our coefficient.

The word "significant" is often used in the discussion of statistical measurements. A statistic (in this case a coefficient of correlation) is considered to be "significant" or meaningful if the probability is that the relationship which it indicates could not have occurred by chance. Note that we said "probability." There is no such thing as absolute certainty. If a statistic is reported as being significant at the .05 level, one interprets the statement as meaning that while the indicated relationship could have occurred by chance, the probability of its having occurred by chance is small, that is of the order of five times in one hundred. A statistic which is significant at the .01 level indicates even greater certainty that the association that has been demonstrated is a true association. There is only one chance in one hundred that the findings may be a result of chance. It is probably not wise to "trust" a statistic unless a test of its significance has been

[*] Correlations high enough to warrant the prediction of speechreading from some other factor or variable have not yet been isolated.

[†] Edwards, A.L.: *Statistical Analysis*, New York, Rinehart, 1946, p. 100.

made and reported. Little confidence is placed in any statistical index of association that could have occurred by chance more than five times in one hundred. There is considered to be too great a chance that the actual correlation in the population from which the sample was drawn might have been zero. Note that when the word "significant" is used in this sense, nothing is being said at the moment about the size or amount of such relationship. The percentage of commonality between two measures is derived from the size of the coefficient and the index of forecasting efficiency. Much confusion can result if one does not understand that the statistical use of the word "significant" has a special connotation. Unfortunately this word is also used to indicate the importance of a relationship. This latter connotation cannot be derived from statistics. It is a value judgment. For example, a finding which is statistically significant might indicate that tall men marry short girls. The trend would be clear. But such a finding is probably of no practical importance or "significance" to you unless you happen to be a tall girl, and of no import at all if you happen to a tall girl who has married a tall man!

4. ORGANIZATION OF THE RESEARCH LITERATURE WITH RESPECT TO THE THEORETICAL CONSTRUCT

The literature concerning the secondary factors will be reviewed first. Our reason for doing so is to present findings in chronological order. Many of the earlier studies dealt almost exclusively with them. By presenting them in this fashion the gradual evolution in research from studying the relationship of general factors to the exploration of more specific factors should become apparent.

In order to organize the literature with respect to primary factors it has sometimes been necessary to take certain liberties. Various psychological subtests from global measures of intelligence have been compared with speechreading skill, but it has not always been clear which attributes or combinations of attributes these subtests purport to measure. It has been necessary for us to intuit the factor or factors that appeared to us to have been measured when the intent has not been explicit or well defined. It should also be noted that our classification of factors measured is not always the same as that of the research workers themselves.

In this chapter studies are rarely reported *in toto*. Various aspects of the same study are reported in various sections with respect to our categorization of the attributes measured. This permits us to tally the results and to indicate the preponderance of evidence when conflicting findings are reported in the research literature. In addition, when results are in conflict we have asked "why" and have tried to find the answers through an analysis of the research designs. In analyzing and evaluating the research, the writer has a bias which should be clearly stated. Research ideas develop out of experience and from logic. The human element cannot be eliminated. Research should serve to verify what is already "known" and to lead to new insights and understandings as well. *The writer has great respect for clinical experience, i.e. for the knowledge that has been accumulated from years of careful observation and analysis of the hearing handicapped in teaching situations and from the subjective reasoning of the hearing impaired. When research findings do not coincide with such experience, the writer is more apt to question the validity of the research than the original postulate itself, and to search for a possible explanation.*

Certain comparisons are not included in our survey because the skills that were tested did not seem to us to be related logically to speechreading. The subtests not included are listed at the back of the chapter along with our reasons for noninclusion. This chapter is written primarily for the nonstatistically oriented reader. An attempt has been made to report and to interpret findings in words in the body of the text, instead of in mathematical formulations or tests of significance. In doing so, the reporting must necessarily be less exact than might be desirable. For the more sophisticated reader statistics are reported in the tables that accompany the text.

One of the major problems that arises in an analysis and evaluation of research findings has to do with the reliability and validity of the measures that have been compared. Do the tests measure what they are purported to measure? This is especially true with respect to the various tests of speechreading.* Only two of them have been evaluated through administration to large populations (Utley Film Test and the Keaster Film Test of Lipreading, John Tracy Clinic Forms A and B.[43, 39] In this analysis we have assumed that all the measuring instruments which have been used are both valid and reliable. Because of such tenuous assumptions, the conclusions that we have drawn are certainly open to question. But in this chapter, we are not attempting to present the "final story." Our goal is the organization of experimental results into a cohesive pattern. We should then be able to examine the pattern and to evaluate it in terms of gaps, errors, and mistaken assumptions.

5. LITERATURE REGARDING SECONDARY FACTORS

Secondary factors are considered to be training, language comprehension, and emotional attitudes or sets.

5.1. Relationship of Speechreading to Training

It was postulated that speechreading skill should improve as the result of training and practice. The research literature appears to substantiate this hypothesis. Four studies have been reported which have dealt directly with the effect of training on improvement in speechreading ability. They are those of Black, O'Reilly, and Peck, 1963; Hutton, 1960; Heiders', 1940; and Lowell, Taaffe, and Rushford, 1959. In all of them significant improvement in mean speechreading scores were found following training.

A number of research workers have correlated chronological age with speechreading skill, using groups of deaf children. One index of the amount of training when considering hearing handicapped children is age. It is assumed that the older the child, the more opportunity he has had to speechread and the more training he has received. This is a fairly safe assumption when

---

* Other factors of equal concern are (a) the correlation of subtests from psychological test batteries with speechreading when the subtest aptitudes are not clearly defined and (b) failure to *control other pertinent variables.*

studying deaf children trained orally since their training is started at an early age. In Table 4-I the results of nine studies are summarized where speechreading skill, as measured by various tests, was correlated with age. Six of them show some measure of positive association.

Another index of the effect of training on speechreading skill is that of grade placement. Children in higher grades are presumed to have had more training than their counterparts at lower grade levels. In Table 4-II four studies are reported which have a bearing on this relationship. All of them show that some relationship does exist.

In contrast to the above are findings that the ultimate level of accomplishment is not closely related to the amount of training, Heider and Heider, 1940, grouped deaf children according to age. Each age group was divided into halves, and then the average amount of training for all of the better and all of the poorer speechreaders was calculated. (See Table 4-III.) No important difference was found between the amount of training of the good and poor speechreaders. They concluded that:[22, p. 133] "These results seems to show that after a certain amount of training there is hardly any improvement in lipreading as such." Similar results were reported by Coscarelli and Sanders, 1968. Two groups of speechreaders who were differentiated in terms of speechreading skill were found not to be differentiated with respect to the amount of training or the duration of hearing loss. In addition, when two groups of hard-of-hearing adults were divided into those who had speechreading instruction and those who had not, the groups were found to be nondifferentiated in terms of age, duration of loss, or visual synthesis skill. The phrase "visual synthesis skill" as used by them is comparable to what we have termed conjectural perception. They found that "... although the highest score on the lipreading test, 90%, was obtained by a subject with 72 months of lipreading training, the next highest score, 75%, was achieved by two subjects, one with normal hearing and one with a hearing loss but no training in lipreading. One of the lowest scores, 27%, was obtained by a subject with 36 months of lipreading training."

TABLE 4-I

SUMMARY OF RESEARCH FINDINGS

CORRELATION OF SPEECHREADING AND CHRONOLOGICAL AGE AS INDEX OF TRAINING

Study	Test of Speechreading	Age Range	Classification	No.	Coef. Corr.	Stat. Sig.	Index of Forecast. Eff.
Conklin[5]	Conklin Test	12 to 21	deaf children	16	No trend		
Reid[37]	Reid Test	10 to 22	deaf children	99	.186 ± .09	N.S.	
Heiders[22]	Heider Test III	9 to 19	deaf children	68	.19 ± .08	N.S.	
Heider[23]	Utley Film Test		deaf children	78	.51	.01	25%
Utley[43]	Utley Film Test	10 to 21	deaf children	737	.383	.01	15%
Craig[9]	Craig Test	6:8 to 16:6	deaf children	164	.51	.01	25%
Craig	Craig Test	6:8 to 16:6	deaf children	79	.43	.01	18%
Evans[13]	Evans Test	8 to 16	deaf children	50	.31	.05	10%
Evans[14]	Evans Film Test	8 to 16	deaf children	64	.67 (eta)		

Speechreading maturity by about age 11; rapid improvement from 8 to 11, but leveling off thereafter.

Summary: While the three earlier studies failed to find a relationship between age (index of amount of training) and speechreading skill, the six later studies found such a trend.

Speechreading

TABLE 4-II

SUMMARY OF RESEARCH FINDINGS CORRELATION OF SPEECHREADING AND GRADE PLACEMENT AS INDEX OF TRAINING

Study	Speechreading Test	Classification	Number	"r"	Sig.	"E" Possible Percent Contrib.
Heiders*	Utley film	deaf children	78	Middle School 37.7 mean	Upper School 58.6 Mean	
				Difference between 34th and 70th in percentile ranks for the two groups.		
				.32 to .65		10% to 42%
Pintner	Utley film	deaf children	606	.552	.01	30%
Utley[43]	Utley film	deaf children	170	.600	2.001	36%
Cavender	Cavender test	normal children	(310 Tests)			

* The percentile rank for Middle School and Upper School was 34 and 70, respectively.

TABLE 4-III
AVERAGE LIPREADING SCORE AND YEARS OF TRAINING FOR
GOOD AND POOR LIPREADERS SEPARATELY*

	Speechreading Test	No.	Average Lipreading Score	Quartile	Average Years of Training
Good Lipreaders	Heiders' Test I	29	30.8	3rd	4.77
Poor Lipreaders	Heiders' Test I	28	22.8	1st	4.95

* Maximum score 55.

5.2. Relationship of Speechreading to Language Comprehension

Language comprehension, i.e. knowledge of structural meanings, vocabulary, and idiomatic expressions, is considered to be the most important of the secondary or "backup" skills. Our speechreading tests have been designed to test the skill of school children. The vocabulary level of currently available tests of speechreading (see section on tests) are all low, most of them requiring a vocabulary commensurate with third grade reading skill or less. In addition, the sentence structure has purposely been kept simple and great use is made of idiomatic expressions. They have been designed to serve as examples of the usual speechreading task—that of understanding "every-day conversational speech." A high level of language comprehension is not required to speechread them. For these reasons one would not expect to find a relationship between speechreading and language comprehension as measured by these tests in an adult population or with children with mild or moderate degrees of hearing loss. The deaf child, however, does not easily attain even a modest degree of language proficiency. Even though he may know the words, problems with idiomatic expressions and structural meanings remain. His speechreading score can be expected to reflect in part his knowledge of language. One would expect on the whole, that the better speechreaders would tend to be those children with greater language proficiency. The research literature substantiates these convictions.

Common indirect indices of language comprehension are reading level, educational achievement, and vocabulary level. The results of studies in which reading, educational achievement, and vocabulary level have been compared with speechreading with

deaf children forming the experimental populations are summarized in Tables 4-IV, 4-V, and 4-VI. Only one study out of
thirteen failed to find a statistically significant correlation. The
remainder of the studies indicate that when studying deaf children, as much as 14 percent to 47 percent of the variability in
scores may be associated with differences in language facility.
While this is a group trend, it is clear from the size of the correlations that not all children made reading, achievement, and
vocabulary scores that paralleled their speechreading scores. An
analysis was made by the Heiders[24] of their data with respect
to speechreading ratings and scores on the Stanford Achievement
Test. They found that *no child who rated low on the speechreading test attained a high score on the achievement test, but
that in* many cases the excellent speechreaders made poor educational scores. They concluded that: *"This implies on the one
hand that a child may become very proficient in speechreading
without having the kind of intelligence that enables him to
succeed in school subjects, but without good speechreading
ability he is seriously handicapped in his school work."*

In Tables 4-VII and 4-VIII the results of research that has
compared reading and vocabulary scores with speechreading
scores, using adult subjects with normal hearing, are reported.
None of the studies found any degree of association that could
not have occurred by chance. As we mentioned earlier, these
results were to be expected considering the nature of our speechreading tests. Had the tests required a highly sophisticated knowledge of vocabulary, it it possible that such a trend might have
appeared.

5.3. *Relationship of Speechreading to Factors Ancillary to Train-ing and Language Proficiency*

Factors ancillary or subordinate to training and language proficiency are those characteristics which can affect learning, such
as *age of onset of hearing loss and duration of loss, extent and
pattern of loss, auditory discrimination,* and *general intelligence.*
It is postulated that they may affect to some extent the improvement in the primary skills that can be achieved through training,
but when studying deaf children their effect will be most impor-

TABLE 4-IV

SUMMARY OF RESEARCH FINDINGS CORRELATION BETWEEN SPEECHREADING ABILITY AND READING
ABILITY—HEARING HANDICAPPED CHILDREN

Study	Reading Test	Speechreading Test	Subjects	No.	"r"	Sig.	"E" Percent Contrib.
Utley	Scores from schools	Utley film	hear. hand.	546	.525	.01	28%
Costello	Gates reading survey	Costello	h.-of-h.	84	.688	.01	47%
	Vocabulary and comprehension		deaf	36	.593	.01	35%
Lowell	Gray-Votaw-Rogers Reading comprehension subtest	Keaster film J.T.C. forms A and B	deaf high school	22	.37	.01	14%

TABLE 4-V

SUMMARY OF RESEARCH FINDINGS CORRELATION BETWEEN SPEECHREADING
AND EDUCATIONAL ACHIEVEMENT

Study	Achievement Test	Speechreading Test	Classification	No.	"r"	Stat. Signif.	"E" Percent Contrib.
Heider and Heider	Stanford Ach.	Heider Film Test III	deaf children	68	$.54 \pm .06$	.01	29%
Utley	Stanford Ach.	Utley Film Test	deaf children	546	.636	.01	40%
Pintner	Pintner Ed. Survey Test		deaf children		.49		24%
Reid	Stanford Ach.	Utley Film Test Sentences—A	deaf children	35	.288	N.S.	
Quigley and Frisina	Stanford Ach.		deaf children	240	.58	.01	33%
Lowell	Lang. Usage Subtest Calif. Ach.	Keaster Film Test. J.T.C. Forms A and B	deaf high school	22	.68	.01	46%
Heiders	Lang. Score Stanford Ach.	Heiders' Film Test III	deaf children	68	.64	.01	46%

TABLE 4-VI

SUMMARY OF RESEARCH FINDINGS CORRELATION BETWEEN SPEECHREADING ABILITY AND SIZE OF
VOCABULARY—CHILDREN

Study	Vocabulary Test	Speechreading Test	Classification	No.	"r"	Stat. Sig.	"E" Percent Contrib.
Quigley and Frisina	Durrell-Sullivan Vocabulary Subtest	Utley Film Sentences Form A	deaf children	240	.58	.01	33%
Lowell	Grace-Votaw-Rogers Vocabulary Subtest	Keaster Film Test J.T.C. Forms A and B	deaf high school students	22	.50	.01	25%

TABLE 4-VII

SUMMARY OF RESEARCH FINDINGS CORRELATION BETWEEN SPEECHREADING ABILITY AND READING ABILITY—ADULTS

Study	Classification	Reading Test	Speechreading Test	No.	"r"	Signif.
Simmons	hard-of-hearing	Iowa Silent Reading Test Comprehension Subtests	Simmons Interview Test	24	.02	N.S.
			Mason Film		.08	N.S.
			Utley Film		.32	N.S.
O'Neill	college students	Robinson-Hall Reading Test Comprehension Subtest	Mason Film No. 410	20	−.21	N.S.
O'Neill and Davidson	college students	Ohio State Psychological Exam. Reading Subtests	Mason Film No. 410	30	−.03	(rho)N.S.

TABLE 4-VIII

SUMMARY OF RESEARCH FINDINGS CORRELATION BETWEEN SPEECHREADING ABILITY AND SIZE OF VOCABULARY—ADULTS

Study	Vocabulary Test	Speechreading Test	Classification	No.	"r"	Stat. Sig.
Simmons	Wech.-Bellevue Adult Scale Vocab. Subtest	Simmons Interview Test	h.-of-h. adults	24	−.05	N.S.
		Mason Film Test			−.03	N.S.
		Utley Film Test			.07	N.S.
Wong and Taaffe	Guilford Vocab. Test. PMA Vocab. Subtest	Keaster Film Test J.T.C. Forms A-B	college students	85	.06	N.S.
		Keaster Film Test J.T.C. Forms A-B		61	−.09	N.S.
O'Neill	Wech.-Bellevue Adult Scale Vocab. Subtest	Mason Film Test No. 410	college students	20	.25	N.S.

tantly related to the attainment of language comprehension. Their effect with respect to training may not be evident unless the subjects used in an experiment can be considered to have comparable language proficiency. It is also true that one ancillary factor can nullify or minimize the effect of another factor or factors. For example, high intelligence may compensate to some degree for a severe loss or an early onset of hearing loss. For this reason it is unlikely that any one factor could serve as an index of either language comprehension or training and hence correlate to any important degree with speechreading attainment unless the other factors are controlled and fairly well equated for the population studied. These assumptions appear to be borne out with respect to hearing loss by the results of various studies. They are summarized in Tables 4-IX and 4-X.

5.3.1 AGE OF ONSET AND DURATION OF LOSS. Age of onset is an indirect measure of the duration of the hearing loss. A severe loss at an early age can seriously interfere with language learning and hence be reflected in speechreading attainment. When considering a group of deaf children, one would expect those children whose losses were incurred at an early age to be less adept at speechreading than their peers who had the opportunity to develop some knowledge of language before their hearing impairments occurred. Utley[43] (see Table 4-IX), when studying a very large population, was able to establish that at least a minimal relationship exists between speechreading skill and age of onset of deafness. It is hypothesized that a greater relationship might have been evident had there been greater differences in age of onset. Most children in classes for the deaf (the larger part of her population) are born with severe losses or acquire them shortly thereafter.

When studying a group of hard-of-hearing children or hard-of-hearing adults, one would expect to find the reverse relationship, i.e. the greater the duration of the loss, the greater the speechreading skill. Basic knowledge of language can be assumed for these latter groups. For them, the longer the duration of the hearing loss, the longer the period in which they have had to depend in part on speechreading. No research was found which

TABLE 4-IX

SUMMARY OF RESEARCH FINDINGS CORRELATION OF SPEECHREADING WITH AGE OF ONSET; DURATION OF LOSS; AUDITORY DISCRIMINATION

Study	Factor	Class Subj's	No.	Speechreading Test	Coeff. Corr.	Stat. Sig.	Percent Variance
Utley	age onset	deaf children	675	Utley Film	.100	.01	1%
Simmons	duration	h.-of-h. adults	24	Intv. Test	.51	.01	26%
				Mason Film	.32	N.S.	
				Utley Film	.29	N.S.	
				Utley Sentence Test, Form B	Z .603	N.S.	
Coscarelli and Sanders	duration	h.-of-h. adults	14	Intv. Test	−.26	N.S.	
Simmons	discrimination	h.-of-h. adults	24	Mason Film	−.001	N.S.	
				Utley Film	−.36	N.S.	

TABLE 4-X

SUMMARY OF RESEARCH FINDINGS CORRELATION OF SPEECHREADING WITH EXTENT OF HEARING LOSS

Study	Classif. Subjects	No.	Speechreading Test	Coeff. Corr.	Stat. Sig.	Percent Variance
Costello	deaf children severely h.-of-h.	36 34	Costello Test	dif. scores t test	.02	Severely hard-of-hearing, the better speechreaders.
Lowell	deaf children and adults	243	Keaster Film Test	−.22	.05	5%
	deaf adults	164	J.T.C. Forms A and B	−.18	.05	
Craig	deaf children	79	Craig Test	−.29	.01	3%
Evans	deaf children	64	Evans Film Test	−.38	.01	8%
Simmons	h.-of-h. adults	24	Simmons Interv. Test	.21	N.S.	14%
			Mason Film Test	.38	N.S.	
			Utley Film Test	.27	N.S.	

reported the relationship between duration of loss and speech-reading skill for hard-of-hearing children. Simmons,[38] and Cos-carelli and Sanders,[6] however, studied this variable with groups of hard-of-hearing adults. No correlation was found by Cos-carelli and Sanders. A positive trend of increased skill with dura-tion of loss was found by Simmons when her Interview Test was used as the speechreading criterion, but not when the Mason or Utley tests were used as criteria.

5.3.2 EXTENT OF LOSS AND AUDITORY DISCRIMINATION. In a deafened population one might expect that individuals with the greater losses and the greater problems in auditory discrimination might be more adept at speechreading because of a greater need for it. The reverse might be expected from children born with severe losses. As was noted before, while they have the greater need for spechreading proficiency, they are handicapped because of their difficulty in acquiring language facility. Costello,[7] 1957, compared the speechreading skill of deaf and severely hard-of-hearing children who had been equated with respect to age, intelligence, eyesight, and onset of hearing loss. The severely hard-of-hearing group was found to be the better speech-readers. Results comparable to Costello's have been reported by three other research workers—Lowell, 1960; Craig, 1964; and Evans, 1965.

Simmons, 1959, studied the relationship between speechreading and extent of hearing loss for an adult hard-of-hearing popula-tion. She was not able to demonstrate a statistically significant trend. However, it should be noted that in making this com-parison her subjects were not equated with respect to duration of loss. For this reason the trend, if it did exist, could have been obscured. Discrimination scores (Table 4-IX), made by the same hard-of-hearing adult group, were also compared with scores made on tests of speechreading proficiency. Again statistically significant correlations were not obtained. But it is interesting to note that, while the correlations could have happened by chance, they were all negative. One would logically expect to find such an inverse trend. The poorer the discrimination score (hearing alone), the greater the need for speechreading skill.

5.3.3 INTELLIGENCE. Generally speaking, there is a relationship between intelligence and learning, and intelligence and language acquisition. The more intelligent children learn faster and tend to acquire more language and knowledge in a given period of time. But when considering a skill-subject, as opposed to a subject matter area, general intelligence may or may not be associated, depending upon the nature of the skill and what, in consequence, is required of the individual. To put it another way, *a skill will be related to intelligence only if certain aspects of what is termed intelligence are needed for the skill.* The relationship of intelligence to speechreading skill has been a puzzle to teachers and research workers alike. It seems probable that deductive reasoning is not closely associated with skill in speechreading, and perhaps is of value to the speechreader only in analyzing or "sizing up" social situations. Since speechreading is a synthetic process, it would seem reasonable to assume that the kind of reasoning required of the speechreader is primarily of the *inductive* or *associative* type. (See Chapter 1 and Table 1-I.) Tests of general intelligence measure many different aptitudes, but they are usually rather heavily weighted in terms of subtests that require analytic reasoning ability. For this reason one would not expect them to correlate to a marked extent. If our line of reasoning is accepted, it should not come as too much of a shock to learn that no association has been found between general or full scale tests of intelligence and speechreading ability. Four research workers have studied this variable. Their findings of no association are reported in Table 4-XI. All of them used normal or hard-of-hearing subjects.

As we said earlier, general intelligence can be expected to relate to the speechreading skill of deaf children (because of the verbal subtests), as an indirect index of language comprehension. There has, however, been no research to confirm this expectation. All of the studies with deaf children have ruled out the factor of language comprehension through the use of nonverbal or performance tests of intelligence.

In Table 4-XII are reported the findings of twelve experiments which have related scores made on performance tests to speechreading ability. Five of them indicate some degree of association.

TABLE 4-XI

SUMMARY OF RESEARCH FINDINGS CORRELATION BETWEEN SPEECHREADING AND MEASURES OF GENERAL INTELLIGENCE

Study	Intelligence Test	Factor Measured		No.	"r"	Sig.
Hard-of-Hearing Adults						
Simmons (1959)	Wechsler-Bellevue Adult Full Scale	IQ	Interview Test	24	.25	N.S.
			Mason Film Test	24	.13	N.S.
			Utley Film Test	24	.21	N.S.
Normally Hearing Children and Adults						
Cavender (1949)	From Schools Grades 6–12	IQ	Cavender Sent. Tests	170	−.02	N.S.
O'Neill (1951)	Wechsler-Bellevue Adult Full Scale, College Students	IQ	Mason Film Test	20	.35 rho	N.S.
O'Neill and Davidson (1956)	Ohio State Psych. Exam.; college students	IQ	Mason Film Test	30	.08	N.S.

TABLE 4-XII

SUMMARY OF RESEARCH FINDINGS CORRELATION BETWEEN SPEECHREADING AND MEASURES OF PERFORMANCE INTELLIGENCE

Study	Intelligence Test	Factor Believed Measured	Speechreading Test	No.	Coef. Corr.	Stat. Sig.	"E" Percent Contrib.
Deaf Children							
Pintner (1929)	Pintner Nonlang. Test of Ment. Abil.	IQ	Pintner	196	.13	N.S.	
		IQ	Day and Fusfeld	212	.02	N.S.	
Reid (1947)	Not reported	MA	Reid Film Test	58	.066	N.S.	
	Not reported	IQ	Reid Film Test	57	.169	N.S.	
Vaughan (1954)	Nebr. Test Learn Apt. Young Deaf Children	IQ	Ranked by Teach. Staff	20	.05		
	Goodenough Draw-a-Man	IQ	Ranked by Teach. Staff	20	−.14	N.S.	
Evans (1960)	Wechsler Adult Performance Scale—Form 1	IQ	Evans Progressive Discrim Test	50	.13	N.S.	
Quigley and Frisina (1961)	From Schools Supplem. by Chi. Nonverb Test	IQ	Utley Film Sent. Form A	240	.16	.05	3%
Craig (1964)	Leiter Internat'l Perf. Plus WISC Perf. Scale	MA	Craig Test, Live	164	.63	.01	40%
	Nebr. Test Learn. Apt. Plus WISC Perf. Scale	MA	Craig Test, Live	79	.58	.01	33%
Evans (1965)	WISC Perf. Scale	IQ	Evans Film	64	.38	.01	12%
Normal Hearing Adults							
O'Neill (1951)	Wechsler-Bellevue Adult Perf. Scale	I.Q.	Mason Film	20	.55 rho	.05	30%

It should be noted that in three of the five comparisons, the performance scale of the Wechsler Intelligence Scale for Children (WISC) was used either alone or in combination with other tests. O'Neill gave a similar test, the performance scale of the adult Wechsler-Bellevue (WAIS), to his group of normally hearing college students. This test was also used by Evans in his earlier (1960) study. Since his experimental population consisted of deaf children, ages eight years, eleven months to sixteen years, zero months (mean age, twelve years, six months), it is possible that the test was too advanced for them.

Why has performance intelligence as measured by the Wechsler Scales and tests analogous to them (Leiter and Nebraska) correlated with speechreading ability when other performance tests have failed to do so? In order to understand this it is necessary to examine the various subtests which compose the scales. In doing so we find that *certain aspects of performance intelligence are directly related to and can be considered to be measures of primary aptitudes.* Three of the subtests of the Wechsler-Bellevue Adult Scale have correlated independently with speechreading. (See Table 4-XIII.) They are Picture Arrangement, Digit Symbol, and Block Design. The Digit Symbol Test would appear to be primarily a measure of visual memory. Both the Picture Arrangement Test and The Block Design Test require powers of deductive reasoning believed to be necessary

TABLE 4-XIII

SUMMARY OF RESEARCH FINDINGS CORRELATION BETWEEN
SPEECHREADING AND WECHSLER'S SUBTESTS OF
PERFORMANCE INTELLIGENCE

Wechsler Performance Subtests—Adults	O'Neill	Coefficients of Correlation				
		Simmons			Costello	
		Intv.	Mas.	Utley	deaf	h.h.
Picture Arrangement	.17	.18	.46†	.48*	.357*	.445†
Digit Symbol	.47*	.42*	.42*	.50†		
Block Design	.38	.44*	.23	.43*		
Picture Completion	−.28	.08	−.04	.00		
Object Assembly	−.14	Not Correlated				
Total Test—Performance Intelligence	.55*					
Total Test—Performance Intelligence	.38** (Evans-Wisc)					

* Significant at the .05 level.
† Significant at the .01 level.

to social awareness—the ability to size up or comprehend a total situation. But, in addition, both tests require much use of abstract inductive (associative) reasoning, believed to be basic to the ability to form perceptual closures. In addition, the Picture Arrangement Test requires keen observation of detail or visual attention. These subtests will be discussed in greater detail later in the section on the relationship of primary factors to speechreading skill.

The WISC performance scale has an additional subtest not found in the adult Wechsler-Bellevue, called "Mazes." It appears to be a test of visual proficiency and perhaps of abstract reasoning as well. An examination of the Leiter International Performance Test and the Nebraska Test of Learning Aptitude revealed that they contain many subtests of visual memory and of abstract inductive reasoning. Because of the extensive "loading of measures of primary factors in these scales, the test results could just as logically be reported as the correlation of speechreading with multiple primary factors, rather than its correlation with performance intelligence. You will find them so categorized in Section 6.6.

5.4. Emotional Attitudes

Emotional attitudes have been listed for ease of discussion as a separate category under the secondary characteristics that are of importance to the acquisition of speechreading skill. It is clear, however, that such factors, as self-concept, reaction toward frustration and failure, and motivation, are factors that can affect learning and as such are ancillary to training and language proficiency. While emotional attitudes are known to affect progress, the adverse effect of negative attitudes may not be apparent in studying a large population which can be expected to vary widely with respect to the primary abilities.

The relationship of emotional variables to the acquisition of speechreading skill has not been studied extensively, (See Table 4-XIV.) Of the five studies which have dealt with the effect of personal adjustment on speechreading skill, three have used normally hearing populations. All correlations were either non-significant or very low. It is unlikely that fear of failure would influence the results of normally hearing subjects to any im-

TABLE 4-XIV
SUMMARY OF RESEARCH FINDINGS—CORRELATION OF SPEECHREADING WITH EMOTIONAL CHARACTERISTICS

Study	Test of Factor	Speechreading Test	Class. Subjects	No.	Stat. Empl.	Sig.	"E" Percent Contrib.
O'Neill 1951	Rotter Incomplete Sentences *Emotional Adjustment*	Mason Film No. 410	norm. hear. coll. stud.	20	−.02 (rho)	N.S.	
	Rorschach—*Rigidity*	Mason Film No. 410	norm. hear. coll. stud.	20	.10 (rho)	N.S.	
	Knower *Speech Attitude Scale*	Mason Film No. 410	norm. hear. coll. stud.	20	−.38 (rho)	N.S.	
O'Neill and Davidson 1956	Rotter Level of Aspiration Test—*Measure of Reaction to Success and Failure*	Mason Film No. 410	norm. hear. coll stud.	30	.122 (Chi. Sq.	N.S.	
Worthington, 1956	Rotter Level of Aspiration Test—*Measure of Reaction to Sucess and Failure*	Mason Film No. 410	deaf, high sch. 14 to 20 yrs.	51	2.02 (Chi. Sq.)	N.S.	
	Mult. Ch. Intell. Test Form A—*Level of Aspir.*	Mason Film No. 410	deaf, high sch. 14 to 20 yrs.	51	2.85 (Chi. Sq.)	N.S.	
	Rotter Incomplete Sentences Test of *Emotional Adjust.*	Mason Film No. 410	deaf, high sch. 14 to 20 yrs.	51	.19 (r)	N.S.	
Elkin 1952	*Personality Characteristics* Rorschach; Selected Thematic Appercep. Test cards; Bibliog. Inventory; questionnaire	Utley Film	h.-of-h. veterans	44	No gross difference	N.S.	

Study	Measure	Subtest	Test	Sample	N	Statistic	Sig.	%
Wong and Taaffe 1958	Guilford-Zimmerman Temperament Survey*	General Activity	Keaster Film Test Liprdg J.T.C. Forms A and B	norm. hear. college students	67 Fe.	.26 (r)	.05	7%
		Personal Relations			67 Fe.	.24 (r)	.05	6%
		Gen. Act. and Person. Rel.			67 Fe.	.31 (r)	.05	10%
		Emotional Stability			95 M.	−.20 (r)	.05	4%
Costello†		Questionnaire to sample Attitudes toward oralism—speech and sp. reading.	Costello Test	deaf children age 11 to 15	30	−.47 (r)	.01	22%
Eisman and Levy		Speaker judged as aggressive, likeable, passive	Keaster Film Test	college students	36	9.2 (Chi. Sq.)	N.S.	
		Speaker roles—moderate and aggressive				.25 (F)	N.S.	

* Subtests from the Guilford-Zimmerman Temperament Survey. The remainder of the subtest were given ("r" range −.07 to +.20, nonsignificant). They are restraint, ascendance, social interest, objectivity, friendliness, thoughtfulness, and masculinity-femininity. Only three out of twenty-one correlations were significant.
† Negative correlation due to method of scoring. Association was found between positive attitudes toward oralism and speech-reading facility.

portant degree. One does not fear failure on a task that is of no practical importance to him and one at which he is not necessarily expected to do well. The results with hearing handicapped populations have been scarcely more rewarding. Worthington,[48] replicated portions of Davidson's work and of O'Neill's, but used deaf high school students. No significant trend was indicated. In a study done by Elkin[12] with hard-of-hearing veterans, it was hypothesized that good speechreaders would manifest greater positive attitudes toward others, the environment, and self. The groups were found not to be grossly different. Another study, Eisman and Levy,[11] dealt with the effect of the way in which the speaker was perceived (likeable, passive, aggressive) on the speechreading skill of the subjects. An interaction was not established.

The one study that has shown a moderately high degree of association between emotional attitude and speechreading skill was reported by Costello.[8] She concluded that her study suggests that attitude toward communication is an important force in the development of skill in speechreading among deaf children. It was found that: (a) A desire to speechread or a liking for speechreading was associated with better skill. (b) Children who considered their parents to prefer the use of signs were among the poorest speechreaders, and in general, those whose parents were believed to prefer them to use speech and speechreading were the better speechreaders. (c) The children who reported positive attitudes among their deaf friends with respect to oral communication also tended to be the better speechreaders.

6. LITERATURE REGARDING PRIMARY FACTORS

The primary factors are visual perceptual proficiency, synthetic ability, and flexibility.

6.1. Relationship of Speechreading to Visual Perceptual Proficiency

Visual proficiency has been subdivided into visual perception, speed of perception, and peripheral perception. No research literature was found that dealt with peripheral perception.

6.1.1 VISUAL PERCEPTION. By visual perception is meant the ability to perceive and identify individual speech sound movements and to discriminate among them. It includes as well the noting of transitional or blending movements. This ability is considered to be one of the most important of the various aptitudes comprising the speechreading act and is basic to all of the rest of them. The more information perceived by the speechreader, the less necessity there will be for him to guess as to elements and words. Despite the obvious importance of this aspect of visual proficiency, it appears that in only three studies has there been an attempt to isolate visual perception from other factors and to assess its contribution to the total skill. (See Table 4-XV.) In all three studies some degree of association was found. Their results indicate that visual perception may be associated with from 14 percent to 46 percent of the total skill.

The low correlations between their consonant and speechreading tests (statistically nonsignificant) were explained by the Heiders as being the result of the homophenity of consonant sounds and of the greater difficulty in recognizing vowel sounds. There was a range in scores on the vowel test from five to thirty-two, out of a possible score of thirty-two; and a range of from twenty to thirty-six on the consonant test, out of a possible score of forty. No allowance was made for the substitution of homophenous sounds. But had this been done, the range in scores for the consonant sounds could be expected to have been still less and the correlation with differences in speechreading skill still less! This can be seen by an examination of Table 4-XVI where the Heiders' data have been regrouped to indicate the percent correct score for homophenous consonant clusters in comparison with the percent correct scores for individual phonemes as scored by them. For example, when this method of scoring is used (homophenes scored as correct) the percent correct score made by their subjects for the consonant cluster /p,b,m/ was 98 percent as contrasted with the reported percent correct scores of 30 percent, 20 percent, and 50 percent, respectively. These results should not surprise us. It has long been known, though not verified experimentally, that individuals with no training in

TABLE 4-XV

SUMMARY OF RESEARCH FINDINGS—CORRELATION OF SPEECHREADING WITH VISUAL PERCEPTION

Study	Test of Visual Perception	Test of Speechreading	No.	Coef. of Corr. "r"	Stat. Sig.	"E" Percent Contrib.
Heiders[22]	Vowel Test*	Heider Test III	81	.68 ± .09	.01	46%
	Consonant Test	Heider Test III	39	.23 ± .08	N.S.	14%
Reid[37]	Consonant and Vowel Test†	Reid Test	99	.375	.01	23%
Evans[14]	Recog. of Designs Test	Sent. and Stories Evans	64	.48	.01	23%

* 16 vowels enclosed by /p/ and then by /f/ e.g., parp, pip, poop, etc: and farf, fif, foof, etc. 20 Consonants followed by /ɔɪ/ and then by /i/.

† 17 vowels presented in isolation. 11 Consonants followed by /i/, /a/, and /u/. A carrier phrase was used, "My sound is——".

TABLE 4-XVI

HEIDER AND HEIDER DATA REORGANIZED TO SHOW PERCENT
CORRECT SCORES OF HOMOPHENOUS CONSONANT CLUSTERS
AS CONTRASTED WITH THEIR NONHOMOPHENOUS SCORING

Homophenous Groups			Fraction Correct	Percent Correct	Order Rank
/p,b,m/			231/234	98%	1
/p/	25/78	30%			
/b/	21/78	20%			
/m/	40/78	50%			
/th/			74/78	94%	2
/f,v/			144/156	92%	3
/f/	68/78	80%			
/v/	48/78	60%			
/r/			70/78	90%	4
/t,d,n,l/			277/312	88%	5
/t/	36/78	40%			
/d/	28/78	30%			
/n/	32/78	40%			
/l/	70/78	90%			
/ʃ,tʃ,dʒ/			185/234	79%	6
/ʃ/	25/78	30%			
/tʃ/	12/78	10%			
/dʒ/	24/78	30%			
/k,g/			114/156	73%	7
/k/	52/78	60%			
/g/	22/78	20%			
/s/			54/78	69%	8
/h/			41/78	52%	9
/j/			12/78	15%	10
/wh/			4/78	.05%	11

speechreading or special skill have no difficulty in recognizing
the visible consonant movements, though they vary in the rapidity with which they can recognize them. See the chapter on
methods for a fuller discussion of this point.

The lower correlation found by Reid (.375) in giving her
combined vowel and consonant test as contrasted with the correlation found by the Heiders for their vowel test (.68) may possibly be due to the test's being weighted in favor of the consonants. The method of scoring was not reported.

What appears to be clear from these two studies is that experienced speechreaders are almost equally proficient in recognizing what we have termed the visible consonant sounds. (See
chapter on visibility.) Their perception, while basic to speech-

reading, will not differentiate among speechreaders with respect to total skill. What has not been established is the importance of the recognition of the obscure consonants, /t,d,n,l/, /k,g/, and /j/, in developing a high degree of speechreading skill. Logic and experience would lead one to believe that this factor is as important as vowel speechreading for two reasons. In the first place, the obscure consonants constitute a high proportion of the consonant information—approximately 30 percent. In the second place, their recognition from a practical point of view is much more important than vowel perception. The hard-of-hearing and severely hard-of-hearing are able to hear the vowel sounds given proper amplification. This is also true of the many children classified as partially or severely deaf rather than profoundly deaf.

6.1.2 Speed of Perception. Because almost all speech is fairly rapid, one would expect the advantage to lie with the individual who is able to focus rapidly. For if the process is slow or slower than average, much important sensory information is bound to be lost to the speechreader. Despite the manifest importance of this aspect of visual proficiency, little attention has been paid to it.

Wong and Taaffe[47] gave the Perceptual Speed Test, a subtest of the Guilford-Zimmerman Aptitude Survey to a large number of college students. It consists of a series of matching problems which require the subjects to note similarities and differences in forms of common objects (spoons, cups, shoes, airplanes, and the like). It is believed by its authors[20] to measure the ability to perceive detailed visual objects quickly and accurately. They note that, since the items are easy, individual differences must be measured mainly in terms of speed. The correlations with speechreading were extremely low and were not statistically significant. No association was found between speed of focusing as measured by this test and speechreading ability. (See Table 4-XVII.)

A study by Byers and Lieberman[3] can be viewed as *an indirect attempt to assess the contribution of speed of focusing to speechreading skill.* Good and poor speechreaders were given speech-

TABLE 4-XVII
SUMMARY RESEARCH FINDINGS—CORRELATION BETWEEN
SPEECHREADING AND SPEED OF PERCEPTION

Study	*Test of Factor*	*Speechreading Test*	*No.*	*"r"*	*"E" Percent Contrib.*
Wong and Taaffe	Percep. Speed Test	Keaster Film Test of Liprdg.	94 M. 88 Fe.	− .02 .19	N.S. N.S.
Byers and Lieberman	Utley Sent. Form A at various speeds	Utley Sent. Form B	48	N.S.	Trend indic.
Frisina and Bernero	Exper. Sent. Test at various rates	Keaster Film Test of Liprdg.	80	N.S.	Trend Indic.

reading tests where the speaker's rate varied from 40 to 120 words per minute. There was no statistically significant improvement in speechreading performance as the rate was lowered for either group. However, their data indicate a trend in this direction. The best mean score for the poor lipreading group occurred when the talker was speaking at the rate of 60 words per minute. *It should be noted that our interpretation of what they were measuring is different from what they purported to measure.* Their purpose was to investigate whether speechreading becomes easier and more proficient as the speaker uses a slower rate of speech. This is a view commonly held by teachers of speechreading and by the speechreaders themselves. Less information can be gleaned when the rate is too fast for ease in focusing. But there are other important variables that obtain when a speaker slows his rate of speech. He articulates more precisely and tends to use more jaw movement. Such changes result in a different motor picture. More information is available to the speechreader with respect to the various speech sounds that have been formed. Byers and Lieberman controlled these variables (leaving only speed of perception) by the nature of their experimental materials. Their talker did not vary her rate. Changes in rate were effected through changes in the rate of photographing and of projecting.

Frisina[16] reported a similar, but unpublished, experiment done by him and Bernero. Subjects were selected for study that had been found not to differ in speechreading proficiency. They were divided into four groups of twenty subjects each, and each group was given the same experimental test, but for each group it was filmed at a different rate. Speech was viewed by the subjects at normal rate; at 0.80, 0.67, and 0.58 of the normal rate. No statistically significant differences between skill and rate were found. However, there was a trend toward higher scores at the rate of speed which was 67 percent of the normal rate. This would appear to be in accord with the trend shown by Byers and Lieberman.

It is understandable that studies such as these have failed to indicate the percent contribution of speed of focusing to speechreading skill despite the fact that their experimental material would appear to measure it. If speechreading is conceived of as a composite skill, it then follows that two individuals might be equally skilled and yet vary in the relative weight of factors contributing toward the skill. More accurate visual perception or greater skill in arriving at conjectural and perceptual closures, good visual memory and the like, may "make up for" lesser ability with respect to speed of perception. *It is impossible to measure accurately the contribution of a single primary factor without equating or controlling the remainder of the factors. It is also possible that the task requirements were not sufficiently stringent* (at least for the good speechreaders) to bring out the importance of fast focusing. Increasing the rate of a filmed test beyond normal rate might be more revealing of differences in speechreading skill as a function of difference in speed of focusing.

6.2. *Factors Ancillary to Visual Proficiency*

Four factors have been postulated as ancillary to visual proficiency. They are visual acuity, visual attention, speed of focusing, and peripheral vision. Two of them have been studied.

6.2.1 VISUAL ATTENTION. In order to speechread, it is necessary to maintain visual attention or concentration for considerable periods of time. Frisina has reported on unpublished experiments dealing with this variable done by him and Cranwill.[17] The Continuous Performance Test (Rosvold, *et al.*, 1956) was used as a test of visual attention, and the Keaster-John Tracy Clinic

Film Test of Lipreading, as the speechreading criterion test. Speechreaders were divided into proficient and inefficient groups. Comparisons were made between two deaf groups and between a deaf group and a hearing group. It was hypothesized that the better speechreaders would make fewer errors of omission or of commission during the sustained attention task. No significant differences were found.

6.2.2 DEPTH PERCEPTION AND VISUAL ACUITY. Two research studies have examined the relationship between visual acuity and speechreading skill. Goetzinger[19] studied the relationship between depth perception and speechreading skill. The Utley Sentence Test Form A, was used as the speechreading criterion. Depth perception was measured directly through the use of Ortho-Rater Vision Test (Bausch and Lomb Optical Co.) and indirectly through presenting the speechreading test binocularly (12 subjects); monocularly-dominant eye (12 subjects), and monocularly nondominant eye (12 subjects). The subjects had normal hearing and ranged in age from eighteen to thirty-seven years. No relationship was found between depth perception and speechreading skill. The twelve binocular speechreaders were examined for evidence of ocular imbalance even after correction with glasses. Five of them showed some indication of imbalance, but it was not reflected in speechreading scores poorer than those made by the remainder of the group. Finally, the visual acuity of the twenty-four monocular speechreaders was measured and compared with their speechreading skill. There was no tendency for the subjects with superior visual acuity to make the better speechreading scores.

Hardick, Oyer, and Irion,[21] gave a group of fifty-three college students the Utley Film Test. They then selected the eight best and eight worst speechreaders for complete optometric examinations. Nine of the sixteen subjects were found to have completely normal vision. Seven of them departed from normality only to a very slight extent (except for one subject) with respect to binocular visual acuity. Nonetheless, significant differences were found between the normal vision group and the visual impairment group on the sentence test portion of the speechreading test and on the test as a whole. Rank order correlations between visual acuity ranking and ranking on the Utley Test were .65 for the Sentence Test and 0.59 for the test as a whole. The relationship between blink rate and speechreading was also investigated, but was found not to be a significant variable.

6.3. *Relationship of Speechreading to Synthetic Ability*

By synthesis is meant the tentative or final identification of a message or any part of it. The process requires the combination of both perceived and conjectured elements and consists of two main stages—perceptual closure followed by conceptual closure. Only certain aspects of the total process have been investigated. They are perceptual closure, conjectural perception, and conjectural closure. We shall begin our discussion with the first of these.

6.3.1 PERCEPTURAL CLOSURE INCLUDING VISUAL PERCEPTION. A word and phrase test (words that go together, but do not constitute a complete message) could be devised to assess the contribution of perceptual closure per se to speechreading skill. But in order to do so, subjects would have to be equated with respect to visual perception and language comprehension, and the other factors which we have listed under visual proficiency would need to be controlled. Credit would also need to be given for the substitution of homophenous words. To date we do not have a pure measure of the relationship of perceptual closure to speechreading skill because no one has devised such an experiment. There have been, however, two studies which can be considered to have measured the contribution of visual perception and at least part of the contribution of perceptual closure to speechreading achievement. Both experiments made use of word tests and compared skill in identifying isolated words with the ability to speechread connected speech—sentences and stories. *Word tests are considered by us not to measure speechreading ability, but only certain aspects which are essential to the process.* If the subjects can be considered to have a knowledge of vocabulary adequate for the task at hand, *then word tests would appear to measure primarily visual perception and perceptual closure.* It is unlikely that the additional subfactors of visual proficiency, namely, speed of perception and visual span play major roles in the recognition of isolated words. Speechreading is the total process. Single words sometimes, but rarely, express complete thoughts. If these premises are accepted, then it follows that the results of studies which have correlated scores from word tests with scores from sentence or story tests can be interpreted as indicating, at least in part, the contribution of visual perception plus perceptual closure to the total process. We qualify our statement to "at least in part" because perceptual closure, as we have defined it, also involves the mental grouping and separation of a string of speech movements, as in a phrase, into a series of words. When given a word test the viewer is cued as to the completion of the word by the talker's presentation.

The two experiments referred to are those of Conklin,[5] 1917, and Utley,[43] 1945. The correlations which they found are presented in Table 4-XVIII.

Conklin combined data from the consonant and word portions of his test and compared the rank order of consonant and word recognition with the rank order of sentence recognition for the group. It is unlikely that the consonant portion of his test contributed appreciably to the variance inasmuch as six of the eight consonants tested (sh, th, s, r, f, p) could be expected to be recognized with ease. The remaining two were /t/ and /l/. Credit was given for homophenous consonants and for homophenous words even when the word written was senseless. He found a correlation of .74 which would indicate that visual perception and perceptual closure might have been associated with as much as 55 percent of the total speechreading score for the population studied. Conklin's finding, however, should perhaps be taken with a grain of salt, since he used only sixteen subjects and the reliability of his speechreading test had not been established. *But if Conklin's findings can be disregarded, Utley's cannot,* and while hers are more extensive, they are remarkably similar to Conklin's. The scores on which Utley's findings are based were made on 761 deaf and hard-of-hearing subjects. Words homophenous to the test words were scored as correct. Her results indicate that visual perception and visual closure are associated

TABLE 4-XVIII

SUMMARY OF RESEARCH FINDINGS—CORRELATION BETWEEN SPEECHREADING AND VISUAL PERCEPTION PLUS PERCEPTUAL CLOSURE

Study	Test of Factors	Test of Speechreading	Classification	Numb. of Subjects	Coef. of Corr. "r"			Stat. Sig.	"E" Percent Contrib.
Conklin	Consonant and Word Test	Conklin Sentence Test	deaf 12–21 yrs	16	.74			.01	55%
Utley	Word Test Form A	Sentence Test Form A	deaf and h.-of-h. 3rd gr. rd.	761	.687	P.E.	.012	.01	47%
	Word Test Form B	Sentence Test Form A	level or better		.687	P.E.	.012	.01	47%
	Word Test Form A	Sentence Test Form B			.705			.01	53%
	Word Tests Forms A and B	Sentence Tests Forms A and B			.778			.01	60%
	Word Test Form A	Stories Test			.560			.01	31%
	Word Test Form B	Stories Test			.616			.01	38%
	Word Tests Forms A and B	Stories Test			.614			.01	38%

with from 45 percent to 60 percent of the differences in speechreading test scores of sentences and from 31 percent to 38 percent of the skill required to speechread stories. One can speculate that the lower correlations with story type material are to be expected inasmuch as the ability to respond to environmental cues are incorporated in the total score. It has long been recognized that speechreaders gain much information from the total setting that is not measured by a test of unrelated sentences.

It is doubtful that language comprehension was a factor in either experiment. Both studies employed simple vocabulary. Utley's words were taken from Thorndike's list of the one thousand most frequently used words in the written language.

A third study, Brannon and Kodman,[2] 1959, made a comparison between the ability of skilled and unskilled speechreaders to speechread a word test. The mean score for the skilled group was 19.75 percent, and for the unskilled group, 12.5 percent, but this difference was not statistically significant (could have happened by chance). *Their results are not included in our tabled summary because no credit was given for the substitution of homophenous words.* They concluded that skill in speechreading "resides in the degree of utilization of contextual, situational, and other cues which are external to the lip movements themselves." On the basis of their data, they speculate that only about 20 percent of the discrete words of conversation can be identified on the basis of vision alone. This would appear to be a conservative estimate. The word test, PB-50 List No. 6, from which their data were derived, contains many words which would not be contained in a word count of the words used most frequently in the English language. Also their test of the effect of familiarity on performance barely missed statistical significance. *It is possible that had they used a list containing more of the familiar words that the percent correct identifications might have exceeded twenty percent.*

6.3.2 CONJECTURAL PERCEPTION. It is believed that the skilled speechreader is more adept at guessing (forming conjectural perceptions) than his less skilled counterpart. Kitson,[27] 1915, believed that this ability might be comparable to that of guessing whole letters when only a portion of the letters was presented. Accordingly, he presented a group of hard-of-hearing adults with the task of completing a group of words and phrases which had been bisected horizontally to show only the upper half. Unfortunately, he combined the scores made on this task with scores made on tasks which were considered by him to measure visual span and speed of apprehension (words and sentences of various lengths) before correlating them with speechreading proficiency. For this reason it is impossible to evaluate his data.

Two research studies, Wong and Taaffe,[47] 1958, and Simmons,[38] 1959, have, however, replicated this aspect of his study and correlated it with speechreading skill. Both studies used the Thurstone Multilated Words Test which consists of twenty-six fragmented one-syllable and two-syllable words. Correlations were low and statistically nonsignificant, (See Table 4-XIX.) In addition, they both gave the Gestalt-Completion Test which consists of thirty fragmented pictures of common objects to their test subjects. Again the association between the kind of skill required for this type of test and speechreading was not apparent. Wong and Taaffe used normally hearing college students, and Simmons, hard-of-hearing adults.

A recent study by Coscarelli and Sanders[6] has attacked the same problem but with somewhat different materials. The three tests used by them were the following: (a) Visual Closure Speed Test,* consisting of twenty-four incomplete pictures which the testee is asked to identify; (b) Disemvowelled Word Test,† consisting of twenty-five words from which all the vowels have been removed, e.g., m-t-l-t (mutilate); (c) Sentence Completion Test—twenty short sentences from which all of the consonants have been removed, e.g. -o-a-e you? (How are you?) Speechreading was measured by means of the Utley Lip Reading Sentence Test (Form B) presented live through the glass window of a sound-isolation booth. "The test-retest correlation co-efficient for a sub-group of the normal hearers was .91 suggesting accept-

* Thurstone, L.L.: and Jeffrey, T.E.: Visual Closure Speed Test, University of North Carolina, 1956. (Chicago Industrial Relations Center, University of Chicago.).

† Hoepfner, R.: Disemvowelled Word Test. University of Southern California.

TABLE 4-XIX

SUMMARY OF RESEARCH FINDINGS—CORRELATION BETWEEN SPEECHREADING ABILITY AND CONJECTURAL PERCEPTION

Study	Test of Factor	Speechreading Test	No.	"r"	Stat. Sig.	"E" Percent Contrib.
Simmons	Mutilated Sentences	Intv. Test Mason Film Utley Film	24 24 24	.32 .28 .24	N.S. N.S. N.S.	
Wong and Taaffe	Mutilated Sentences	Keaster Film Test J.T.C. Form	94 M. 88 Fe.	.05 .08	N.S. N.S.	
Simmons	Street-Gestalt Completion	Interview Mason Film Utley Film	24 24 24	.38 .25 .29	N.S. N.S. N.S.	
Wong and Taaffe	Street-Gestalt Completion	Keaster Film Test J.T.C. Form	94 M. 88 Fe.	−.05 .12	N.S. N.S.	
Coscarelli and Sanders	Visual Closure Speed Test	Utley Sent. (B) Live	24 (N) 24 (H.H.)	.68 .63	<.001 <.001	47% 40%
	Disemvowelled Word Test	Utley Sent. (B) Live	24 (N) 24 (H.H.)	.52 .48	<.02 <.02	27% 23%
	Sentence Completion Test	Utley Sent. (B) Live	24 (N) 24 (H.H.)	.64 .45	<.001 <.05	41% 20%

able reliability for the live method of presentation." Their results are presented in Table 4-XIX. All correlations were significant. In addition, the seven best speechreaders in each group (hard-of-hearing and normal) made significantly better scores on all three of the aptitude tests than did the seven poorest subjects.

Why were Simmons, and Wong and Taaffe unable to find a correlation between conjectural perception and speechreading, while Coscarelli and Sanders found such a relationship? When we attempt to do some "Monday morning quarterbacking," we arrive at two possible reasons. (a) Perhaps the tests used in the first two research studies were not difficult enough for the populations studied to differentiate subjects with respect to conjectural perception. Such a possibility was not reported, however, in either research study. But an examination of the subtests used clearly indicates that they were easier than those used by Coscarelli and Sanders. More visual information was available to guide the testee in arriving at the Gestalt. For example, with respect to the Thurstone Mutilated Words Test, fragments of letters usually give some cues as to the specific letters. There is a fragment for each letter, and the consonants, when identified, serve as cues to the particular vowel represented by a letter or letter combination. The difficulty of the Gestalt Completion Test would also appear to be of a low order. (b) It is also possible that conjectural perception was not one of the factors which differentiated the subjects used by Simmons, and Wong and Taaffe since it is but one of the many primary factors which are believed to contribute to the total speechreading score.

6.3.3 CONJECTURAL CLOSURE. By conjectural closure is meant the ability to fill in missing words. It is part of the process of arriving at a conceptual closure, the identification of the message or thought that the speaker wishes to convey.

Two studies, by Kitson, 1914, and Simmons, 1958, have attempted to measure the contribution of conjectural closure to speechreading ability. (See Table 4-XX.) Both used the same kind of material. Kitson[27] described his Completion Test as consisting of a printed story, with certain letters, syllables, words, and

TABLE 4-XX

SUMMARY OF RESEARCH FINDINGS—CORRELATION BETWEEN SPEECHREADING AND MEASURES OF CONJECTURAL CLOSURE

Study	Test of Factor	Speechreading Test	Classification	No.	"r"	Sig.	"E" Percent Contrib.
Kitson	completion test	subj. ranking	hearing handicapped adults	15	.65	.01	42%
Simmons	fragmentary sent.	interv.	h.-of-h. adults	24	.06	N.S.	
		Mason Film		24	.44	.05	19%
		Utley Film		24	.40	.05	16%

phrases left out. The number of elisions correctly filled in in five minutes was the score for the test.

Simmons[*] used a Fragmentary Sentences Test which consisted of one hundred sentences requiring completion. Examples are the following: "Here's nice quiet place rest." "Should we let little children go movies themselves?" "Put that cookie back box." "Morning paper didn't say anything rain this afternoon tonight." Positive associations were found between this test and speech-reading skill.

Kitson's and Simmons' studies indicate that from 16 percent to 42 percent of the ability to speechread may be associated with skill at filling in words that are not perceived. The more recent and presumably more reliable study indicates the lower percent involvement. A word of caution is probably in order. It is recognized that the speechreader's task is not completely comparable to that of filling in missing parts or words on a printed page. The speechreader must possess a good visual memory and may, in the process of "filling in" and arriving at a conceptual closure, be forced to shift or modify his original perceptual closures. On the other hand, the words not missing on a fragmentary sentence type test are established and, hence, serve as fixed guides to the guessing process.

There have been no studies which have attempted to measure the contribution of conceptual closure *in toto* to speechreading skill. One can conjecture, however, that for anyone who knows the English language, the process of concluding what was said, once the original associations and conjectural closures have been made, might be a fairly easy task. For this reason the final step, conceptual closure or identification of the message, should perhaps not be expected to discriminate among speechreaders, other than prelingually deaf children.

6.4. Relationship of Speechreading to Flexibility

We have defined this factor as the aptitude for revising tentative closures, (sounds, words, phrases, and message), and shifting to different sets or closures when a meaningful or appropriate

---

[*] From original data which the author most graciously sent to us for examination and evaluation.

message cannot be synthesized on the bases of the original decisions. Because so many sounds are homophenous and so much information is missing, flexibility is required with respect to all of the three basic closures: visual perception—which sounds; perceptual closure—which words; conceptual closure—what was the message. In order to be flexible with regard to the first two it is postulated that one must have a good visual memory. But a good memory does not necessarily insure rapid shifts in conceptual association. Given language proficiency adequate for the task at hand, the ability to revise conceptual closures is probably predicated primarily upon aptitude for verbal reasoning.

There has been no research dealing directly with the relationship between flexibility (as we have defined it) and speechreading skill. Its importance to the task can, however, be inferred from relationships established between speechreading skill and the factors listed above as well as other factors listed as ancillary to flexibility on our theoretical construct. They were abstract inductive and deductive reasoning and rhythm. The research is reported in the succeeding section.

6.5. Relationship of Skill to Factors Ancillary to Synthetic Ability and Flexibility

Factors ancillary to the synthetic process and to flexibility are those aptitudes, apart from those related to visual proficiency, which underlie the individual's ability to form and to revise perceptual and conceptual closures. There would appear to be at least five such aptitudes: (a) visual memory, (b) rhythm, (c) abstract inductive reasoning, (d) verbal inductive reasoning, and (e) social awareness-abstract deductive reasoning. The first three aptitudes are believed to underlie the ability to form and revise perceptual closures, and the fourth and fifth, to the formulation and revision of conceptual closures. Visual memory, as was stated heretofore, is believed to be most importantly related to the ability to revise perceptual closures.

6.5.1 VISUAL MEMORY. By visual memory is meant the ability to retain, at least briefly, the sensory information, i.e. the sequence of motor movements, on which the visual percepts are based. It is reasonable to assume that visual memory should play an important part in speechreading achievement. The individual needs to retain the visual imagery long enough to enable him to decide what he has seen—in our jargon, to arrive at a perceptual closure, or a series of perceptual closures—and also long enough to permit him to be flexible and to form different associations if the first associations cannot be combined into a meaningful message.

Three research studies in investigating the association between visual memory and speechreading achievement have used a visual digit span test, not as a test of visual span, but as a test of visual memory. Their findings are summarized in Table 4-XXI.

Costello[7] used a printed test consisting of sequences of from four to eight digits. The digits were exposed one at a time at the rate of one per second. After exposure, each digit was withdrawn from view. The subject responded by reproducing each series from a set of cards before him. A positive association between skill in this test and skill in speechreading was found for both deaf and hard-of-hearing groups. In addition, the same test was given using spoken, rather than printed numbers. The only digit omitted was *eight*, because of its close visual similarity to the digit *nine*. The children were able to speechread all of the symbols used. This type of presentation would appear to be superior to the printed form because it replicates the exact task of the speech-reader. Similar results were found. The children with the better memories tended to be the better speechreaders.

Both O'Neill and Davidson,[34] and Simmons[38] used printed visual digit span tests similar to the one used by Costello with the exception that their sequences were on slides and exposed for only .1 second. The visual digit span test, when presented in this fashion, would appear to measure speed of perception as well as retention. Both studies reported low and nonsig-nificant correlations between visual retention scores and speech-reading.

It is difficult to understand this divergence in results. Why did Costello find visual memory to be importantly associated with speechreading achievement when O'Neill and Davidson, and Simmons were unable to demonstrate such a relationship? Actu-

TABLE 4-XXI

SUMMARY OF RESEARCH FINDINGS CORRELATION BETWEEN SPEECHREADING AND VISUAL MEMORY

Study	Test of Factor	Time	Speechreading Test	No.	"r"	Sig.	"E" Percent Contrib.
Costello	Visual Digit Span 4–8 digits	1 sec. per digit	Costello Test	36 deaf ch.	.511	.01	26%
				34 h-of-h. ch.	.548	.01	30%
Costello	Verbal Digit Span 4–8 digits	1 sec. per digit	Costello Test	36 deaf ch.	.594	.01	35%
				34 h-of-h. ch.	.584	.01	33%
O'Neill and Davidson	Visual Digit Span 4–8 digits	0.1 sec. per slide	Mason Film	30 normal h.	.168	N.S.	
Simmons	Visual Digit Span 3–7 digits	0.1 sec. per slide	Interview Test	24 h-of-h. adults	.04	N.S.	
			Mason Test	24 h-of-h. adults	.38	N.S.	
			Utley Test	24 h-of-h. adults	.06	N.S.	
	Object Span	0.1 sec. per slide	Interview Test	24 h-of-h. adults	.50	.01	25%
			Mason Film	24 h-of-h. adults	.42	.05	18%
			Utley Film	24 h-of-h. adults	.57	.01	32%
			Mason Film	20 normal h.	.47	.05	22%
O'Neill	Digit Symbol Subtest W.B.		Interview Test	24 h-of-h. adults	rho .42	.05	25%
Simmons	Digit Symbol Subtest W.B.		Mason Test		.42	.05	18%
			Utley Test		.50	.01	32%

ally one might expect the latter studies to have shown higher correlations because two aptitudes combined, visual memory and speed of focusing, should logically result in a higher correlation than visual memory alone. Their time requirement does not appear to be unreasonable. It is, nevertheless, possible that the short time requirement contaminated their data. They may have been measuring a more rapid rate of focusing than was required by their speechreading criterion tests, or the very brief exposure period may have interferred with the measurement of true differences in visual memory. *One cannot retain material that he has not seen.* Substantiation of this latter hypothesis is perhaps given by the results found by Simmons on a somewhat different test of visual memory and speed of focus.

An Object Span Test was presented to the same subjects. Twenty-one slides of two or more common objects, were projected on a screen. The time element per slide was the same as before, .1 second. Subjects were required to write down the names of the objects. Correlations between this test and speechreading were found to be significant. (See Table 4-XXI.) These findings are very much like those found by Costello on her printed visual digit span test. It is likely that the rapid recognition of objects is an easier task than the rapid recognition of digits. The more familiar the material, the more quickly it can be perceived. One can reason that the focus rate did not interfere with perception on this task.

The Wechsler-Bellevue Digit Symbols subtest was given by both O'Neill[33] and Simmons[38] to their groups. There are ten numbers and ten symbols, one for each number. The numbers are printed in random order. The subject's task is to match each number with its appropriate symbol and to do it as rapidly as possible. While visual perception and motor skill are involved, they are not of a high order. For this reason it can be considered to be essentially a test of visual memory for the groups involved. The better the subject's memory, the faster the task can be completed and the higher his score, because there is less need for him to refer back to the key. Both O'Neill and Simmons found a positive association between scores made on the Digit Symbol Subtest and measures of speechreading achievement.

6.5.2 SENSE OF RHYTHM. It seems reasonable to assume that a sense of rhythm should be of help to the speechreader in recognizing phrasing and the end of thought units. The results of two studies are reported in Table 4-XXII. The Heiders[22, p. 143] found "that the children who can follow a rhythm better are also better lipreaders." The subjects were rated on a scale of from 0 to 4 on ability to follow rhythms by the teachers of gymnastics and dancing.

Simmons[38] gave the Seashore Rhythm Tests, Forms A and B. The tests require the individual to listen to two recorded rhythmic patterns and to decide if they are the same or different. Form A is the easier test. As can be seen from the Table, an association was found between skill in speechreading and rhythm for Form A, but not for Form B. Perhaps one can conclude that while a good sense of rhythm aids one in speechreading, that an excellent sense of rhythm is not a requisite. The size of the coefficients of correlation indicate that approximately 20 percent of the variation in scores was associated with differences in rhythmic sense.

6.5.3 OVERVIEW—RELATIONSHIP OF REASONING TO SPEECHREADING ABILITY. As was noted earlier, since general intelligence has not been demonstrated to be associated closely with speechreading skill, research workers have turned their attention to the exploration of the contribution of various specific cognitive aptitudes. Among these have been abstract or nonverbal reasoning and verbal reasoning. There are basically three kinds of reasoning, whether the reasoning is abstract or verbal—inductive, deductive, and intuitive. By inductive reasoning is meant the reasoning from a part to a whole. It is a synthetic or associative process. Deductive reasoning on the other hand proceeds in the opposite direction from the whole to the part and involves an analysis of either the total situation or the part which is to be subdivided into even smaller parts or elements. The third kind of reasoning, intuitive reasoning, is described as immediate apprehension or knowing without recourse to an analytic or deductive process. It is apparently an unconscious process. The person "grasps the idea" or "knows the answer" without either conscious analysis or synthesis.

TABLE 4-XXII

SUMMARY OF RESEARCH FINDINGS—CORRELATION BETWEEN SPEECHREADING AND SENSE OF RHYTHM

Study	Test of Factor	Speechreading Test	Subjects	No.	"r"	Stat. Sig.	"E" Percent Contrib.
Heiders	Teacher Ratings 1 to 4	Heider Test I Heider Test II	deaf ch. deaf ch.	81 60	Children who ranked higher in rhythm, also the better speech-readers.		
Simmons	Seashore Rhythm Test A Seashore Rhythm Test B	Interview Test Mason Film Utley Film Interview Test Mason Film Utley Film	h.-of-h. adults	24	.31 .47 .46 .03 .30 .29	N.S. .05 .05 N.S. N.S. N.S.	22% 21%

Implicit in the task of speechreading would appear to be the need for associative and intuitive reasoning as opposed to deductive or analytic reasoning. It is postulated that skill in deductive reasoning will be of little help to the individual in achieving proficiency, except as it enables him to analyze a social situation and, hence, anticipate what may be said. Unfortunately the research literature does not lend itself easily to this type of analysis. Tests of reasoning have been correlated with speechreading skill, but for the most part no special attempt has been made to choose instruments which measure primarily associative reasoning or, on the other hand, primarily analytic reasoning. Possible exceptions to this statement are those studies reported in Section 6.5.4. Nonetheless, in reporting the literature an attempt will be made to classify the various tests of reasoning first with respect to whether they are tests of abstract or verbal reasoning and secondly as to whether they appear to measure primarily inductive, deductive, or intuitive reasoning, or combinations thereof.

6.5.4 ABSTRACT INDUCTIVE REASONING. Nonverbal inductive reasoning and its product, concept formations, are believed to be most importantly related to one aspect of perceptual closure, namely, the ability to combine elements into parts and patterns, and may perhaps be conceived of as an indirect measurement of this aspect. Two psychological performance tests which appear to measure primarily inductive concept formation have been correlated with scores made on various tests of speechreading aptitude. (See Table 4-XXIII.) In the Hanfmann-Kasanin Test the subject is required to sort into four categories, twenty-two blocks of five different colors and four different shapes. O'Neill and Davidson found an association between scores made on this test and speechreading ability, while Simmons did not. O'Neill and Davidson's better speechreaders scored higher on this test than the less skilled subjects and also required less time than the poorer speechreaders to complete the task. As a consequence of this finding they concluded that skill in speechreading appears to involve the recognition of configuration or form patterns and suggested that it might be good to give training in this skill.

TABLE 4-XXIII

SUMMARY OF RESEARCH FINDINGS—CORRELATION BETWEEN SPEECHREADING AND
NONVERBAL INDUCTIVE REASONING

Study	Test of Factor	Speechreading Test	Subjects	No.	Stat.	Sig.	"E" Percent Contrib.
O'Neill and Davidson	Hanfmann-Kasanin Test	Mason Film	adult normal hearing	30	rho .39	.05	15%
Simmons	Hanfmann-Kasanin Test	Interview / Mason Film / Utley Film	adult h.-of-h.	24	"r" -.34 / "r" -.36 / "r" -.29	N.S. / N.S. / N.S.	
Costello	Progressive Matrices	Costello Test	deaf / h.-of-h.	36 / 34 / 34	"r" .178 / "r" .514 / "r" .373*	N.S. / .01 / .05	26% / 14%
Vaughan	Progressive Matrices	Subj. Rank.	deaf ch.	20	"r" .24	N.S.	
Evans	Progressive Matrices	Evans Film Test	deaf ch.	64	"r" .27	.05	7%

* Partial "r"

It can be argued, however, that one must recognize forms and patterns (words and phrases) in order to speechread, and that such training is implicit in any material (other than isolated sounds) that may be presented to the student.

The second test, The Raven's Progressive Matrices, consists of a series of geometric designs from which one piece is missing. Below each design are six to eight pieces, one of which completes the design. *In three of the five comparisons, an association was found between this test and speechreading ability.* More association was found for hard-of-hearing than for deaf subjects.

The two tests of abstract reasoning ability discussed above have correlated with speechreading skill for some groups of speechreaders but not for others. One can speculate that the variables which can becloud the picture were perhaps "unintentionally controlled" in some experiments but not in others. If subjects are not controlled with respect to the other factors that affect the ability to close, the importance of grouping or organizational ability to the total skill may be obscured. The grouping of visual elements is only a part of the process of forming perceptual closures. In addition, the ability to form perceptual closures is affected by such factors as visual proficiency and visual memory. It is also possible that some of the controls instituted in certain experiments have influenced adversely the degree of association found. For example, Costello equated her subjects with respect to intelligence and then gave them a test of one aspect of intelligence—abstract reasoning.

6.5.5 ABSTRACT DEDUCTIVE REASONING PLUS ABSTRACT INDUCTIVE REASONING. It is postulated that deductive reasoning may be of help to the speechreader in gaining information from nonverbal environmental cues. However, correlations between abstract deductive reasoning alone and speechreading are not to be found. Some indirect evidence of its relevance can perhaps be gleaned from correlations between speechreading and tests which require both deductive and inductive reasoning. (See Table 4-XXIV.) The Picture Arrangement Test may in part measure the kind of facility that is implied by the term "social awareness," the ability to deduce the topic of conversation from

TABLE 4-XXIV

SUMMARY OF RESEARCH FINDINGS—CORRELATION BETWEEN SPEECHREADING AND ABSTRACT DEDUCTIVE-INDUCTIVE REASONING

Test of Factors	Study	Speechreading Test	Subjects	No.	Stat.	Sig.	"E"
W.B. Picture Arrangement	O'Neill 1951	Mason Film	col. stu.	20	rho .17	N.S.	
	Costello 1957	Costello	deaf ch.	36	"r" .357*	.05	12.7%
			h.-of-h. ch.	34	"r" .445*	.05	19.8
	Simmons 1959	Part Costello	h.-of-h. adult	24	.509	.01	25.9
		Intv.			.18	N.S.	21.2
		Mason F.			.46	.05	23.0
		Utley F.			.48	.05	
W.B. Block Design	O'Neill	Mason F.	col. stu.	20	rho .38	N.S.	
	Simmons	Interv.	h.-of-h. adult	24	"r" .44	.05	19.4
		Mason F.			.23	N.S.	
		Utley F.			.43	.05	18.5
Bruner, Goodnow† & Austin Test	Tiffany and Kates	Heider, Film and Clarke School Sp. Percep. Tests	deaf high school	24	F4.59	.05	

* Partial "r"

† Believed to require intuitive reasoning as well.

situational and environmental cues. The test "consists of a series of pictures which, when placed in the right sequence, tell a little story." According to Wechsler,[46, pp. 87,88] ". . . it is the type of test which effectively measures a subject's ability to comprehend and size up a total situation. The subject must understand the whole, must get the 'idea' of the story before he is able to set himself effectively to the task." A positive association was found between the Picture Arrangement Test and speechreading in four of the six comparisons that have been made.

The WAIS Block Design Test has been described as a timed colored block assembly for designs. The pattern to be duplicated is printed in red and white on a card which is left in front of the subject. The task consists of mentally analyzing a pattern into its components and then synthesizing the blocks to duplicate the pattern. Neither O'Neill[33] nor Simmons[38] was able to demonstrate an association between this test and speechreading as measured by the Mason Film Test. Simmons, however, found a correlation between it and speechreading as measured by her Interview Test and the Utley Film Test. Unlike the Mason Test, both of these tests permit the speechreader to appraise the social situation and to guess as to what may be said. This is true of the Interview Test as a whole and of the Story Test portion of the Utley Film.

A third test, presumed also to require powers of nonverbal analytic reasoning, the Knower-Dusenbury Test of Ability to Judge Emotions, was given by O'Neill.[33] No relationship was found between it and speechreading ability.

6.5.6 ABSTRACT DEDUCTIVE, INDUCTIVE, AND INTUITIVE REASON-ING. The Bruner, Goodnow, and Austin Test, a test of nonverbal concept attainment, would appear to require all three kinds of reasoning—deductive, inductive, and intuitive. This test was given by Tiffany and Kates[42] to twenty-four subjects who had been divided into two subgroups of twelve each, good speechreaders and poor speechreaders, on the basis of speechreading test scores. The two groups were equated with respect to intelligence, age, years of training, hearing loss, and socioeconomic status. Both groups used the same intellectual approach to the problems, successive scanning, which consists of testing one single hypothesis as to the correct concept at a time. This is in contrast to the mental process labeled "conservative focusing" which consists of choosing cards so that only one attribute is changed on each successive choice. There was also no significant difference in the number of guesses as to correct concept made by each group. These findings can perhaps be interpreted to mean that the study provided no evidence of good speechreaders being more willing to gamble than their less skilled counterparts.

Additional results indicated that the poor speechreaders required significantly more choices (card selections), and more total time than good speechreaders to attain the solutions.

It is possible that the difference between the two groups, good speechreaders and poor speechreaders, might have been even more dramatic had not the subjects been equated with respect to intelligence (Wechsler Performance scale) before given a test which would appear to measure an important aspect of it—namely, reasoning.

6.5.7 VERBAL INDUCTIVE PLUS DEDUCTIVE REASONING. Verbal inductive reasoning is considered to be primarily ancillary to the formation of conceptual closures. It is involved in deciding which words go together and which words should be filled in when one must construct a message from limited information. But it will affect perceptual closure and flexibility as well. Since words look alike, associative reasoning is involved in identification as well as conceptualization.

The importance of verbal associative reasoning, by itself, to the speechreading process cannot be deduced from the research literature. Only one research project, Wong and Taaffe, has studied the association between verbal reasoning and speechreading ability. But in it no attempt was made to study associative reasoning separately from analytic reasoning or from general knowledge.

Wong and Taaffe gave five tests of verbal reasoning to groups of subjects and then correlated them with speechreading skill. One of the tests was the Reasoning Subtest from the SRA Primary Mental Abilities. Reasoning is measured by such items as: e f e f c d g h g h c d i j. The letters form a series based on a rule. The problem is to mark the letter that should logically come next in the series, in this case "i." The examinee must discover the pattern, i.e. he must associate the letters that go together and then fill in the letter that should logically come next. Wong and Taaffe gave this test and the Keaster Film Test of Lipreading, John Tracy Clinic Forms A and B, to a large group of normally hearing college students. An association between reasoning and skill in speechreading was found for their female subjects, but not for the males. The subjects were separated with respect to sex because it had been found that females make somewhat better scores than the males on the speechreading criterion test which they used. Wong and Taaffe,[47, p. 5] felt that the task required on this test "is analogous to the lipreading situation where missed (unseen or invisible) elements must be fitted into the lipreading sequence." In our view it is more comparable to the task of filling in missing words, though the grouping or visual organization of the letters is essential to the process. Analytic reasoning is probably involved in the latter process.

Two additional tests which appear to measure verbal inductive reasoning in part, though they surely measure knowledge as well, are the Brick Uses, Fluency, and the Brick Uses, Flexibility. They were developed by the University of Southern California Aptitudes Research Project. The first task is to list as many uses as one can think of for a brick. It is considered to be a measure of ideational fluency. The score for the second test, Brick Uses, Flexibility, is obtained for the data on the first test. A point is given everytime there is a shift from one category of use to another. For example, from construction to destruction—"to build a house" followed by to "throw at a dog." It is considered to measure spontaneous flexibility. Neither of these tests were found to be associated with speechreading when correlated independently, but when combined, were found to be associated with skill for female subjects.

Controlled Associations is another test developed by the University of Southern California Aptitudes Research Project. It consists of four words—quiet, angry, funny, and feeble. The task is to list as many words similar to the given words as is possible in the time allotted. It is believed to measure associational fluency.

TABLE 4-XXV
SUMMARY OF RESEARCH FINDINGS—CORRELATION OF SPEECHREADING WITH VERBAL REASONING

Study	Test of Factor	Speechreading Test	No.	"r"	Sig.	"E" Percent Contrib.
Wong and Taaffe*	PMA—Reasoning; Inductive-Deductive	Keaster Film	95 M.	.09	N.S.	7%
		J.T.C. Forms	67 Fe.	.27	.05	
	Brick Uses, Fluency	J.T.C. Forms	85 M.	.15	N.S.	
	Verbal Association	J.T.C. Forms	61 Fe.	—.20	N.S.	
	Brick Uses, Flexibility	J.T.C. Forms	85 M.	.16	N.S.	
	Change Verbal Set	J.T.C. Forms	61 Fe.	.09	N.S.	
	Controlled Associations	J.T.C. Forms	85 M.	.12	N.S.	
	Inductive Reasoning	J.T.C. Forms	61 Fe.	.13	N.S.	
	Brick Uses, Fluency, and Flexibility	J.T.C. Forms	61 Fe.	.41	.01	17%
	Brick Uses, Fluency Plus Controlled Associations	J.T.C. Forms	61 Fe.	.31	.05	10%
Simmons	Iowa Silent Reading Test	Simmons Interview	24 h.-of-h.	.02	N.S.	
	Sentence Meaning—Deductive	Mason Film	24 h.-of-h.	.33	N.S.	
	Reasoning	Utley Film	24 h.-of-h.	.44	.05	19%

* Subjects were college students with normal hearing.

The test failed to correlate independently with speechreading achievement, but when combined with Brick Uses, Fluency, a multiple correlation was found for female subjects.

6.5.8 VERBAL DEDUCTIVE REASONING. A test which appears to measure verbal deductive reasoning as well as common knowledge is the Iowa Silent Reading Test of Sentence Meaning. It is placed under this section because it was correlated with adult rather than child speechreading ability. The assumption is made that the knowledge required would be held by most adults. The testee marks "yes" or "no" in response to each question. Some sample items are the following:

Should one be constantly changing his decision concerning his life work?
Is a flat-topped roof usually desirable in a land of heavy snowfall?

More advanced items require a knowledge of vocabulary as well— example: Do carnivorous animals live exclusively upon vegetables? The speechreading criterion tests, however, did not require a high-level knowledge of vocabulary. For these reasons it is assumed that the association with speechreading skill would be predicated upon both tasks requiring some measure of analytic reasoning ability. Simmons[38] found a correlation between this test and Utley Film Test of speechreading ability. As we said previously, deductive reasoning ability may be of value to the speechreader in understanding the Story Test portion of the Utley Test. If the social situation is analyzed properly, one may be able to predict what may be said.

6.6. Relationship of Speechreading to Multiple Factors

Many of the psychological subtests which have been correlated with speechreading can be presumed to measure more than one ability. They were classified as best as possible with respect to the primary aptitude that appeared to be measured. There were other tests, however, which appeared to measure multiple factors, but in which no one factor seemed to predominate. These are reviewed in this section. (See Table 4-XXVI.)

Simmons[38] compared age and speechreading skill for a group

TABLE 4-XXVI

SUMMARY OF RESEARCH FINDINGS—CORRELATION OF SPEECHREADING WITH *MULTIPLE FACTORS*

Study	Test of Factors	Class Subjects	No.	Speechreading Test	"r"	"E" Percent Contrib.
Simmons	Age as index of visual proficiency	h.-of-h. adults	24	Interview	−.19	
				Mason	−.25	
				Utley	−.22	
	Key Words—reasoning, spd. of focus, memory	h.-of-h. adults	24	Interview	.04	
Goetzinger	Age	normal hear adults ages 18–22 and 25–37	36	Mason	.53*	28%
				Utley	.58*	34%
				Sent. A	−.3369	11%
Kitson	Tachis. Test. Visual span; spd. of perception; conjectural closure	18–22 and 25–35 hearing hand. adults	16 15	Subject Ranking	−.6977 .67*	46% 45%
O'Neill	W.B. Adult Perf. Scale. Visual memory, abstract reasoning, social awareness	normal adults	20	Mason Film	.55†	30%
Evans	WISC Perf. Portion. Visual memory, abstract reasoning, social awareness	deaf ch.	64	Evans Film	.38*	14%
Craig	WISC Perf. Portion, plus Leiter Internat'l Perf. Test	deaf ch.	164	Craig Test	.63*	40%
	WISC Perf. plus Nebr. Test Learning Apt. visual memory, abstract reasoning (Induc. and Deduc.), social aware.	deaf ch.	79	Craig Test	.58*	33%

* Significant at the .01 level
† Significant at the .05 level.

of hard-of-hearing adults with a mean age of 47.13, S.D. of 9.64. The exact range was not reported. Age is expected to be related to speechreading skill, as it can serve as an index of proficiency. As people grow older their eyesight, attention span, and memory often diminish. While none of the correlations reached statistical significance, a trend was apparent for the older subjects to be the poorer speechreaders.

Goetzinger[19] also compared age and speechreading, but with younger and normally hearing subjects. They were found to be negatively associated; the older subjects made the poorer speechreading scores. From these data, it would appear "that subtle changes are taking place which have a deleterious effect on ability to lipread." Differences in visual proficiency between the older and younger subjects could not be demonstrated with the Ortho-Rater.

Another test which appears to measure multiple skills is Key Words, a subtest from the Iowa Silent Reading Test. Under each question are printed four words or phrases. Three of the words would be of help in locating information regarding the question in an index. One would not. The testee's task is to locate the one word or phrase that would not help. Examples of items are the following:

How long has the income tax law been operating in the United States?
1. income tax   2. tax act   3. salary   4. government income
When was the transatlantic cable laid?
1. transatlantic cable   2. radio   3. Atlantic   4. telegraph
The test is believed to measure knowledge, reasoning, and since it is timed, it probably also measures speed of focusing and memory. This test was found to be associated with scores made on two speechreading tests (Mason and Utley) but not with the Interview Test.

Kitson[27] gave a tachistoscopic test consisting of four kinds of material—long words, e.g., superintendent, sentences containing from three to six three-letter words, the letter "a" printed from four to seven times, and words and phrases bisected horizontally showing only the upper half. The number of exposures necessary before all the sixteen cards were correctly perceived represented the score for the individual. The test is believed to measure visual span, visual memory, speed of perception, and conjectural perception. A correlation was obtained indicating that 45 percent of the variation among the test scores was attributable to these factors.

Three research workers[14,9,33] have given the Wechsler Performance Scales either by themselves or in combination with other performance tests, and have correlated scores with tests of speechreading skill. Their studies were reported under the section on intelligence, but are repeated here because these performance measures can also be considered as measures of multiple primary factors. Three of the Wechsler subtests have correlated independently with speechreading. They are picture arrangement, digit symbol, and block design. They have been classified by us as measures of social awareness, visual memory, and abstract reasoning (deductive plus inductive), respectively. The Nebraska Test of Learning Aptitude contains many subtests of visual memory and nonverbal inductive reasoning.

7. TESTS GIVEN BUT NOT CLASSIFIED

The following psychological tests have been correlated with speechreading. They could not, however, be classified with respect to our theoretical construct because they did not appear to measure the factors considered to be important to speechreading ability. For this reason they were not included in the body of this chapter. Nonsignificant correlations with speechreading were found for all of them with the exception of the Knox Cube Test which correlated only with the word portion of Costello's test and only for deaf children. They are presented here in order to report a complete picture and to enable the reader to judge for himself as to whether they measure the kind of task (and aptitudes) required of the speechreader.

TEST	*REASON NOT INCLUDED*
Case-Ruch Test of Spacial Relations. Timed design assembly. N.S. cor.[33]	The test requires only gross visual perception and perceptual closure. The speechreader must perceive and associate fine motor movements.

TEST	REASON NOT INCLUDED
Primary Mental Abilities— Space. Task: To mark every figure in a row that is the same as the first figure though subsequent figures have been rotated in space. N.S. corr.[47]	Visual perception, but not the kind required of the speechreader. The speechreader identifies motor movements, but does not rotate them or manipulate them in arriving at a Gestalt.
Wechsler Bellevue Picture Completion Subtest. Task: Draw the missing part, e.g., ship's funnel. N.S. corr.[33,38]	Gross Conjectural Perception. Not closely related to the speechreader's task of guessing as to missing sounds.
W.B. Object Assembly Subtest. Task: To assemble simple puzzle, e.g., manikin, hand, head. N.S. corr.[33]	Gross Perceptual Closure. Not closely related to the speechreader's task of associating and identifying motor movement sequences.
Knox Cube Test. Examiner taps out on 4 cubes a series of movement sequences which must be replicated, e.g., 1 3 1 2 4. N.S. corr.,[7] with total speechreading test for hard-of-hearing and deaf. Sig. Corr. for deaf on word test. Partial "r," .44, sig. at .01.	Visual memory for gross movement patterns. Not considered to be comparable to the speechreading task of retaining a complex movement pattern.
P.M.A.—Number Subtest. Items consist of addition of 4 two-digit numbers. N.S. corr.[47]	Appears to be unrelated to the speechreader's task.
W.B. Arithmetic Subtest. Simple arithmetic calculations. N.S.[33]	Appears to be unrelated to the speechreader's task.
W.B. Information Subtest. Ques Questions,[25] for range of information. N.S. corr.[33,38]	Extensive information is not required for performance of any of the speechreading criterion measures.

TEST	*REASON NOT INCLUDED*
W.B. Comprehension Subtest, e.g., "Why does the state require people to get a marriage license?" N.S. corr.[33,38]	Test would appear to measure knowledge plus verbal deductive reasoning. This kind of knowledge and reasoning is not required in order to speechread.
W.B. Similarities Subtest. Item: "In what way are an orange and a banana alike?" N.S. corr.[33,34,38]	Verbal deductive reasoning. Not the kind of reasoning required of the speechreader. The speechreader engages in verbal inductive reasoning.
Match Problems, Aptitudes Research Project U.S.C. Drawings of matches laid out in multiple squares. Task: To form new patterns as per instruction. E.G., two six-square diagrams given. Cross out 4 matches; leave 3 squares. A different solution of the same problem must be found for the second diagram. N.S. corr.[47]	Appears to measure ability to visualize patterns within patterns and to engage in deductive reasoning of a high order. Task appears to be quite unlike that required of the speechreader.
Word Checking II, Aptitudes Research Project, U.S.C. Items consist of 4 listed objects, e.g. car, bun, horse, ear of corn. Task: To select the word which represents an object that is not growing and is smaller than a football. N.S. corr.[47]	Score may also be influenced by visual span and speed of perception since the test is timed. Analytic reasoning of this sort is not part of the speechreading task.
Letter Prediction Test. Testee is given one word from a sentence. He is then asked to predict each letter in the sentence starting from the first letter;	The task does not appear to be closely related to the kind of prediction, (conjectural perception), that is required of the speechreader.

TEST

15 seconds per letter. When the guess is incorrect, the tester supplies the latter. N.S.[41]

SUMMARY OF RESEARCH LITERATURE ORGANIZED WITH RESPECT TO A THEORETICAL CONSTRUCT

An analytical collation and interpretation of the research literature and its organization with respect to a theoretical construct should serve a number of purposes. In the first place, it should permit us to see what factors have been found to be associated with speechreading and which factors that appear reasonably to be associated are in need of further investigation. And in the second place, it should give some indication of the relative weight or importance of aspects to the total process.

Secondary Factors

The secondary factors that have been found to be associated with speechreading are presented in Table 4-XXVII. In addition

TABLE 4-XXVII
ASSOCIATION OF SECONDARY FACTORS WITH SPEECHREADING
ABILITY—COMBINED RESULTS OF ALL STUDIES REVIEWED

Factor	No. Stat. Sig. Comparisons to Total	Range of Pearsons "r's"*	Percent Total Variance†
Training	4/4		
Indices: Chronological age and grade placement	10/13	.31–.65	10%–42%
Language Comprehension—Children Indices: Reading and ed. achievement; vocabulary level	12/13	.37–.688	14% to 47%
Emotional Attitudes	5/15	−.20 to .31	4% to 10%
Ancillary Factors—Training and Language Comprehension Age of onset; duration, extent of loss; discrim.	7/16	.10–.51	1% to 14%
General intelligence	0/6		
Performance intelligence (WISC and W.B. Adult)‡	5/12	.38–.63	14% to 40%

* All r's significant at .01 or .05 levels.
† Estimates based on Index of Forecasting Efficiency, "E".
‡ Because of the nature of three of the subtests, Performance Intelligence as measured by the Wechsler Scales is believed to be more importantly associated with Primary rather than with Secondary Factors.

to presenting the range of the statistical indices of association, "r," we have also indicated the range of the percent association, "E," of factors with variation in speechreading scores. The importance of two of the secondary factors—training and language comprehension appear to be well established. Improvement in speechreading skill occurs as the result of training,[1,4,5,9,13,14,22,23,25,29,35,37,43] but there is a limit to the amount of improvement that can be effected through training.[20,21] There is evidence which indicates that basic skill may be achieved in three years.[14] Large individual differences in speechreading skill exist among individuals with equal amounts of training and with no training at all. Expert and poor speechreaders are found in both categories.[6,22,23,24,43]

The speechreading skill of deaf children is associated with their language comprehension and can be expected to improve with growth in comprehension.[7,22,28,35,36,37,43] On the other hand, the unimportance of language comprehension to speechreading skill, (at least for the tests used), when considering the adult population, is also well established. No significant relationship was found in a total of 11 comparisons.[33,34,38,47]

When studying deaf children, one finds the extent of the loss to be negatively correlated with speechreading skill, (the greater the loss, the poorer the speechreading), in five out of five comparisons.[7,9,14,28]

The association between emotional attitudes or sets and speechreading skill has not been studied extensively, but some evidence of association is indicated.[8,47]

It is postulated in the theoretical construct that intelligence might be associated with language acquisition and, hence, with speechreading when considering the deaf child. There is no evidence from the research literature that this may be so. All comparisons, where deaf children have been used as subjects, have ruled out the factor of the relationship of intelligence to language acquisition through using performance tests of intelligence. In the six comparisons between general intelligence and speechreading ability[4,33,34,38] the subjects were either hard-of-hearing adults or normally hearing subjects. No relationship was established.

However, five of the twelve comparisons between performance tests of intelligence and speechreading indicated a relationship.[36,9,14,33] When we asked "why" and investigated the studies in somewhat more detail, an interesting fact emerged which may well explain the relationship of intelligence to speechreading skill. We found that in four of the five comparisons either the WISC, or in one instance, the W.B. Adult Performance Scale, had been used by itself or in combination with other performance tests. An examination of the subtests revealed that three of them (Digit Symbol, Block Design, and Picture Arrangement) could be considered to be measures of such aptitudes as visual memory and nonverbal analytic and nonverbal associative reasoning. Moreover, these three subtests had been found by other research workers to correlate independently with speechreading ability. (See Table 4-XIII and Sections 5.3.3, 6.5.1, and 6.5.5.) An examination of the scales used in conjunction with the WISC (Leiter International Performance Test and the Nebraska Test of Learning Aptitude) also indicated that many of their subtests could be considered to measure primarily visual memory and nonverbal associative reasoning.

The research literature indicates that performance tests of intelligence will correlate with speechreading ability providing enough of their subtests measure aptitudes postulated as being ancillary to the primary factors. To state this another way: A skill, such as speechreading, will be related to intelligence only to the degree that certain aspects of what is termed intelligence are needed for the skill.

Primary Factors

Research with regard to the primary factors—perceptual proficiency, synthetic ability, and flexibility—is indeed meager. (See Table 4-XXVIII.) None of them has been studied in its totality. Nonetheless, certain subfactors under each main factor or category have been explored to some extent, and occasionally trends have emerged which can be viewed with reasonable certainty.

One of these is visual perception—the ability to associate motor movements with speech sounds. Its importance has been indicated in three out of four investigations,[22,47,14] The better speech-

TABLE 4-XXVIII
ASSOCIATION OF PRIMARY FACTORS (BELIEVED TO DETERMINE
SPEECHREADING ABILITY) WITH SPEECHREADING

Factor	No. Stat. Sig. Comparisons to Total	Range of r's	Estimated Percent Total Variance†
Perceptual Proficiency	0/0		
Visual perception	3/4	.38 to .68	14% to 46%
Speed of perception	0/4		
Peripheral perception	0/0		
Ancillary Factors—Perceptual Proficiency			
Visual acuity	2/3	.59 to .65	45% to 42%
Visual attention	0/1		
Speed of focusing	0/0		
Peripheral vision	0/0		
Synthetic Ability	0/0		
Perceptual closure (plus visual perception)	8/8	.56 to .778	31% to 38% (stories) 47% to 60% (sentences)
Conjectural perception	6/16	.45 to .68	20% to 47%
Conceptual closure	0/0		
Conjectural closure	3/4	.40 to .65	16% to 42%
Flexibility	0/0		
Ancillary factors—synthesis and flexibility			
Visual memory	11/15	.42 to .594	18% to 35%
Rhythm	4/8	.46 to .47	21% to 22%
Abstract reasoning	12/21	.27 to .514	7% to 26%
Verbal reasoning	4/13	.27 to .44	7% to 19%

* All R's significant from .01 to .05 level.
† Estimates based on Index of Forecasting Efficiency "E."

readers were also the subjects with the greater skill in identifying speech sounds[22,37,14] We place this subfactor in the established category because in the one comparison in which a significant correlation was not found, the lack of association was apparently due to the fact that the subjects did not differ in their ability to speechread the visible consonant sounds. The importance of their recognition to speechreading skill can scarcely be denied. The remaining subfactors of perceptual proficiency have either not been studied or need further investigation. They are speed of perception, peripheral perception and the ancillary factors, visual attention, visual acuity, and speed of focusing. Another possible ancillary factor is depth perception.[19] There is some indication of the association of visual acuity with speechreading skill.[21]

There have been no studies which have attempted to assess the importance of perceptual closure as a whole. To do so one would have to control conceptual closure as well as the other primary factors. There have been, however, eight comparisons which can be said to have investigated the combined skills of visual perception and perceptual closure, i.e. the identification of isolated words.[5,38] All eight were found to be statistically significant. The findings also indicate that the ability to identify words was more important in speechreading sentences than in understanding connected speech-stories. This finding was perhaps to be expected inasmuch as situational and environmental cues were available to the subjects when speechreading the stories.

Conjectural perception, a subfactor under perceptual closure, has received some attention. It can be defined as the ability to fill in mentally missing speech sounds, often a necessary step in the identification of words and phrases. Significant associations were found between this skill and speechreading ability in six out of sixteen comparisons.[6] Perhaps more credance can be given to the six positive associations than to the ten comparisons where no association was found because the subtests used in the former appear to more closely relate to the actual task of the speechreader. (See Section 6.3.2.)

The ability to fill in missing words (conjectural closure) has been found to be associated with speechreading skill in three out of four comparisons.[24,34]

There have been no direct measurements of flexibility, defined by us as the ability to revise tentative closures or decisions with respect to words, phrases, or message. Its importance to the speechreading process, if not established, can, nonetheless, be said to be strongly indicated because of the establishment of the ancillary aptitude that we have postulated as being essential to it, namely, visual memory. Visual memory was found to be associated with speechreading ability in eleven out of fifteen investigations.[7,33,34,38]

Other aptitudes believed to be basic to both synthetic ability and flexibility are rhythm and reasoning.

A good sense of rhythm may be of help in speechreading. Positive correlations were found in four out of eight comparisons.[22,38]

There is some evidence of the importance of abstract reasoning to speechreading ability—8/15 comparisons;[34,7,14,38,42] but very little evidence of the role which verbal reasoning may play—4/13 comparisons.[38,47] Evidence of the importance of reasoning in general to the speechreading process was found in the one study which has employed factor analysis in an attempt to isolate factors basic to speechreading skill. "Lipreading reasoning" was isolated as a factor.[40]

Reasoning is believed by us to be ancillary or basic to two of the primary factors—synthetic ability and flexibility. The research is too limited to give any evidence with regard to our four hypotheses, which are the following: (a) that speechreading should correlate more highly with associative than analytic reasoning; (b) that abstract inductive reasoning is basic to and should be most closely associated with the ability to form and revise perceptual closures; (c) that verbal inductive reasoning should play the same role with respect to conceptual closures; and (d) that abstract deductive reasoning will only be of importance provided the environment provides clues as to what the speaker or speakers may be expected to say.

It is impossible at this stage to ascribe definite weightings to the three primary factors and the various aptitudes believed to be basic to them. This is true for at least six reasons.

1. There has been little research. Some facets of the process have not been explored at all and others but barely.

2. The research that has been done has not always been clear-cut. Most of the investigators have failed to control other major variables when attempting to isolate the importance of a particular variable. Speechreading is a composite skill consisting of many subskills. It is impossible to arrive at any correct idea of the contribution of a particular aspect to the total unless all other aspects are controlled or are studied simultaneously and their relative contributions assessed by means of statistical techniques.

3. The relative importance of the primary factors and the aptitudes basic to them can be expected to vary to some extent with the speechreading milieu (availability of environmental cues), with the visibility of the language used, and with the language proficiency of the speechreader. With respect to the

latter, for example, one might predict that perceptual proficiency might contribute relatively more to total score, and synthetic ability and flexibility, relatively less for a population of deaf children as compared with a hard-of-hearing or normal population. In order to synthesize effectively one must have a well developed knowledge of language. Without it the effect of aptitude for associative and intuitive reasoning cannot be apprehended.

4. The psychological tests used to measure various aptitudes are not pure measures in the sense that they can isolate independent variables.

5. There is a need to develop tests that measure directly the various aspects of the speechreading process. Psychological subtests designed for other purposes, e.g., perception of memory for *printed symbols*, are at best indirect measures of the tasks confronting the speechreader.

6. The relative weighting or contribution of each of the primary factors to the total task can be expected to vary with the individual and with the relative strength of the ancillary aptitudes that he brings to the task. It is possible that greater insight into the speechreading process might be gained through studying individuals rather than groups. Another possibility would be to analyze the relative importance of the primary factors and/or their ancillary aptitudes in a group that had been equated with respect to speechreading skill.

It is possible, however, to conjecture as to the relative weight of the primary factors that will eventually be established through research. Our conjecture is that "in general" perceptual proficiency will be found to contribute approximately 40 percent to the total task, and synthetic ability and flexibility, the remaining 60 percent. This estimate is based in part on the research findings and in part on knowledge of the limited sensory information available. In Chapter 2 we estimated that under usual viewing conditions the speechreader could not expect to receive more than from 10 percent to 25 percent of the information available through the auditory channels, and under the best conditions, no more than approximately one third. The 40 percent is basic or subordinate to the 60 percent. *Without the ability to perceive and retain sensory information, skill in association, whether abstract or verbal, cannot come into play.* The contribution of associative skills becomes more evident when some measure of auditory sensory information is available to supplement the limited visual information.

BIBLIOGRAPHY RESEARCH LITERATURE CITED

1. Black, J.W., O'Reilly, P.P., and Peck, L.: Self-administered training in lipreading. *J Speech Hearing Dis, 28:*183–186, 1963.
2. Brannon, J.B., Jr., and Kodman, F., Jr.: The perceptual process in speechreading. *Arch Otolaryng, 70:*114–119, 1959.
3. Byers, V.W., and Lieberman, L.: Lipreading Performance and The Rate of The Speakers. *J Speech Hearing Res, 2:*271–276, 1959.
4. Cavender, B.J.: *The Construction and Investigation of a Test of Lip-Reading Ability and a Study of Factors Assumed to Affect the Results.* Unpublished M.A. thesis, Indiana University, 1949.
5. Conklin, E.S.: A method for the determination of relative skill in lipreading. *The Volta Review, 19:*216–219, 1917.
6. Coscarelli, J.E., and Sanders, J.W.: The relationship of skill in visual synthesis to lipreading ability. Paper presented at the 44th Annual Convention of the American Speech and Hearing Association, Denver, Colorado, November 16, 1968.
7. Costello, M.R.: *A Study of Speech Reading as a Developing Language Process in Deaf and Hard of Hearing Children.* Unpublished Ph.D. Thesis, Northwestern University, 1957.
8. Costello, M.R.: Individual difference in speechreading. *Report of the Proceedings of the International Congress on Education of the Deaf and the Forty-First Meeting of the Convention of American Instructors of the Deaf.* Washington, D.C., United States Government Printing Office, 1964, Document No. 106, pp. 317–321.
9. Craig, W.N.: Effects of preschool training on the development of reading and lipreading skills of deaf children. *Amer Ann Deaf, 108:*280–296, 1964.
10. Edwards, A.L.: *Statistical Analysis.* New York, Rinehart, 1946.
11. Eisman, B., and Levy, J.: Interpersonal factors related to lip reading performance; performance as a function of characteristics of known communicators. In Lowell, E.L. (Principal Investigator): *Pilot Studies in Lip Reading, John Tracy Clinic Research Papers VIII.* Los Angeles, John Tracy Clinic, 1958.
12. Elkin, V.B.: *The Relationship between Personality Characteristics and Efficiency in the Use of Aural Sensory Aids by Groups of Acousti-*

cally Handicapped Patients. Unpublished Doctoral dissertation, New York University, 1952.

13. Evans, L.: Factors related to listening and lip-reading. *The Teacher of the Deaf,* 58:417–423, 1960.

14. Evans, L.: Psychological factors related to lipreading. *The Teacher of the Deaf, LXIII (no. 371):*131–137, 1965.

15. Frisina, D.R.: Speechreading. *Report of the Proceedings of the International Congress on Education of the Deaf and the 41st Meeting of the Convention of American Instructors of the Deaf.* Washington, D.C., United States Government Printing Office, 1954, Document No. 106, pp. 191–207.

16. Frisina, D.R., and Bernero, R.J.: A study of the effect of rate of speech in lipreading proficiency in hearing impaired subjects. Unpublished data. Cited in Frisina, *op. cit.,* Washington, D.C., United States Government Printing Office, 1954, Document No. 106, pp. 191–207.

17. Frisina, D.R., and Cranwill, S.: A comparison of sustained visual attention in two groups of hearing impaired lipreaders. Unpublished data. Cited in Frisina, *op. cit.,* Washington, D.C., United States Government Printing Office, 1954, Document No. 106, pp. 191–207.

18. Gault, R.H.: On the identification of certain vowel and consonantal elements in words by their tactual qualities as seen by the lipreader. *J Abnorm Psych,* 22:33–39, 1927–1928.

19. Goetzinger, C.P.: A study of monocular versus binocular vision in lipreading. *Proceedings of the International Congress on Education of Deaf and 41st Meeting of the Convention of American Instructors of the Deaf.* Washington, D.C., United States Government Printing Office, Document No. 106, pp. 326–333.

20. Guilford, J.P.: *Psychometric Methods.* New York, McGraw-Hill, 1936.

21. Hardick, E.J., Oyer, H.J., and Irion, PE.: Lipreading performance as related to measurement of vision. Paper presented at the 44th Annual Convention of the American Speech and Hearing Association, Denver, Colorado, Nov. 16, 1968.

22. Heider, F., and Heider, G.: An experimental investigation of lip reading. *Psychol Monogr,* No. 232, pp. 1–153, 1940.

23. Heider, G.M.: The Utley Lip Reading Test. *The Volta Review,* 49:457–458, 488, and 490, 1947.

24. Heider, F., and Heider, G.: *67th Annual Report Clarke School for the Deaf,* Metcalf Printing and Publishing Co., 1934.

25. Hutton, C.: A diagnostic approach to combined techniques in aural rehabilitation. *J Speech Hearing Dis,* 25:267–272, 1960.

26. Jeffers, J.: The process of speechreading viewed with respect to a theoretical construct, *Proceedings of International Conference on Oral Education of the Deaf, II:*1530–1561, 1967.

27. Kitson, H.D.: Psychological tests for lip-reading ability. *The Volta Review,* 17:471–476, 1915.
28. Lowell, E.L.: Research in speechreading: Some relationships to language development and implications for the classroom teacher. Proceedings of the 39th Meeting of the Convention of American Instructors of the Deaf, Washington, D.C., United States Government Printing Office, 1960, pp. 68–75.
29. Lowell, E.L., Taaffe, G., and Rushford, G.: The effectiveness of instructional films on lip reading. *Western Speech,* Summer 1959, pp. 158–161.
30. Miller, J., Rousey, C.L., and Goetzinger, C.P.: An exploratory investigation of a method of improving speechreading. *Amer Ann Deaf, 103:* 473–478, 1958.
31. Nitchie, E.B.: Tests for determining skill in lip-reading. *The Volta Review,* 19:222–223, 1917.
32. Nitchie, E.B.: *Lip-Reading Principles and Practise.* Lippincott, Philadelphia and New York, 1930.
33. O'Neill, J.J.: An exploratory investigation of lipreading ability among normal hearing students. *Speech Monographs,* 18:309–311, 1951.
34. O'Neill, J.J., and Davidson, J.L.: Relationship between lipreading ability and five psychological factors. *J Speech Hearing Dis,* 21: 478–481, 1956.
35. Pintner, R.: Speech and speechreading tests for the deaf. *Amer Ann Deaf,* 74:480–486, 1929; also *J App Psychol,* 12:220–225, 1929.
36. Quigley, S.P., and Frisina, D.R.: Institutionalization and psychoeducational development of deaf children. *CEC Res Monogr, No. 3,* 1961.
37. Reid, G.: A preliminary investigation in the testing of lip reading achievement. *J Speech Hearing Dis,* 12:77–82, 1947.
38. Simmons, A.A.: Factors related to lipreading. *J Speech Hearing Res,* 2:340–352, 1959.
39. Taaffe, G.: A film test of lip reading. In *John Tracy Clinic Research Papers II,* Los Angeles, John Tracy Clinic, 1957.
40. Taaffe, G.: *An Investigation of the Cognitive Domain of Lipreading.* Final Report, Project No. 7-E-048, U.S. Dept. H.E.W., Office of Ed., Bureau of Research, March, 1968.
41. Tatoul, C.M., and Davidson, G.D.: Lipreading and letter prediction. *J Speech Hearing Res,* 4:178–181.
42. Tiffany, R., and Kates, S.L.: Concept attainment and lipreading ability among deaf adolescents. *J Speech Hearing Dis,* 27:265–274, 1962.
43. Utley, J.: *Development and Standardization of a Motion Picture Achievement Test of Lip Reading Ability.* Unpublished Ph.D. Thesis, Northwestern University, 1945.
44. Utley, J.: A test of lip reading ability. *J Speech Dis,* 11:109–116, 1946.

45. Vaughan, V.D.: *A Study of the Value of Certain Tests in Predicting Success in Speech Reading.* M.A. Thesis, University of Oklahoma, 1954.

46. Wechsler, D.: *The Measurement of Adult Intelligence,* Third Ed. Baltimore, Williams and Wilkins, 1944.

47. Wong, W., and Taaffe, G.: Relationship between selected aptitude and personality tests and lip reading ability. *John Tracy Clinic Research Papers VII.* Los Angeles, John Tracy Clinic, 1958.

48. Worthington, A.M.L.: *An Investigation of the Relationship between the Lip Reading Ability of Congenitally Deaf High School Students and Certain Personality Factors.* Unpublished Ph.D. dissertation, Ohio State University, 1956.

49. Wright, J.D.: Familiarity with language the prime factor. *The Volta Review, 19:*223–224, 1917.

Chapter 5

METHODS

The methods used to teach speechreading that are presented here are organized with respect to the basic philosophy given in Chapter 1 regarding the factors believed to be important in the attainment of speechreading skill. They consist of exercises and materials, including instruction in how to use them, which have been designed to improve visual proficiency, flexibility, and skill in arriving at perceptual and conceptual closures.

1. EXERCISES FOR VISUAL PROFICIENCY

1.1. Perception and Speed of Perception

There are two goals, improvement in visual perception and improvement in speed of perception. These goals can be achieved through Quick Recognition Exercises. The exercises are a modification and extension of the "movement word" exercises that were developed by Nitchie.* There are basically four kinds or four variations of the Quick Recognition Exercise: exercises for recognition of visible consonant movements in the initial position in a word, visible consonant movements in the final position, obscure consonant movements in both initial and final positions, and vowel speech reading movements.

The speechreading movements, *recognizable visual patterns*,

---

* The Quick Recognition Exercises differ from Nitchie's Movement Words in three respects: (a) All visible consonant movements occur in each exercise. (b) The obscure consonant movements are not combined with the visible consonant movements, but instead are practiced separately. The movement for "l" is considered to be homophenous with that for "t," "d," and "n." The Obscure Consonant Exercises are intended only for advanced speechreaders. (c) Vowel Exercises are based on the Vowel Chart and represent true visual contrasts. They are intended for use only with the deaf.

usually common to two or more speech sounds, are presented again for easy reference in Table 5-I.

TABLE 5-I

SPEECHREADING MOVEMENTS°

Ideal Viewing Conditions

Visible Movements	*Obscure Movements*

Consonants

1. Lip to teeth—/f,v/
2. Lips puckered—narrow opening—/w,hw,r/
3. Lips together—/p,b,m/

4. Tongue between teeth—/θ,ð/
5. Lips forward—/ʃ,ʒ,tʃ,dʒ/
6. Teeth together—/s,z/

7. Lips back—narrow opening—/j/
8. Tongue up or down—moderate opening—/t,d,n,l/
9. Tongue back—moderate opening—/k,g,ŋ/

Vowels

1. Lips puckered—narrow opening—/u,ʊ,oʊ,ɝ/
2. Lips back—narrow opening /i,ɪ,eɪ,ʌ/
3. Lips rounded—moderate opening /ɔ/

4. Lips relaxed—moderate opening—/ɛ,æ,ɑ/

Diphthongs

1. Lips relaxed—moderate opening to lips puckered—narrow opening—/aʊ/

2. Lips rounded—moderate opening to lips back—narrow opening—/ɔɪ/
3. Lips relaxed—moderate opening to lips back—narrow opening—/ɑɪ/

° Note that consonant movements 2 and 7 are the same as vowel movements 1 and 2.

The speechreading movement for /j/ is not seen unless the sound is followed by a high back vowel.

Consonant movements 8 and 9 cannot be seen unless the mouth is opened fairly wide.

The homophenes for which each movement serves as a cue are presented in parentheses following the description of the movement.

1.1.1 QUICK RECOGNITION EXERCISE—VISIBLE INITIAL CONSO-NANTS. Three examples of this type of exercise are given below. More of them will be found in the section on practice materials.

1. fish	wish	pitch	(fɪʃ	wɪʃ	pɪtʃ)
sin	chin	thin	(sɪn	tʃɪn	θɪn)
2. gem	web	pep	(dʒɛm	wɛb	pɛp)
fan	than	sand	(fæn	ðæn	sænd)

| 3. judge | budge | fudge | (dʒʌdʒ | bʌdʒ | fʌdʒ) |
| sing | thing | wing | (sɪŋ | θɪŋ | wɪŋ) |

Notice that all of the words in a given line look alike *except for the beginning consonant.* Another way of stating this is to say that the initial consonant movement is varied in each word, but the remainder of the visual pattern is held constant.

An easy way to see that these requirements have been met is to transcribe the words using I.P.A. symbols. It is not necessary for the words to rhyme.

It is possible to substitute for any given sound, a sound homophenous to it, providing the resulting combination is meaningful. For example, in the first line, the second word, *wish,* could just as well have been *whish* or *witch,* but *vish* could not have been substituted for *fish.* It is also not necessary to retain the same vowel sound in a given line, providing the vowels used are recognized on the basis of the same visible movement. Possible substitutions for *chin* in the second line are *chill, chit, cheat, chain, sheet, sheen, shirt, shut, Jill, Jane, jail,* and *jade.* All thirteen words will look alike as they are spoken. Usually, however, it is better to retain the same vowel sound, because it enables the pupil to respond more rapidly and the teacher to use reduced voice in giving the drill, if he wishes to do so. It should be noted, however, that these exercises are easy enough to be given without voice.

Notice, also, that *all six visible consonant movements* are used in each exercise—one movement per word.

All visible consonant movements are introduced through this technique in the very first lesson. Discrimination is taught through contrast. If the pupil identifies the words correctly, he does so through observing differences in the appearance of the three initial consonants in each of the two lines of the exercise. He is not told *how* they are different—instant unconscious recognition is the aim.

1.1.2 QUICK RECOGNITION EXERCISE—VISIBLE FINAL CONSONANTS. An example of this type of exercise is given below. More of them will be found in the section on practice materials.

rope	rose	rove	(roʊp,	roʊz,	roʊv)
match	math	map	(mætʃ,	mæθ,	mæp)

Notice that one of the speech movements, in this instance *lips together*, has been repeated in order to balance the exercise. There are only five visible final consonant movements. The glide consonants /w/, /hw/, /r/, and /j/ do not occur in the final position. All five movements must occur in each exercise. The rules given before, regarding the use of homophenous sounds apply here also. Each word must look the same except for the final consonant movement. Practice in recognizing visible consonant movements in the final position in the word is of special importance to the hard-of-hearing. Sounds which can be heard in the initial position are often missed when they occur at the end of a word or phrase because they are spoken more softly.

1.1.3 QUICK RECOGNITION EXERCISES—OBSCURE CONSONANTS. Two examples of this kind of exercise are given below

1. town	cowed	sound	(taʊn,	kaʊd,	saʊnd)
balk	paws	mall	(bɔk	pɔz	mɔl)
2. let	set	get	(lɛt,	sɛt,	gɛt)
jet	chess	check,	(dʒɛt,	tʃɛs,	tʃɛk)

In the first line of each exercise the contrastive movements are presented in the initial position. In the second line the contrastive movements are presented in the final position.

Observe that only low vowel movements, those that we have labeled "obscure," have been used in this exercise. This is because the mouth is often opened moderately wide in saying the low vowels, permitting the speechreader to see the tongue up and down, and the tongue back movements characteristic of /t,d,n,l/ and /k,g,ŋ/, respectively. The third obscure consonant speechreading movement, lips back, narrow opening, which is the cue to /j/, has not been included for two reasons. The first reason is that the lip movement for the beginning /i/ position—lips back—is usually not visible unless /j/ is followed by a high back vowel. The second reason is that when the movement is from /i/ to a low vowel, the tongue movement may be seen, but is confused with the movement for the /t,d,n,l/ sounds. When the obscure consonant "tongue" movements are to or from a high vowel, they are not seen at all and hence are logically confused with each other and with the consonants /s,z/ or /θ,ð/. The sounds /s,z/ or the sounds /θ,ð/ are used to complete the exercise and also to give the pupil practice in distinguishing between either of these movements and the tongue down or up, and the tongue back movements under conditions where it is possible to do so.

1.1.4 QUICK RECOGNITION EXERCISE—VOWELS AND DIPHTHONGS. The hearing handicapped individual who can hear vowel and diphthong sounds will usually have no need for training of this sort. It should be reserved for the deaf and for those severely hard-of-hearing individuals who cannot (often because of an inadequate hearing aid) hear the vowels unless they are very close to the speaker. It can also be used with the relatively few hard-of-hearing adults who evince *phonemic regression*—the inability to discriminate among sounds although they receive the necessary sensory information.

Three or occasionally all four of the vowel movements have been combined in the same exercise. It is not too difficult to distinguish between speechreading movements from the two major categories, i.e. front versus back vowel movements, or even the high back movement, lips puckered, from the low back movement, lips rounded. The real problem lies in distinguishing high front from low front vowels—lips back, narrow opening from lips relaxed, moderate opening. For example, there is usually little difference between "bait" and "bat."

The Vowel Movement Exercises must be given slowly and with more than the average amount of lip and jaw movement for the distinctions between words to be made.

Two examples of vowel exercises are given below.

1. bit	bat	boat	(/bɪt/ /bæt/ /bout/)
feet	fat	fought	(/fit/ /fæt/ /fɔt/)
2. rip	rap	rope	(/rɪp/ /ræp/ /roup/)
tea	toy	too	(/ti / /tɔɪ/ /tu/)

1.1.5 MODIFICATION OF EXERCISES FOR YOUNG CHILDREN. Recognition of consonant movements through contrast can be taught to young hearing handicapped children who cannot read, but it must be done through the use of objects, pictures, or actions. Because of the limitations in vocabulary imposed by these materials, it is not possible to vary just one speech movement per word. An example of such an exercise might be:

fish   ball   thumb

shoe   wash   soap

Just make sure that the words used are within the child's experience and represent a true visual contrast. For example, (drʌm) drum, (tɑp) top, and (ɑɚm) arm should not be used together because they look too much alike. The vocabulary should be based on the names of things—parts of the body, clothes, furniture, foods, simple actions, (run, walk, swim) etc.

1.1.6 HOW TO USE THE Q.R.E.'s. The Quick Recognition Exercises are used, as previously stated, to improve visual perception and speed of perception. Of the two aims, the former is the more important in training for recognition and identification of obscure speech movements, and the latter, for the visible movements. Most students are able to perceive immediately differences among the visible speech movements, but they will need training to achieve maximum speed. Despite the fact that the immediate goals are more limited, recognition of the whole word pattern or Gestalt is used in these exercises for two reasons. The first reason is that the formation of all but the most stable speech movements are modified to some extent by the sounds which precede or follow. The second reason is that there is no need to use diacritical markings when words, rather than nonsense syllables, are used in the drills. As far as the speechreader is concerned, he is speechreading *words,* not *visible movements* or even speech sounds. It *is not necessary* for him to be told *what* he is doing, and *he should not* be told *how* he is doing it. The association of speech movements with sounds is accomplished rapidly and without conscious analysis—eye to mind. *The analysis and description* of speech movements given in Chapter 2 and in this Chapter *are for the teacher, not for the student.* Only in the very rare case (once in the writer's experience of over 20 years), is it necessary to tell a pupil *what* to look for.

Another important use of the Quick Recognition Exercises is as a *diagnostic tool.* When the exercises are given individually, the teacher can quickly spot those pupils who need to improve their skill in fine focusing and speed of focusing. They are the pupils who cannot discriminate among the words unless they are given slowly and are carefully articulated with more than the usual amount of lip, tongue, and jaw movement. *The teacher's first task is to determine the initial ability of each member of his class.* From then on he is able to meet individual needs and to vary his technique depending on which student is being asked to respond. The same exercise can be given slowly and with careful articulation to the poorer pupils and quite rapidly for the more advanced. Individual instruction is given within a group setting. The individual needs of each pupil are recognized and provided for. As each pupil progresses, the rate used in giving the quick recognition exercises is increased, accompanied by less lip and jaw movement. At no time is the amount of lip and jaw movement exaggerated beyond that found in normal speech.

One of the aims of all speechreading instruction is to increase the pupil's confidence in his ability to speechread through providing successful experiences. When the Quick Recognition Exercises are given properly, they will further this aim. The exercises are, for the most part, easy, and success for each pupil can be insured through the method of presentation.

Where Quick Recognition Exercises are used, it is not necessary to "introduce one movement at a time," or to load associative material with specific speechreading movements. Ample practice will have been given in recognizing all speechreading movements through the use of these exercises alone.

Not more than five to ten minutes per lesson should be spent on these exercises. While there is a certain physical satisfaction and enjoyment in parroting, and especially in group response or "choral speaking," it quickly pales. Further practice has all of the satisfaction of practicing piano scales ad infinitum to the point of nausea. Maximum skill in recognition and speed of focusing is gradually developed over a series of lessons. It does not need to be achieved before proceeding to connected speech materials. As a matter of fact, it can be argued that this type of exercise is not necessary, because all speechreading practice material serves to improve the visual skills. But without some sort of direct approach, the instructor has no way of checking on each pupil's initial level with respect to fine focusing and speed of focusing, nor no easy way of providing for individual differences or of being able to note improvement as a result of practice. As soon as a satisfactory level of proficiency has been achieved by the class members, the exercises should be dropped and no longer constitute a part of the lesson plan. If necessary, slower pupils can be given five minutes or so of instruction before the class meets as a whole.

The exercises are usually taught in the order presented above: (a) visible consonant movements—initial position, (b) visible consonant movements—final position, (c) obscure consonant movements—initial and final positions, and finally, and *only,* if there is need for such instruction, (d) vowel movement exercises. The teaching procedures are as follows: *

1. The exercise is written on the board.

> fish   wish   pitch
> sin   chin   thin

2. The teacher points to the first line and says, "Watch me." He then says the words aloud, pointing to each word as he does so. It is usually necessary to use a pointer, because the teacher must be facing the class at all times, body parallel to the blackboard (but not in front of the writing) to permit full view of his lips. Never *unintentionally* turn your side to the viewers.

3. The teacher then says, "Say them with me," and again

* Many of these procedures were first suggested in *New Aids and Materials for Teaching Lip-Reading.*⁶ The "talk with me" technique is found in a number of sources, but appears to have been first described in *Speechreading—Jena Method,*¹ 1932 edition.

points to each word in turn and in reverse and scrambled order. Emphasis is placed on the *with*. The pupils are to say the words *with*, not *after* the teacher. This requires that they pay close attention to the teacher's lips and imitate his speech movements. A possible order for giving the words is as follows:

fish	wish	pitch
pitch	wish	fish
wish	pitch	fish
fish	pitch	wish
pitch	pitch	fish, etc.

4. The teacher then says, "Watch me again." He again points to each word in turn in the order given above, but this time he says them *silently*. Reduced voice, rather than silent speaking can be used if preferred, but the beginning exercises are easy enough to permit them to be given without sound.

5. After this orientation he says, "Repeat after me, all together," and gives the drill (silent voice) without pointing to the words, three words at a time. The pupils repeat the three words of a given line in the order presented. As the pupils become more adept, the teacher gradually increases his speed of presentation. Actually, for most groups it is possible to use a rapid rate in giving the exercises for visible consonant movements right from the start. The teacher should have the exercises written on a piece of paper which he can hold in front of him and glance down at when needed. If he has to glance at the board to decide his order of presentation, his eye movements will be distracting and may also cue the pupils as to the order.

The basic exercise is never erased from the board. To do so would result in confusion with respect to response. The same visual word pattern can often represent more than one word. For example the speechreading movement pattern for the word "*wish*" is the same as that for "*witch*" or "*which*."

6. Following the group practice the teacher says, "All right, now we'll take turns. I'll start with the people in the front

row, (or back row)." He then speaks directly to the person who is to respond, and points to him or calls him by name, if necessary. This step should not be omitted, because it is through individual response that the teacher is able to note differences in ability. Since the good speechreaders always "sing out loudly," in group practice, it is very easy for the instructor to be misled and to assume that everyone in the class is recognizing the material. If the individual who is called upon can not repeat the word orders accurately at the "going rate," the teacher will first indicate the correct order by pointing to the words written on the board and then give them to him again, this time using a slower rate and more articulatory movement. Another reason for giving the exercises individually, is that it is important to establish the practice of individual response from the first lesson so that the shyer pupils will become accustomed to it and will not become flustered when called upon.

7. The procedures outlined above are then repeated for the second group of three words.

1.1.7 VARIATIONS IN PROCEDURE.

1. The amount of orientation practice can be varied according to the needs of the group. Once the pupils understand the nature of the exercises and what is expected of them, it can usually be drastically reduced.

2. The teacher can use different rhythmical patterns in speaking the words, e.g. (accented words, underlined).*

<u>fish</u>	wish	pitch
fish	wish	pitch
fish	<u>wish</u>	<u>pitch</u>

3. Four, five, or even six words can be given at a time. The exercise in this instance is being used to improve visual memory.

4. The pupils can take turns at "playing teacher," and giving the drills. This variation is an important one, because it is

---

* This is a modification of a Jena Method technique.[1]

necessary to learn to speechread many people, not just the teacher.

5. The class can be divided into two teams and scores kept. If a pupil on one team misses the correct word order, someone on the other team is given a chance to give the correct response and so score an additional point for his team.

6. The pupils can work in pairs for two or three minutes, each pupil having a turn to give a line to his partner in scrambled order. This enables the student to see at closer range all speechreading movements. When the teacher again gives it to the group as a whole, recognition is much more rapid.

1.2. *Visual Memory and Flexibility*

Facility in making rapid shifts from a mistaken perceptual closure (i.e. a decision as to a word or phrase) to another more applicable one is an important skill. The ability to make rapid shifts is probably principally dependent on the speechreader's grasping the sense of the context or on his knowledge of the emotional or social milieu in which it was said. (See the following section for an expansion of this idea.) But it is also true that flexibility is enhanced if one can retain the visual imagery or sound movement pattern which was the basis of the original closure. For example, let us say that the speaker said, "In a year like this one, it is necessary to conserve water for the crops." A pupil speechread, "In a year like this one, it is necessary to conserve water for the robins." Now it is true that *crops* and *robins,* /krɑps/ and /rɑbɪnz/, may look alike to anyone who is depending solely on visual cues. The /k/ was missed; the lips together movement was interpreted as /b/; the teeth together movement, as /z/, and the /n/ was filled in to make a sensible word. Nonetheless, the context alone should have prevented this nonsensical mistake or permitted a quick shift in thought. (But it did not—this actually happened.) In order to correct his mistake, the student had to see the last word again. Once he had made the perceptual closure, "robins," he forgot the visual imagery on which it was based, and had no information to guide him to a better choice. In some sentences neither the context nor the situation may be of help. The speech-reader *must remember the word pattern* in order to correct, or at least to understand, his confusion. "Do you like your job?" could just as well have been, "Do you like your chop?" "Where is that park?" could be, "Where is that bark?" and "He dined at home last night," could be, "He died at home last night."

1.2.1 QUICK IDENTIFICATION EXERCISES. The following type of exercise is designed to improve retention of visual imagery and permit quick association of a pattern with the various homophenous words for which it serves as a cue. For ease in discussion we shall label them *Quick Identification Exercises*. The speechreader is required to answer these subconscious queries: "what is it?" "what else could it have been?" There are three levels of quick identification exercises—beginning, intermediate, advanced. Some examples are given below. More of them will be found in the materials section, pp. 276–278.

Beginning Exercises	*Intermediate Exercises*	*Advanced Exercises*
1. bath, math, path	1. dirge, lurch	1. face, vase, phase, fizz, fuss
2. face, vase, phase	2. make, bake— also accepted: mate, made mail, main, may, bay	2. shag, shack, jag, jack, jog, chock, shock, check
3. chews (choose), juice, shoes, Jews	3. sit, sin, sill, sinned—also accepted: sick	3. sack, sag, sank, sock, soggy
4. Amuse, abuse, muse	4. bead, bean, beet, mean (mien), meat (meet), meal, peat, also accepted: bee, me, pea, beak, meek, peek (peak)	4. peg, peck, pack, pang, pike, beg, beck, back, bang, bank, bock, bike, mock

The Quick Identification Exercises are graded with respect to visibility. Only words containing visible consonants are included in the beginning group. Obscure consonants along with visible ones are used in the intermediate group. When the vowel in an intermediate exercise is from one of the high groups, the tongue down or up /t,d,n,l,/ and the tongue back /k,g,ŋ/ movements *will usually not be seen* and must be mentally filled in or partially heard by the speechreader. It is for this reason that words in the "also accepted" category are included in the exercises. The beginning and intermediate exercises are to be given with reduced voice. The same vowel is used throughout each exercise. The advanced exercises, on the other hand, include homophenous vowels as well as homophenous consonants and are given without voice. When obscure consonants are used in the advanced exercises, they are always associated with low vowels to permit recognition of their movement patterns.

1.2.2 Procedure in Giving Quick Identification Exercises.

1. The words of a given exercise are *not* written on the board. The instructor says, "See if you can speechread this word," and then speaks one of the words of a homophenous group. Regardless of whether the student responds with the word presented or one of its homophenes, the response is correct.
2. The instructor says in full voice, "That's right." Now close your eyes and see if you can imagine my saying the word again. Without repeating the word, he then asks, "What else could it have been?"
3. This process is continued until all of the homophenes have been elicited from the group. The instructor has a check list and notes all identifications. The word is *not repeated* after the initial presentation unless there are remaining homophenes which have not been identified.
4. If the class is unable to think of all of the homophenes, even after the word has been repeated a second or a third time, the instructor will put the remaining words in sentences. For example he might say (reduced voice):

"The bell in the church tower *pealed* twelve o'clock," or "You have such a pleasant *mien* that I'm sure that you're a very happy person."

5. When all of the homophenes have been identified, the words are written on the board and members of the class are asked to select a word, without revealing which one it is, and make up a sentence using it.

6. The same exercises are reviewed in succeeding lessons until the pupils are able to recall quickly all possible associations.

The technique or method of presentation is considered *to be important and should be followed as outlined above.* If the wording is not natural to the teacher, he may make minor changes in the phrasing of instructions. If the homophenous word is repeated after each correct response, the pupils will not receive training in retaining visual imagery. Likewise, if the words are written on the board before all homophenes have been associated with the pattern, the student does not have to remember how the words looked, but can resort to an analytic process of figuring out possible changes in sound pattern. The pupil should not be told which sounds look alike. He should arrive at this intuitively and preferably without verbalizing it to himself. When speechreading, he does not have time to do any conscious reasoning. He does not have time to say to himself, "Hm, the lips came together. Well that could have been /m/, /p/, or /b/."

As with the Quick Recognition Exercises, these Quick Identification Exercises also have little innate interest and should constitute only a small portion of any given lesson. The use of one exercise per lesson should be sufficient. Students will gradually develop improved visual memory and flexibility of association over a series of lessons. Improvement in *verbal memory*, i.e. retention of recognized material, is best achieved through connected speech material. The amount of information that the pupil is expected to retain is gradually increased. "Story-type" material which will be presented in a later section is particularly useful in this respect.

2. MATERIALS TO IMPROVE SYNTHETIC ABILITY AND FLEXIBILITY

2.1. *Overview*

Perceptual closure, conceptual closure, and flexibility are interrelated and interdependent processes which are not separated in time but occur almost simultaneously. Except for the probable importance of visual memory to flexibility, the keys to all of them would appear to be *context* and *setting*. It is not possible to isolate each process and teach it independently of the others. The same materials are used to effect training in all three areas.* To simplify matters we shall call this kind of training, *training in association*. Certain premises or general rules underline both our choice of materials and the gradual introduction or grading from easy to difficult, i.e. from beginning to advanced instruction. The general rules are as follows:

1. That which is most familiar is most easily identified.†
2. That which is most visible is most easily identified.
3. That which is cued by the language structure is most easily identified.
4. That which is cued by context is most easily identified.
5. That which can be anticipated because of known topic or social situation is most easily identified.‡

---

* Note that no attempt has been made to introduce one movement at a time or to load materials artificially with particular movements. When this is attempted, speechreading material is often stilted and is difficult to grasp because of its divergence from normal conversational patterns. Adequate practice in achieving greater visual proficiency is provided for through the use of the Quick Recognition and Quick Identification Exercises.

† Lloyd, L., and Price, J.: "Sentence Familiarity as a Factor in Visual Speech Reception (Lipreading) of Deaf College Students." Paper presented at the 44th Annual Convention of the American Speech and Hearing Association, November 16, 1968, Denver, Colorado. Lloyd and Price found that the speechreading test sentences rated most familiar also tended to be the ones most easily speechread. Deaf college students served as raters and subjects (r, .34, significant at less than .01 level of confidence). They concluded that sentence familiarity is an important variable in successful speechreading.

‡ Arthur found that speechreaders performed significantly better on a speechreading test where nonverbal cues were available as compared to the

Training in Association

2.2. *Beginning Speechreading Materials—Recognizing the Familiar*

The beginning speechreader like the beginning silent reader is expected, for the most part, to recognize only vocabulary, sentence structure, and ideas that are highly familiar to him. Beginning speechreading instruction and beginning silent reading instruction are comparable in other respects as well. Both make use of much reinforcement—repetition and elaboration of the basic ideas presented. Both also make use of titles as well as pictures which suggest the content to follow. And as in silent reading, the beginning speechreader is not expected to read a whole story before he is made aware of the correctness of his response, but only a phrase or a story sentence. But unlike silent reading, the materials are written with the view in mind of visibility as well as familiarity. Little emphasis is placed on recognition of isolated words.

The types of materials used in beginning speechreading can be described as: *overlearned speech, simple stories,* which can also be described as a series of closely related sentences, *colloquial sentences,* where the content can be cued by the presentation of a *clue word* before each sentence is given, *conversations or skits* involving two people, *games and quizzes* which make use of known vocabulary and knowledge.

There are roughly two categories of beginning speechreading materials—beginning speechreading for ages five through ten, and beginning speechreading for older children and adults. Most of the speechreading materials presented in this text assume

---

same test when such cues were eliminated. By nonverbal cues were meant such factors as environmental setting and the employment by the speakers of appropriate facial expression, gestures, and properties. Average percent change in scores was from 15 percent to 19 percent improvement in word accuracy, from 22 percent to 28 percent improvement in ability to guage the thought expressed, and from 48 percent to 57 percent improvement in ability to summarize the content of the conversations. (Arthur, R.H.: *The Effect of Contextual and Non-Contextual Motion Pictures on the Speechreading Proficiency of Comparable Adult Males.* Ph.D. Dissertation, University of Florida, 1962.)

an aural recognition vocabulary comparable to that of at least a third grade reading level. When used with younger children, the materials become lessons in vocabulary development as well as speechreading.

2.2.1 OVERLEARNED SPEECH. The simplest form of overlearned speech has often been called automatic speech. By automatic speech is meant the speech we use when we wish to convey our feelings of friendship or good fellowship. No information is conveyed—only feelings. Good examples of such speech are greetings and the weather. When we meet an acquaintance or a friend, we all tend to use the same stereotyped expressions. We say such things as "Hello," "Hi," "How are you?" "What do you know?" And the replies are equally stereotyped and predictable, "Fine," "Fine, Thank you," "Nothing," "Nothing much," and so on. Woe be to the person who takes the question, "How are you?" literally and proceeds to tell you. As the old ditty goes, "Don't talk about your indigestion. 'How are you' is a greeting, not a question." Once the initial noises have been made and we have nothing more to say, we comment on the weather. There is some variation here, depending on the actual weather, but not much. Such expressions are used as, "Isn't it a beautiful day?" "Yes, this is a perfect day," "Is it hot enough for you—or cold enough for you?" "Do you think it's going to rain?"

At the next higher level, by overlearned speech is meant speech that is heard so frequently that one can anticipate and predict what the speaker will say. The speechreader need see only a portion of the information to enable him mentally to fill in the rest. It consists of commonplace expressions—phrases, statements, questions, and commands—that are regularly said on certain occasions. They are the obvious or conventional things to say in a given situation or about a given topic. Also included under this category are words "that go together," the word order and tense that are set by the structure and grammar of the language. And not excluded are cliches and trite, hackneyed, and banal expressions as well as the more useful ones. Overlearned speech differs from automatic speech only in that the content as well as the noise has some significance. Both consist of stereotyped expressions. The words and the sentence structure vary only slightly from one speaker to another. This kind of language, "things that people say," is understood by most of us by the time we are eight years of age or even younger. It is the kind of language that is used much of the time by all of us regardless of our age, sex, or education. Once the topic has been set, or the situation specified, much of the language can be anticipated. It is probably because so much that we say is patterned as well as redundant that speechreading is possible, despite the limited sensory information available.

Here are some examples of "overlearned" speech where the things that people say are related to an overall topic or situation. Once the topic is known, the listener is able to anticipate what may be said. More examples will be found in the materials section.

A. *Topic Centered Familiar Sentences*

Topic: Health

1. What's wrong with you?
2. You don't look at all well.
3. You don't look like you feel well.
4. I don't feel very well.
5. I don't feel very well today.
6. I was sick last night.
7. I think I may be catching cold.
8. I have a cold.
9. I have a toothache.
10. I have a stomachache.
11. My eyes are bothering me.
12. I guess I must be allergic to something.
13. Why don't you take some aspirin?
14. You had better go home and go to bed.
15. You had better stay in bed and get plenty of rest.
16. You had better take care of yourself.

17. Can I do anything to help you?
18. Shall I call a doctor for you?
19. Do you want me to call a doctor for you?
20. I'm sorry you feel so bad.
21. I wish there were something I could do to help you.
22. I wish I could help you.
23. I wouldn't come to work tomorrow if I were you.
24. Is there anything I can do to help you.
25. How long have you been sick?
26. Are you running a temperature?
27. (To a child). I had better send you home.
28. I had better notify your parents.
29. Is there someone at home to take care of you?
30. I wouldn't come to school tomorrow if I were you.

Command and Admonitions—Adult to Child

1. Go wash your face.
2. Go wash your hands.
3. Did you wash behind your ears?
4. When did you last take a bath?
5. Did you wash your hands before dinner?
6. Keep your elbows off the table.
7. Don't eat with your knife.
8. Put your napkin in your lap.
9. Don't interrupt mother when she is talking.
10. Have you had enough to eat?
11. You don't eat enough to keep a bird alive.
12. Finish your vegetables before you can have dessert.
13. When you have finished you may excuse yourself and go outside and play.
14. Don't forget to brush your teeth.
15. It's time for your nap.
16. It's time to get ready for bed.
17. Get ready for bed now.
18. It's time for you to go to bed.
19. It's your bedtime.
20. Take a bath before you go to bed.

21. I'll read you a story if you get in bed fast.
22. You just had a drink of water.
23. You don't need any more water.
24. Settle down and go to sleep, or I'll spank you.
25. For the last time—Good Night!!

Procedure.

1. The instructor introduces the exercises by saying (Full Voice):

   "What are some of the things that you say or are said to you when you don't feel well?

2. After eliciting a few of the commonplace remarks he then says:

   "Here are some more. Raise your hand if you can tell me what I'm saying."

3. *Teacher Presentation.* The sentences are given one at a time, in reduced voice. After each sentence is presented, pupils are called upon to respond in the manner designated by the instructor. If the pupils are not seated in a semicircle where they are clearly visible to each other, the respondee must walk to the front of the class and face it before replying.

   Possible ways of responding are the following:

   a. Repeating what the instructor has just said.
   This is the kind of response elicited from young children or from older children and adults in their first few lessons. A literal response is not required, but the gist of the idea must be clear.

   b. Repeating statements but answering questions.
   For example, in response to the query, "What's wrong with you?," the pupil might reply, "I don't know what's wrong with me. I just don't feel well."
   Pupils must be trained to repeat enough of the query so that it is clear, that it was understood. Response is always in full voice.

c. Commenting on statements and answering questions.

The student answering responds as though he were in a two-way conversation. For example, in response to the statement, "You don't look at all well," an appropriate reply might be, "Well I'm not surprised that I don't look well because I certainly don't feel well."

d. Acting out the response in addition to responding verbally.

This is a favorite of children, but adults enjoy it as well. To the query, "Do you have a toothache?" the pupil can respond by clutching his jaw and moaning before replying, "Oh yes, it hurts something awful."

e. Quiz—written response

After each statement the pupil writes down what he thinks the instructor has said. It is scored by recording either the number of words correct or the number of sentences with the correct idea but not necessarily the exact wording.

f. Simple contest—two teams.

When a pupil misses a member of the opposing team has first chance at responding and scoring an additional point for his team.

4. *Pupil Presentation.* The sentences are written on separate cards and the cards shuffled. Each pupil is dealt a certain number of cards. Pupils then take turns. Each pupil presents one of his cards at a time and calls on another pupil to respond in any of the ways suggested above.

In order to turn the exercise into a contest the instructor gives the card to the pupil who responds correctly. The winner is the person who has the most cards at the end of the game.

B. *Familiar Phrases*

A slightly more difficult form of overlearned speech (more difficult because the topic is not set) is familiar phrases or "words that go together." The speechreader with a basic knowledge of language is able to guess and to fill in mentally words that he may not see. While this kind of exercise may be more difficult than familiar sentences (centered around a known topic), it is possible to obviate the difficulty if the speechreader initially has prior knowledge of the phrases that he will be expected to speechread.

Dr. James R. McDearmon* has compiled such a list of familiar phrases and developed a method of using them based on programmed learning principles. The programmed learning principles are as follows: (a) small, sequential steps toward the goal, (b) learner response and immediate reinforcement at each step, (c) enough assistance to the learner at each step to assure success, (d) thorough mastery of all steps covered before beginning the next step, and (e) gradual reduction of assistance to learner as progress decreases his need for it. Some of his materials are presented here. The remainder will be found in the materials section. The following expressions contain all the words comprising 50 percent of written English.

1. Sunday	11. April	(The following ex-
2. Monday	12. May	pressions contain all
3. Tuesday	13. June	the words compris-
4. Wednesday	14. July	ing 50% of written
5. Thursday	15. August	English.†)
6. Friday	16. September	20. It's for you.
7. Saturday	17. October	21. Who was that?
8. January	18. November	22. with that in
9. February	19. December	mind
10. March		23. up and down

* James R. McDearmon, Ph.D., is Director, Speech and Hearing Clinic, Washington State University, Pullman, Washington. The teaching of two hundred or more short everyday expressions constitutes Phase I of his method of speeching instruction based on programmed learning principles. Phase II, appropriate for the intermediate or advanced speechreader, makes use of less familiar material. Content sentences are used. The material in Phase II is simple, but not "overlearned." See materials section for explanation.

† Dewey, G.: *Relative Frequency of English Speech Sounds.* Cambridge, Massachusetts, Harvard University Press, 1923.

24. I'm going to
25. Come in.
26. as a matter of fact
27. on second thought
28. by that time
29. not at all
30. what of it
31. not at this time
32. Are we going?
33. but will they all
34. I had it with me.
35. There were some.
36. Has he seen it?
37. I saw him.
38. What's it for?
39. Which is it?
40. Where are you from?
41. one of ours
42. Where have you been?
43. Do you know?
44. Is that my pen?
45. if that were true
46. He said to me.
47. What would you do?
48. Do you hear them?
49. I asked her.
50. He wore it.
51. Where is your car?
52. Do you have any more?
53. Now it's time to go.
54. Things are looking up.
55. Do you think so?
56. We went out.
57. How can that be?
58. later than you think
59. I only hope so.
60. What did she say?
61. He made it.
62. Is there any more?
63. Let's not get into that.
64. those men
65. It must be.
66. a lot of people
67. May I say this?
68. It's a man's voice.
69. what about
70. Look it over.
71. There are some more.
72. I like these two.
73. Very well, thank you.
74. Please do.
75. as I said before
76. I feel great.
77. How could you?
78. such a thing
79. He was first.
80. only once
81. only one time
82. every little thing
83. Can you come?
84. Tell us about it.
85. Shall we go?
86. What should I do?
87. then I said
88. The paper's here.

Procedure.

General Instructions

Begin with two expressions. Teach until the two can be easily distinguished. Then add a third expression. Teach until all three expressions can be identified on the lips and "read" with the help of memory. Add one new expression at a time, continuing in the same manner. Always vary the order of presentation during review, practice, and testing. Never add a new expression until the previously taught expressions have been thoroughly mastered. If an expression is found to be too difficult or too easily confused with another, withdraw it.

In the application of programmed learning principles, *responsibility for successful response by the student falls on the teacher.* Both teacher and student must thoroughly accept this principle. A mistaken response is, actually, a "mistake" on the part of the teacher. It is the teacher's responsibility to discover what he, the teacher, has done wrong. He may have permitted the student to move too fast, left out needed substeps, neglected to assure mastery at each point, or neglected to provide enough forms of assistance *to assure* successful response.

In saying the phrases, the instructor should speak naturally and colloquially. For example, he should not say "up and down," but "up'n down."

Specific Instructions

1. Type or print each new expression to be taught, after its number, at the top edge of a 3 × 5 card.
2. Teach expression #1 and #2 until mastery is attained. The expressions, of course, are practiced and tested in random order. First, the student has the appropriate cards before him during practice; then he is assisted by recall without the cards being visible.
3. Teach expression #3.
   a. Practice with #1 and #3 until mastered.
   b. Practice with #2 and #3 until mastered.
   c. Practice with #1, #2, and #3 until mastered. *This step is essential.*
4. Teach expression #4. Select and use only as many substeps below (from a to f) as are helpful in preparation for the final substep (g).
   a. Practice #1 and #4 until mastered.
   b. Practice #2 and #4 until mastered.
   c. Practice #3 and #4 until mastered.

    d. Practice #1, #2, and #4 until mastered.

    e. Practice #1, #3, and #4 until mastered.

    f. Practice #2, #3, and #4 until mastered.

    g. Practice Expression #1 and #4 until mastered. *This step is essential.*

5. Continue in this manner. Use only those substeps that will be helpful in preparation for each final substep. Faster learners will need fewer substeps. Slower learners will need more. *An incorrect response probably indicated the need for more substeps.*

6. A new expression should never be added until thorough mastery of all previously taught expressions is attained. Neglect of this rule results in failure. Strict conformity to this rule assures success.

7. To assist the student to speechread the expression being formed on the lips of the teacher, the cards for the expression being practiced with at a given time may need to be visable to the student. Practice should continue until the student can do without them. Memory will then serve to assist him in speechreading the expression.

8. Withdraw any expression proving difficult to teach in this phase.

2.2.2 SIMPLE STORIES—A SERIES OF CLOSLEY RELATED SENTENCES. The next stage of difficulty is following a series of closely related sentences or a simple story. This type of story has a number of characteristics. Both the vocabulary and the ideas presented are highly familiar. Basic vocabulary and concepts that are "common knowledge" are adhered to. Pupils *are asked to recognize only what they already know.* Whenever possible the vocabulary is selected for its visibility as well as its familiarity. Ideas are logically related. It is possible to anticipate the next statement. The following idea is either a restatement or an extension of the previous one, or is suggested by it. Beginning pupils respond after each sentence. After the sentences are given one by one, the material is repeated as a whole in story form. An example of this type of material is given below. The topic is given before any of the sentences are presented.

My Dog

1. I have a dog.
2. His name is Butch.
3. Butch is a very big dog and has lots and lots of long thick hair.
4. He is always getting fleas and then he scratches like everything!
5. It makes you itch just to watch him.
6. But he hates to take a bath.
7. He seems to know when I want to give him a bath.
8. As soon as he sees me coming, he runs like mad.
9. I usually find him hiding under a bed—way back against the wall.
10. I have to drag him out, and it's quite a job, because he's very heavy.
11. My sister usually has to help me.
12. It takes two of us to drag him to the bathroom and put him in the bathtub.
13. One of us holds him down while the other uses a scrub brush and special soap.
14. If he gets a chance he'll jump out of the water and run away as fast as he can.
15. But first he shakes himself and water flies all over the bathroom.

Notice that in addition to one idea being suggested by the previous one, that the sentence structure was simple and followed, for the most part, a subject, predicate, object order. Colloquial, i.e. conversational, language was used throughout.

The pupils should be seated in a semicircle. The teacher, using reduced voice, gives the sentences one at a time starting at the left of the semicircle. If a pupil misses, another pupil is permitted to give the correct response. The teacher then repeats the sentence before going on to the next one.

2.2.3 COLLOQUIAL SENTENCES—CLUE WORDS.* In the course of a normal conversation individuals often change the subject. They make remarks without elaborating on them or ask questions. And they expect a response! The speechreader needs training for this kind of situation. In the sentences to be presented the topic changes with each sentence. The speechreader is expected either to make an appropriate remark or to answer the question. If the pupil does not understand, he is given a *clue word* in full voice, and then the sentence is repeated. The word used must be truly a clue to either the topic or the meaning of the sentence and not just one of the words in the sentence. If desired it can be a word or phrase not found in the sentence.

These sentences differ from the ones given in overlearned speech in an important respect. The content *cannot be predicted as easily* from the milieu. They are things which may be said in a given setting, but not things that we necessarily *expect to hear* in that setting.

Some examples of unrelated sentences that might be appropriate at a beginning level for older children and adults follow.

1. I think I'll take a ride down to the ocean tomorrow.
   The clue word should be *ride,* or if necessary, two words, *ride* and *ocean.* It should not be *tomorrow* or *take.* If given to a group of children *bicycle* could be used as a clue in place of *ride.*

2. I saw an old W. C. Fields movie on T.V. last night.
   The clue words should be either *W. C. Fields* or *W. C. Fields Movie.*

3. Did you finish your homework before you went to bed last night?

---

* The term "clue word" appears to have been used for the first time in *New Aids and Materials for Teaching Lip-Reading.*[6] It refers to a technique first introduced by Sarah Fuller and later used extensively by Nitchie of using a single word as a clue to the meaning of the sentence to follow. The lessons were organized around lip movements and the clue word contained the movement in question. Because of this restriction a particular clue word often revealed little about the sentence which followed. Our use differs from theirs in that the word used as a clue is not illustrative of a speechreading movement, does not necessarily occur in the sentence, and, most importantly, is truly a "clue" to the meaning of the sentence.

The clue word is *homework,* not *bed, last night,* or even *finish.*

4. How's about going sailing with me tomorrow?
   The clue word is *sailing.*

5. Did you see that nasty expression on her face when I told her I had changed my mind?
   The clue word, in this instance, should suggest the topic of conversation, i.e. the person being talked about. The best word for a clue might be *salesgirl.*

6. I'm expecting company day after tomorrow.
   The clue word is *company.*

7. You're not going to eat three hamburgers and drink a double malted milk, are you?
   The best clue in this instance is probably the topic—*enormous appetite* or *teenage appetite.* If the pupil still misses the question after being given the clue words, the sentence should be restated, but in a more visible form. The phrase "double malted milk" could be changed to "two malted milk shakes," or to "two milk shakes."

Difficult vocabulary or concepts can also be established through elaboration, using a series of clue sentences. For example the teacher might say:

1. You must be very hungry.
2. How many hamburgers can you eat?
3. What do you want to drink with your hamburger?
4. Do you always have a "coke" with your hamburger?

This kind of material, unrelated sentences, cued by clue words, is very useful in teaching a heterogenous group. The poorer students can be given the clue word before the sentence is presented. It is given to the better members of the class only when they miss the information. Or the student can decide for himself whether he wishes a clue before attempting to speechread the sentence. All the instructor has to say is, "Do you want a clue?"

2.2.4 GAMES AND QUIZZES. A game, in the sense of a contest, can be made out of almost any speechreading material. Games are popular with both children and adults. This mode of response should be used frequently in giving speechreading instruction. Quizzes, on the other hand, are short examinations that are given "for the fun of it"—the fun pupils have in displaying their knowledge or guessing ability. Quizzes provide variety in a speechreading lesson and have the added advantage of focusing the pupil's attention on getting the answer and away from concern about himself and his speechreading ability. It also tends to equalize the class. It is not enough to speechread the question. One must also know or guess the answer.

An example of a quiz suitable for beginning children or adults is given below. Note that, as in previously presented beginning level speechreading material, only basic vocabulary and simple grammatical structure are used. Words and phrases were selected for visibility as well as familarity. The "add a phrase" technique is also employed. The speechreader has the security of knowing what the first seven words will be—"What is a three letter word meaning?"

Three Letter Word Quiz

What is a three letter word meaning:

1.	A man's best friend?	dog
2.	Something we wipe our feet on before we enter the house?	mat
3.	Something we use when we play baseball?	bat
4.	A toy that spins around?	top
5.	Something that is worn on the head?	hat
6.	Something that looks like water, but is found in trees?	sap
7.	Something we like to put on our bread?	jam
8.	A farm animal?	cow
9.	One of the colors found in our flag?	red
10.	Something we use in the summer when we are too warm?	fan
11.	Something we use when we scrub the kitchen floor?	mop
12.	A popular name for a sailor?	Gob
13.	To feel blue and unhappy?	sad
14.	The same as happy?	joy

15. Something we ride in? car
16. A green vegetable? pea
17. Something a child receives at Christmas? toy
18. Something we use when we put a diaper on a baby? pin
19. Something placed across a river to hold
    the water back? dam
20. A household animal that purrs? cat

Procedure.

1. *Instructor Presentation*

   The instructor writes the title on the board—Three Letter Word Quiz

   He then turns to the pupils and says in full voice, "We are going to have a quiz. If you know the answer to a question, raise your hand. The answer to each question will be a three letter word."

   Before giving the quiz, the instructor makes it clear to the pupils what they are to do. Possible responses are the following:

   a. The pupil repeats the content of the query before giving his answer. For example, he might say, "A three letter word meaning a man's best friend is dog."
   b. The pupil responds as in (a) and then gives the group a sentence which he has made up incorporating the three letter word answer. For example he might say, in a soft voice, "I wish I had a dog."
   c. Group contest. The groups are divided and the quiz is given as a contest between two teams.
   d. Individual contest. Pupils write the answers down. The papers are scored and the winner receives some simple prize.
   e. The instructor writes all of the answers in scrambled order on the board before giving the quiz. Before answering the question the pupil points to the correct answer and then crosses it out or erases it. This method of response is by far the easiest. Pupils are able to anticipate the answers and hence are cued to some extent as to

what the question may be. As words are eliminated the possible questions and answers become narrowed.

2. *Pupil Presentation*

The questions are written on strips of paper and given to members of the class. In order for pupil presentation to be successful the instructor must have previously trained the class members to speak in such a fashion that they can be understood. Emphasis will have been placed on natural speech using adequate lip and jaw movement and a reduced or soft level of voice.

2.2.5 CONVERSATIONS AND SKITS. At the beginning level this type of material consists of a simple dialogue between two people. When presented to a group, it becomes a skit. Conversations are true to life situations and, as such, are considered to be one of the best kinds of speechreading material. Care must be taken, however, to structure the material so that it can be followed easily. Conversational language must be used; the vocabulary must be highly visible; the topic must be limited and known in advance. And, as in the Simple Story, the following idea must evolve from the preceding one. An example is given below:

Topic: What do you want in your lunch?
Participants: mother and child

M. 1. You didn't eat your apple yesterday. Do you want another one today or would you rather have an orange?
C. 2. I'd rather have an orange than an apple. Do we have any bananas?
M. 3. Yes, why?
C. 4. Could I have a banana instead of an orange?
M. 5. All right.
C. 6. Will you put in an extra piece of cake for Charlie? His mother never gives him anything but a sandwich and a piece of fruit.
M. 7. Perhaps he shouldn't have cake.
C. 8. Well he is kind of fat.

M. 9. Well you are too. Why don't you give him half of your piece if you are so worried about him.

C. 10. Gosh Mom, I'm not *that* worried about old Charlie.

Procedure.

1. *Skit* (Reduced Voice)

   The instructor is one of the "actors" in beginning instruction. Through his participation he can guide the conversation and elaborate on an idea that has been missed by the audience. (He is cued through puzzled expressions.) As the pupils become more skilled both in acting and speechreading the instructor need no longer assign himself a part.

   When presented as a skit the conversation is first given in its entirety. Following this it is presented line by line, and the members of the audience are called upon to repeat what was said. It is then given once more as a whole.

   The participants turn toward each other as they would in a normal conversation. The class gains experience in speechreading from the side and also from a three quarter view.

   The dialogue is practiced in advance of its presentation. Each actor has the complete script.

2. *Conversation* (Reduced Voice)

   Pupils practice in groups of two. Each pupil is given a script which contains only his part of the conversation.

   Each participant must make sure that his partner has finished talking before interrupting or responding, as in a normal conversational situation. If he does not understand what his partner said, he tells him so and asks him to repeat or to elaborate. This procedure has two corollary advantages. The hard-of-hearing individual is being trained not to interrupt and hog the conversation and to ask for help instead of pretending that he understood.

   "Conversations" can follow the group or skit presentation and make use of the same material for the slower pupils and fresh material for the more advanced.

After practicing the prepared script, the pupils are asked to make up a spontaneous conversation of their own on the same topic. The teacher illustrates this procedure using one of the members of the class as a partner.

2.3. Intermediate and Advanced Speechreading— Recognizing the Less Familiar

2.3.1 DIFFERENCE BETWEEN INTERMEDIATE AND ADVANCED INSTRUCTION. After the speechreader has mastered the recognition of highly familiar or overlearned speech, he is considered to be ready for intermediate or advanced materials. The distinction between intermediate and advanced is often more in the method of presentation than in the nature of the materials themselves. For the intermediate group more clues are used, and the rate of speech is slower. The materials differ from those used for beginning pupils in that the obvious and trite things are not said, or not said as often. The speechreader cannot anticipate what will be said on the basis of past experience. New information is given, and the vocabulary becomes increasingly more advanced. Four kinds of associational materials are used—stories (connected speech), topic sentences, games or quizzes, and multiple or cross conversations.

2.3.2 STORIES—CONNECTED SPEECH. The word *story* is used as a general term to indicate that the material to be presented is connected speech, as distinguished from independent statements or questions, that there will be only one speaker, and that the pupil will be expected to watch the entire monologue, or a good portion of it, before he will be asked to recall what he has understood. Examples of forms: information story, humorous story, narrative story, and descriptive story.

There are important values to be gained from this kind of experience. For one thing, material of this sort forces the student to be emotionally less dependent on immediate knowledge as to the correctness of his speechreading. He is on his own for five to ten minutes at a time with no reassuring help or verbal pat on the back from the instructor. After the initial introductory or orientation clues as to the topic or content, no additional clues are given. Another value is that the pupil is forced to depend on contextual clues, as he must often do in a real-life situation. He gradually learns that if he does not fully understand a statement or misses it altogether, he is not to panic and close his eyes, or look off "into the wild blue yonder." Instead, he must continue watching until he begins to understand a phrase or two. He will be surprised and delighted at the sudden flashbacks he has which will make clear ideas that he thought he had missed entirely. It is somewhat comparable to the experience we have all had in understanding under adverse listening conditions. The listener thinks he has not understood the message. Just as he is about to open his mouth to say, "I did not understand you," the message is clear to him. He did not understand immediately because he had not heard all that was said. It took a few seconds for the "wheels to whirl around," and for his mind to fill in for him the missing information, without, of course, any conscious effort on his part. Good speechreaders do not expect to understand everything that is said, or even anything at all, if the topic is not known, when they first begin to watch the speaker. But they continue watching, picking up words and phrases here and there until they become aware of the larger pattern or topic. Only then can they follow and understand the ideas that are being expressed.

A third important value is that experience with this kind of material should result in improvement in both visual memory and verbal or recall memory. The speechreader must retain visual imagery which he could not immediately identify (perceptual closure) long enough to obtain clues as to the meaning from the content which follows. Verbal or recall memory is also gradually improved. It is not unusual to have students who are new to story-type materials, when quizzed with respect to some specific point, say, "Well you know I understood it as you were giving it, but I can't remember it now. Say it for me again." And the instructor does just that, providing no other member of the class could remember it either.

The amount of preparatory information that is given before a story is greater than that for a sentence, but as with a sentence the amount will vary with the difficulty of the material (familiarity, visibility, and associational clues) and the skill of the pupils. There are in general four ways of introducing stories.* One of the ways can be used at a time or any combination that appears to be desirable. They are the following:

1. Discussion of the general topic from which the story is abstracted.
2. Presentation of a series of clue words.
3. Presentation of a series of clue sentences.
4. Presentation of visual aids.

Excerpts from stories which will be found in the section on materials will be used to illustrate these approaches.

A. Discussion of the Topic

It is often helpful to set the stage for what is to follow by discussing the topic with the group. The instructor first writes the topic on the board. He may then present information which will not be in the story, will respond to questions, and will urge the class members to volunteer any information which they may have. The discussion or orientation is always given in *full voice*. Every instructor will of course put the orientation material in his own language, but a suggested orientation to the story, "A Beeline for Home," is as follows:

When we say we make "a beeline for home," we mean that we go directly home in as straight a line as possible. Scientists say the bee does this. Every movement in the flight of a bee has meaning. This is a story of a beeline and the flight of this insect.

B. Series of Clue Words

A simple and effective way to introduce a story is through a series of clue words. The script is first examined to locate the words that are apt to give the speechreader difficulty. These are the words that are low in visibility or are not especially familiar. Included in this category are names of people or unfamiliar places. After the topic is given and written on the board,

---

* Originally collated in an organized fashion in *New Aids and Materials for Teaching Lip-Reading.*[6] Number three is a Mueller-Walle technique;[2] Number two is a Kinzie technique.[4]

the words are presented in *sequential order* as they appear in the story. The order is important because it gives the pupils additional information, as to the content of the story. The instructor writes the phrase, *clue words,* on the board and says, "These words are difficult to speechread. See if you can guess any of them." Each word is given in reduced voice. If no one responds, it is immediately said in full voice and then written on the board. This procedure is continued until all the words are placed on the board. They can be practiced further by the instructor presenting words selected from the board at random and continuing until they have all been identified. A modification of this is to indicate the word by pointing to it and then putting it into a simple sentence. By the time there has been adequate practice in speechreading the *clue words,* the pupils should be ready to follow the story. They have foreknowledge of the difficult and unfamiliar words, and since the words have been presented in sequential order, they have some notion of the ideas which will be developed. The meaning of unfamiliar words should be discussed before the presentation of the story. An example of this kind of introduction is given for the story which follows.

Title: Story of Pearls

Clue Words.

mollusk	layer	irritated	harvested
shell	hard	sand	natural
fluid	colors	rid	cultured
lining	nacre (neɪ-kɚ)		bead

A mollusk is a water animal that lives in a shell. The animal secretes a kind of fluid which covers the inside of its shell. The purpose of the fluid is to make a smooth lining to protect the mollusk from the rough shell. As soon as the first layer becomes hard, another layer is formed. Then the lining, which we call mother of pearl, becomes smooth. It is very beautiful. If you look carefully you can see many different colors. Another name for mother of pearl is nacre. Pearls are formed from nacre. An oyster is a very sensitive mollusk. He doesn't like to have his skin irritated. Have you ever had a stone in your shoe? You know how it hurts, but you can take your shoe off to get rid of it. If a piece of sand gets into an oyster's shell, he can't get rid of it. But he can cover it up. And he doesn't know when to stop. He keeps adding layer after layer of nacre until a pearl is formed. We can say a pearl is formed because the oyster was irritated! Many oysters must be harvested to find one which holds a pearl. This is why natural pearls are so expensive. Today we can buy cultured or cultivated pearls. Cultured pearls are made by putting a very small round bead into the oyster's shell. The oyster doesn't like this very much so he covers it up with nacre and forms a pearl. Cultured pearls are as beautiful as real pearls, but they are not so expensive. The only way to tell them apart is through x-raying them. Pearls are found in many parts of the world.

The story presented above is for an intermediate group of speechreaders, students who have finished their practice on "over-learned" speech. If the story is used with a group of children, any words that are not familiar should be defined and discussed. It is possible to use it with very young children by making certain vocabulary changes. For example, the words *spit out* or the word *produces* could replace *secrete* in the sentence, "The animal secretes a kind of fluid which covers the inside of its shell." "An oyster is a very sensitive mollusk," could be replaced by, "An oyster doesn't like to get hurt." Likewise, the word *scratched* could be used in place of *irritated* in the sentence, "He doesn't like to have his skin irritated." After the story is told, there should be some form of follow-up. A pupil can be asked to tell it in his own words, or a series of questions can be asked about it. Another device is to give the story again as a *series of related sentences*. Each sentence is repeated by a member of the class. Most groups will enjoy having the entire story repeated. Regardless of the technique that is used, the instructor must make certain that every member of the class understands the material before he goes on to something else.

The suggested clue words are those that would be most likely to be missed if the pupils are depending solely on vision. Fewer clue words are necessary if the students have vowel-hearing and if a combined approach, sight and sound, is used. In this case the words, *shell, layer, hard, sand, natural,* and perhaps others, will probably not need to be practiced in advance of the story.

C. Series of Clue Sentences

Another way of introducing a story is through a series of clue sentences. When using this technique, it is not necessary to practice clue words separately from the clue sentences, since they will be incorporated in the sentences. The sentences are based in part on the content of the material to follow and are designed either to bring out or to contain some of the more difficult words that will be found in the story. The sentences are *not,* however, *taken from the story.* The purpose is to prepare the pupils to follow the story, but not to give it to them piece-meal. If the story is a funny story or has a punch line, the clue sentences should not give it away. This is a modification of a method suggested by Bruhn in one of her earlier texts on the Mueller-Walle Method.[2, pp. 27-28] The preliminary sentences were considered to be an exercise, and the whole, sentences and story, was termed an *exercise-story.*

This method will be illustrated through basing the sentences on part of the story of the sea horse. After each sentence is given, a member of the class responds either by answering the question, repeating the statement, or commenting on it.

The title of the story (but not the sentences) is written on the board as before.

Title: The Sea Horse

Visual Aid.
Picture of a sea horse.
Clue Sentences.
  1. How do you suppose the sea horse got its name?
       Answer: *Head* shaped like a horse: has a *tail.* (Teacher
            repeats the answer)
  2. What do we call a mosquito?
       Answer: insect.
  3. Does part of the seahorse look like an insect?
       Answer: Yes, the body.
  4. The body of the sea horse is made from small bony plates.

5. Sea horses are hatched from eggs just like chickens.
6. How does a baby drink its milk?
   Answer: sucks it.
7. What is a word that means the opposite of giant?
   Answer: pygmy
8. Can you whinny like a horse?

The clue sentences are given in reduced voice. Any sentence or word that is not understood by at least one of the class is repeated in full voice. Words that may be new to the pupils should be written on the blackboard, even when they are correctly identified. An example of such a word might be *pygmy*.

Story

The sea horse has a head shaped something like that of a horse. It has the body of an insect. It has no scales on its body like a fish. It has very small bony plates on its body which overlap. This makes it look like an insect. The sea horse has a pouch like a kangaroo. The pouch holds the eggs before the babies are hatched. The tail of the sea horse is something like a monkey's tail. It can wrap its tail around a piece of seaweed. It uses it for an anchor. Its mouth is very small. It has no teeth. It sucks its food in the same way that we drink from a straw. The pygmy sea horse eats very tiny sea animal life. It swims in an upright position, but it cannot go very fast. This tiny animal does not whinny like a horse! But at times it does make some sound. It is a very soft, humming noise.

The information story presented above is part of a longer story for an intermediate group of children. It can, of course, also be used with adults. The remainder of the story will be found in the section on materials.

The clue sentence technique is probably the best single way of introducing a story to a group of pupils who have just reached the intermediate stage of their training. By the time the students have finished the clue sentences they should have little difficulty in following the story because a good deal, but not all, of the content has been conveyed.

Observe that the clue sentences followed the story in sequential order. Notice also that much of the vocabulary was repeated and that very easy sentences were included as well as more complex sentences. This is done deliberately in order to insure participation of the poorer speechreaders.

The method chosen for introduction will depend in part on the content of the story that is to be presented. Not every story is equally adaptable to all methods of introduction. Stories that contain a good deal of information and many words which may be new to the pupils are often best introduced through the clue word technique, while the narrative form of story adapts well to the use of clue sentences. In the two stories just presented, if only one technique of introduction is to be used, the "Story of Pearls" is perhaps best introduced by the clue word method and the "Sea Horse" through the use of clue sentences.

D. Visual Aids

To create interest in a topic much use is often made of such visual aids as objects, pictures, actions, maps, and flannel board charts. They may also be necessary in order for the pupils to get a clear understanding of material which may be new to them. When used for these two purposes, visual aids serve as adjuncts to other preparation techniques. But when dealing with known vocabulary they can often serve as the sole preparation technique making it unnecessary for the pupils to repeat clue words or respond to clue sentences. An example of this is the material entitled a *Story Picture* which will be found on page 298. The picture is complete in itself and actually tells a story. After the class has had ample time to examine the picture, they should be able to speechread whatever the instructor wishes to say about it. It can also serve as preparation for a story which departs somewhat from the content given by the picture. For example, the instructor might say:

This picture reminds me of my own son. He is simply car crazy. All he can think about is cars. He begged us to buy him one, but we told him that we couldn't afford it. So he got himself a job working in a grocery store after school and all day Saturday. He saved his money for six months until he had enough to buy an old wreck of a car. As soon as he bought the car, he quit his job at the grocery store so that he could spend all of his spare time fixing it up. Actually, this is about all that he does. He doesn't drive it very often. He can't. He usually has it apart. And he can't even take a girl to a movie or out for a Coke because he doesn't have any money. I don't think this bothers him very much. He's car crazy, not girl crazy. Every cent of his allowance is spent on parts for his car. And all he wants for his birthday or for Christmas is cash to buy more parts.

For younger children picture books can be found that are so well illustrated as to suggest the content. Familiar examples are the story of *The Three Bears* and *Little Red Riding Hood*. After each picture is shown the instructor tells that part of the story which was illustrated.

Picture	*Script*
Picture of the three bears.	Once upon a time there were three bears. There was a papa bear, a momma bear and a little baby bear.
Picture of bears in a big house in the woods.	The three bears lived in a big house in the woods.

And so on until the story is completed. The important thing to remember is not to ask the pupils to look at the pictures and to speechread at the same time. The picture is first shown. It is then turned over or put aside and attention is directed to the speaker by some such simple phrase as, "Did you all get a good look? All right, now watch me." The instructor must never *read* a story, but always *tell* it—usually in his own words. If he is following a script, the same technique is used as in good oral interpretation. He glances at a sentence, reads it, remembers it, and then looks up and talks directly to his audience. He should never be caught with his eyes down! And certainly never with his eyes down and his mouth open! The speechreader depends on a full view of the speaker's mouth and facial expression.

2.3.3 TOPIC SENTENCES—CUED BY CLUE WORDS AND CLUE SENTENCES. Unrelated sentences are also used in giving intermediate and advanced instruction. The sentences convey information and are the kind that might be heard in a school or lecture situation or in a private conversation when the participants are exchanging information as well as expressing feelings, attitudes, or making requests. The clue word or words are *always* given before the presentation of the sentence because the speechreader must know the general topic if he is to speechread material taken from a broader context. Such material is appropriate for, and presents a challenge to, the more advanced speechreaders. It can, however, be used with intermediate speechreaders or in a mixed skill class (the usual situation), providing that after the original sentence is given, a number of clue sentences are provided for the benefit of those pupils who did not understand the original sentence. Examples of this kind of material are given below.

1. Did you know that around Times Square the streets are cleaned twelve times a day?

The logical clue words to use are either *Times Square* or *New York* since these would refer to the general topic from which the sentence is assumed to be abstracted and represent more nearly the amount of information which the speechreader would have in the real setting. But if the instructor so desires, he can substitute the less visibile and familiar words, *clean streets*. Whether he does so or not will probably depend upon whether any of the members of the class are deaf. If the pupils can hear the vowel energy, the substitution will not be necessary because they will hear and speechread /sis/, /ɑɚ/, /in/, for streets are cleaned, and should be able to reach a perceptual closure from this much information.

Suggested clue sentences are as follows:
a. Have you ever been to New York?
b. Did you visit Times Square? Times Square is the area around Broadway and Forty-Second Street.
c. Did you think that the area around Times Square was as clean as it could be expected to be?
d. Believe it or not, the streets around Times Square are cleaned very often.

2. The first *lamps* were made out of pottery and were filled with vegetable oil.

The clue word is *lamps* because this word suggests the topic. The clue sentences are the following:

    a. Have you ever seen an old-fashioned oil lamp?
    b. The oil used is kerosene, but it would be possible to use vegetable oil.
    c. The lamp itself is made out of metal.
    d. Would it be possible to make a pottery or ceramic lamp?

3. It's been estimated that at Christmas time the average woman shopper walks about eleven miles a day.

The clue word is shopping. Possible clue sentences are these:

    a. Almost everyone goes shopping now and then.
    b. Women usually do most of the shopping.
    c. Most of us shop at least at Christmas time.
    d. Do you think you walk very far when you go shopping?
    e. You probably walk further than you think you do.

Procedure.

1. The clue word or words are given in full voice and written on the blackboard.

2. The instructor says to the group: "This is going to be a difficult sentence. Maybe you'll understand it. If you do, raise your hand to let us know, but I won't call on you until we finish the clue sentences."

    The original sentence is then given, in reduced voice.

    The first clue sentence is given (reduced voice) and repeated (full voice) by a member of the class.

3. The second clue sentence is given, and so on, until the content of all clue sentences has been established. Pupil participation can be provided for by having the students, rather than the instructor, give the clue sentences.

    By the time the last clue sentence has been repeated, most of the vocabulary of the original sentence will have been practiced. By then, it is highly probable that all members of the group have sufficient information to enable them to read the original sentence.

4. The instructor says: "Original (or first) sentence again," and gives it with reduced voice.

5. One of the pupils, who understood the original sentence the first time it was given, is then called upon to repeat it before the group as a kind of recognition or reward.

In the material given above, did you notice that the clue sentences, for the most part, did not give additional information, but were intended instead to establish certain concepts and words in the original sentence that would have been difficult to speechread? This same material could be used for a beginning class if the procedures were reversed and the clue sentences were given before the original sentence. In this case the material could be described as a series of related sentences.

Did you also observe that all of the original sentences had inherent interest? One of the aims of speechreading instruction is to entertain as well as to instruct, i.e. to make it a pleasant as well as a profitable learning experience. The material that the pupils are asked to speechread should so far as possible be something *worth* speechreading. After the pupil has progressed from the beginning to the intermediate stage, commonplace expressions and trite material should be avoided. He should be able to carry back to his classroom or home with him some new and interesting information, which he can have the joy of sharing with others. The pupil should look forward eagerly to his next speechreading class, rather than feeling that it is something which he dreads but must attend because it is good for him. This attitude of eager anticipation is fostered by the kinds of materials the instructor uses, and by his insuring that each student meets with success, and feels good about his progress. Of course, the instructor must also be enthusiastic and enjoy his work. Good material and methods can be ruined if presented by a cranky or depressed teacher.

2.4. *Games and Quizzes—Intermediate and Advanced Levels*

Games and quizzes at the intermediate and advanced levels are used often to provide pupil participation. They also develop knowledge and can be used at the intermediate and upper school levels to provide a review of subject matter at the same time that speechreading skill is being increased. Geography, history, and arithmetic facts lend themselves well to this kind of presentation. Another important objective for the school-age child is the development of a more extensive vocabulary. The chief difference between beginning games and intermediate or advanced games is that the former are based on everyday conversational commonplaces; the latter require some degree of knowledge.

An example of a geography game is the one that follows our story, "A Beeline." Students are supplied with individual maps of North America. They follow the speechreading directions and are also permitted to "take notes." An excerpt from this game is as follows:

1. Cross only one state in a beeline from Missouri to Minnesota.
2. You would cross a state best known for the production of corn.
3. You could visit the state capital at Des Moines.
4. Name the state you cross.
   Answer: Iowa

A volunteer is called on to give the name of the state and summarize the rest of the information—in full voice. For example, he might say, "The name of the state is Iowa. I made a beeline from Missouri to Minnesota. Iowa is known for the production of corn. Its capital is Des Moines." The complete game will be found in the materials section.

A game designed to build vocabulary is called "Find the Twin." An excerpt from it follows:

appropriate   Do you have an appropriate costume for
                     the Halloween party?
                     Be sure to wear the *proper* mask with your
                     costume.

The teacher writes the word *appropriate* on the board and explains that he will give a sentence using the word. Immediately following he will give a second sentence which contains a word which means the same as the first word. The pupils task is to find the synonym. In this case, the word is "proper."

These games and many more like them will be found in the materials section. It is expected that the teacher will be able to devise more of them to suit the needs and interests of the particular group he is instructing.

2.5. *Conversations and Skits—Intermediate and Advanced Levels*

Colloquial language is used at all levels in designing conversations and skits, but the situation is increased in complexity. At the beginning level only two actors take part in a conversation or skit, and what they say to each other is closely related. There are no abrupt changes in topic. At the intermediate level changes in topic similar to what might occur in a normal conversation are incorporated. And at the advanced level the conversation is not limited to two individuals, but may include three or more speakers. The speechreader is required to be alert and to look for the next speaker. At the beginning level the topic of the conversation or skit is given the speechreader; at the more advance levels, only the general social milieu. A very useful exercise for the advanced level is what we have termed "cross conversation." Several conversations are going on at the same time independently of one another. To create this situation in a speechreading class partners are seated facing each other at a distance of approximately six to eight feet. The partners must talk to each other and ignore the remainder of the partners that are also talking at the same time. A party setting—one of the most difficult for the speechreader—is created. He must concentrate on what is being said to him and ignore the conversations around him. Because this is most tiring, it is recommended only for advanced speechreaders and for short periods of time. All speakers use full voice—the amount they would normally use in such a setting. A collection of skits and topics that can be used in this fashion will be found in the materials section. When the speechreaders become proficient at this kind of exercise they will be able to say what comes naturally to them and will not need to rely on prepared materials.

3. RESPONSIBILITY OF THE TEACHER

The various "please do's" and "please dont's" have been elaborated in some detail both in the chapter on principles of speechreading and in this chapter on methods. In this section we shall try to restate them as best we can.

3.1. Psychological Problems

The teacher needs to be sensitive to the emotional problems and needs of his pupils. This is just a formal way of saying that he must not forget that he is dealing with people who are hearing handicapped and who do not like it! There is bound to be some measure of insecurity—some loss of ego strength, some feelings of inadequacy. The reactions take a number of forms, but are fairly predictable. Some children (and adults too) react by attempting to deny the problem. They decide that they do not need a hearing aid or that they do not need speech-reading instruction. They tend to be very sensitive to failure and easily discouraged. Sometimes the reaction is excessive bravado—"I'm very good at this"—when the facts are otherwise. Or the reverse, discouragement and depression, "I just can't learn to speechread; there's no sense trying." Often anxiety is expressed through a demand to know *right now* whether a particular response was correct or not. Bodily signs of unease are sometimes apparent—fidgeting, squirming, looking away, clock watching, expressions of embarrassment, all saying eloquently, "Let me out of here." The reverse is neuresthenia. A bright alert person suddenly becomes overwhelmed with fatigue and lethargy and must fight to keep awake. Frequently the hearing handicapped person seeks to be master of the situation. He may attempt to "hog the conversation." If he is doing the talking, he is spared the embarrassment and discomfort of not understanding someone else. A child will sometimes reject any activity or game planned by the instructor, regardless of how interesting it may be, and announce that he would rather do something else, something that he has decided on, where he will set the rules and have the situation well in command. Adults sometimes give the impression that they doubt the competency of the instructor. But the impression is often a false one. They may demand to know the total plan, the structure of succeeding lessons, and the procedures that will be used in advance of the lessons themselves. They wish to be reassured that things will proceed in an orderly fashion and to know the reasoning behind each activity. They are attempting to set themselves to anticipate each task and, hence, if possible, to avoid failure.

All of this sounds like speechreading is an onerous task. But it is not. It can be and should be high fun for the teacher as well as for the pupils. Most of the unpleasant emotional reactions described above can be avoided. The basic principle is that "nothing succeeds like success."

3.2. *Preparation of the Teacher*

In order to provide for success the teacher must have a thorough knowledge of the speechreading process. (See Chapter 2.) Specifically, he must "know" without having to think about it which sounds are visible, which are obscure, and which are invisible. This knowledge permits him to substitute quickly a visible word for an invisible one and to amplify and restate when necessary. By his management of the speechreading materials, he prevents student errors. A knowledge of the International Phonetic Alphabet is an invaluable aid. When a pupil has "apparently" made a mistake, this knowledge permits him to transcribe quickly what he said and what the pupil said and to compare the two. Frequently it will then be obvious that the two are almost identical. He can then show the older pupil or tell the younger one that he really did not make a mistake, adding immeasurably to the feelings of confidence and well-being of the individual.

Part of the preparation of the teacher should also include the development of good speaking habits. (See Chapter 1.) He must learn to use adequate lip, tongue, and jaw movement and to make the speech sounds in the conventional manner. He must also learn how to vary his rate and to use reduced voice while at the same time maintaining normal patterns of rhythm stress and enunciation.

Another important aspect of his training is learning how to write and rewrite materials for speechreading instruction. This will be discussed in more detail in a succeeding paragraph.

3.3. Analysis and Diagnosis of Learning Difficulties

Our "good" teacher recognizes from the start that he is not teaching a method or a series of lesson plans, but individuals who will vary markedly in their aptitudes. If he is to modify his materials to meet the problems he must know what the problems are. The Quick Recognition Exercises and the Quick Identification Exercises can be used for diagnosis as well as remediation. The former can be used to measure visual perception and speed of perception; the latter, visual memory and flexibility. The pupils need not know that they are being diagnosed. The teacher simply calls on the pupils in turn rather than asking for volunteers or for a group response. Tests of speechreading (see Chapter 7) can be used to measure synthetic ability. Again the students need not know that they are being tested, if this is deemed desirable, providing the teacher has made use of written responses as a regular part of his instruction.

3.4. Planning for Individual Needs, Interests, and Background

The teacher plans for the individual within the group situation, by varying the way in which he presents materials and the difficulty of the materials themselves. The Quick Recognition Exercises, for example, can be given very slowly or very rapidly depending upon who is being asked to respond. More visible and familiar material is given to the poorer students, and more difficult material, to the more skilled. When pupils have developed adequate skill in the exercises designed to improve visual proficiency, they are no longer used. The speechreading lesson is used for remedial and language enrichment tutoring for children who are already skilled speechreaders.

The most effective teaching of adults is often done with material planned specifically for them in view of their work and hobbies. Students are requested to list their hobbies and to bring fairly extensive lists of the kinds of things they say to others and the kinds of things that are said to them in the course of their work. If it is a group situation, other members of the group will be delighted to learn the technical vocabularies of fields other than their own, while the individual for whom the material is designed is getting much needed practice.

3.5. *Selection and Development of New Materials, Including Rewriting*

The teacher of speechreading should cast an analytic and critical eye at any "canned" materials, including our own, and be prepared to rewrite or revise them in accordance with his needs. He should also develop skill in writing original materials for his class. Much of the best material is based around current happenings in the community and in the world.

There are a number of principles that are followed in writing materials for speechreading. Perhaps the most important one to keep in mind is that all material must be written in a conversational style. One of the best ways to achieve this style is through the use of a tape recorder. First one masters the information which he wishes to present. He then puts it aside, imagines that he is talking to a friend, and speaks into a tape recorder. The material is then transcribed and rewritten, when necessary, to make it useful material for speechreading practice. The material is examined to see if a simple syntactical structure has been followed. The easiest order for the speechreader to follow is subject-verb-predicate. Long and structurally complex sentences should be avoided. Next it is checked for *visibility* and *familiarity*. Is it possible to substitute words that are either more visible or more familiar than those originally used? Should certain portions be *restated* or *elaborated* to provide more *contextual* and *situational* clues? Has provision been made for *association* of ideas? Is the following idea often cued by the previous one? And finally, after all of this revision, is the "story" still interesting and something that you would enjoy giving, and the pupils "hearing?" If not, by all means scrap it and start again—perhaps on another day!

To illustrate this procedure we will rewrite a short story. The original was as follows:*

> Command Performance. Tourists jammed the shops on Michigan's Mackinac Island, and keeping offsprings corralled was a problem. But one father had the situation under control. When he turned to leave a shop, he simply said, "Heel," and his four children obediently fell in behind him.

Imagined Conversation.

I read an interesting story in *The Readers' Digest* the other day. It seems that a guy was out shopping with his four children in one of those crowded shopping centers where there are numerous stores. He really had his kids trained. Everytime he was ready to leave a store he would say "Heel," and the kids would fall in line right behind him.

Revision.

Shopping With Children

Have you ever gone shopping with your children? It can be murder. Especially if you're in a crowded shopping center where there are many different shops. You look around, and all of a sudden Johnny is missing. What to do? The other day I saw a man who had it all figured out. He was shopping with his wife and four children. They were browsing around and going from one shop to another. They didn't have their dog with them, but obviously this man knew all about how to train dogs—and also how to train children, too. Whenever they were ready to leave a shop, he quietly said, "Heel," and all four children fell into line right behind him.

A title was given the story to set the scene. It was further elaborated through association with common experience. These aspects were missing in the imagined story. The 'wife' was added to add visibility and familiarity. "Shopping with his wife" is more commonly heard than "shopping with four children." Other changes to provide higher visibility were: "man" for

* *The Readers Digest.* August, 1966, p. 110. Contributed by Mrs. John Pittenger.

"guy;" "children" for "kids;" "shop" for "store;" "browsing around," and "quietly." To prepare the students for the punch line, through association of ideas, the story was amplified further to bring in the idea of dogs and training of dogs.

3.6. *Varying Pupil Participation and Response*

It is important to train one's pupils to participate in the instruction process. They need to learn to read each other's lips as well as the instructors. It is sometimes necessary to spend a period or two on good speech habits. The pupils must learn, as the instructor has, how to be understandable without mouthing or exaggeration. Since many hard-of-hearing individuals cannot do a good job of monitoring or changing the intensity levels of their voices, it is often better to let them use full voice and ask the other pupils to turn their hearing aids down a bit. To make the lessons interesting and fun the method of response required of the students is varied. The teacher should require a good deal of individual response, calling on each pupil in turn. This permits him to vary his materials in relation to the skill of the respondee and insures participation from everyone. The people who "volunteer" are usually the better speechreaders. There are basically two kinds of responses—verbal and motor. Verbal responses consist of (a) repeating what has been said, (b) answering questions, and (c) commenting on statements. After the introductory or beginning lessons the pupils are gradually weaned away from parroting back and are asked to respond most frequently as they would in a normal social situation. Motor responses consist of (a) writing or (b) some other form of physical action. Pupils can be asked to write their answers at their desks or on the board. There are many other forms of physical action and most of them are very enjoyable. The pupil can indicate that he has understood in the following ways: placing a pin in a chart, selecting the correct lotto piece, putting the correct part on a flannel-board chart, drawing a picture, completing a picture, moving doll furniture or other objects, finding something that is hidden, acting out a part— "and then the lion roared," etc.

3.7. *Changing Material to Insure Correct Response**

When a student misses a question or statement, it is often considered to be a better tutorial and psychological technique to revise the material to insure his success rather than just giving him the correct answer or calling on another pupil for it. The same principles are used that were described under the previous section on writing materials for speechreading. The essential difference is that the revision is done on the spot. Words and phrases are changed to provide higher visibility and greater familiarity. Association is built through elaboration, restatement, and the introduction of related ideas. Examples have already been given on pages 239–241. Here is another one.

Let us imagine that the "small story" on an early American nutcracker from Our American Heritage (see materials section) was being given sentence by sentence to members of the class as a review, and to make certain that the less skilled speechreaders understand the story and are not being left out. The teacher gives this sentence: "It was placed on the table when nuts were served as dessert." The pupil has missed the sentence. The teacher must now quickly decide how to get him to see it. In this instance, if the topic "nutcracker" has already been established, probably all the teacher would need to do would be to repeat the statement, but replace the word "it" by "the nutcracker." But what if the topic has not been established or the pupil still does not understand? The teacher realizes that the source of the trouble is probably two words that are low in visibility and not as familiar as "placed" or "table." They are "nuts" and "dessert." Since the words cannot be replaced, recognition of them must be developed through association. The procedure might be as follows:

To the pupil:

1. Do you like apple pie?

The words "apple pie" are used because of their high degree

---

* A number of these techniques appear to have been first suggested in *New Aids and Materials for Lip-Reading.*[6]

of familiarity. If the answer is in the affirmative, the teacher proceeds to the next sentence.

2. Do you like apple pie for dessert?

   If the pupil understands, the word "dessert" has been established.

This may be all that is needed, but if necessary, the teacher can next establish understanding of the word "nut." In order to do this he might say:

3. Do you like cashews?

   The word "cashews" is selected because of its high visibility.

4. A cashew is a kind of a nut.

5. Do you ever eat nuts for dessert?

The teacher then says, "This is the sentence you missed. Watch it again." He pauses and then says, "It was placed on the table when nuts were served as dessert."

It should be added that the whole problem could probably have been avoided in the first place had the original sentence been: "It was placed on the table when nuts were served after the meal." This is the way it would have been written for a beginning intermediate group. A good part of the problem was due to the fact that nuts are rarely served alone as dessert nowadays. The speechreader did not expect this statement and so could not anticipate it. Another minor improvement with respect to visibility would be to use the word "for" in place of "as" in the phrase, "as dessert." The original material should not be revised, however, for more advanced students. An interesting point would have been missed.

When a procedure such as this is written out, it sounds impossibly long and tortuous. It is not, however, in the actual situation. Understanding is established very quickly. The three keys to easy understanding are *visibility, familiarity,* and *association.* Immediate revision and elaboration of material is one of the most important skills of the speechreading teacher. Because of this skill, no one is left in the dark and made to feel inadequate. It becomes second nature to the experienced teacher. He quickly revises without having consciously to plan his method. Until the beginning teacher has established this ability, he should anticipate difficulties and be prepared in advance with "back-up" sentences such as those described above.

3.8. Mental Hygiene

The teacher of speechreading is in a sense an educational psychologist or therapist. He works indirectly to dispel feelings of anxiety, frustration, and inadequacy through insuring that each student meets with success. The best mental hygiene in this situation is relaxed, happy, and learning pupils. To accomplish this goal, the teacher, when teaching a group, must be firmly committed to the idea that he is giving individual lessons within a group setting. It cannot be emphasized too strongly that there is no such thing as a homogenous group of speechreaders. While we have attempted to grade our materials, the grading should serve only as a guide. It is assumed that the teacher who uses them will select materials from various levels for the same class period. In addition, as he teaches, he will modify the more difficult materials for the less skilled members of his class. Positive attitudes are developed toward speechreading and toward self by the teacher's sensitivity to his pupil's feelings and needs, by the use of multilevel materials in the same period, and by anticipating difficulties and providing for them. Problems are largely avoided through skillful manipulation of materials. Advanced pupils must not be bored by having to endure a lesson based entirely on skills which they have long mastered; less skilled students must not be frustrated by being expected to speechread materials too difficult for them. The teacher must know the strengths and weaknesses of each pupil. He does not try to hide this knowledge from the students (they know it anyway), but neither does he seek to impress it upon them. Such simple phrases as, "This is for Jean," serve to direct the material to the right person. It is important in terms of emotional well-being for everyone to understand, at least eventually, everything that has been said. There is nothing more devastating than to have missed the point and never to learn what it was. This happens often enough in real-life situations to the hearing handicapped person. Do not let it happen in your classroom.

It can be easily prevented. The respondee is asked to use full voice and face the other students so that they may speechread as well as hear. The teacher then repeats the answer in reduced voice or the original question or statement. Through this procedure the less skilled pupils are speechreading the more difficult material *after* they have learned what it is. If the group is composed of deaf students or there are some deaf members in the group, it is sometimes necessary before repeating to write a key word or two on the board. Do not be afraid to repeat material. The better speechreaders will actually enjoy seeing the more difficult material over again.

Another way in which the speechreading teacher helps to establish self-confidence in his pupils is through his attitude toward them. It is one of respect. Respect for their knowledge and for their insights. After he has worked with a group of older children or adults for awhile he will seek their positive criticisms and suggestions. The teacher can often gain important insight from such questions as the following: Am I easy to speechread? Is there anything about the way I talk that makes it difficult for you to follow? Do I repeat too much or not enough? Are these the kinds of materials that you need? When do you have difficulty in understanding? Are there special vocabularies that you would like us to cover? And, we might add, if a warm climate of mutual acceptance has been established, the teacher will not have to ask such questions. The students will volunteer suggestions.

The teacher also respects his students' "right to know." Questions regarding goals and the rationale for certain materials or procedures are answered. As mentioned earlier, such questions often arise when teaching adult speechreaders. Some of the students will probably have had prior instruction from someone who may not have taught in the same fashion as you do. If the student has had silent instruction before, he will wish to know why you use reduced voice. He may feel that if he hears some voice that he is not really learning to speechread. If he has been taught by the method of introducing one speech movement at each lesson, he may wonder why you are not doing this. He may need to be reassured that you are giving him training in visibility as well as association. It does no harm to point out the reason for the various activities, for example, that the Quick Recognition Exercises are for training in visibility and include all of the speech movements; that the Quick Identification Exercises are for visual memory and flexibility; and that the sentences, games, skits, and stories are designed to improve association. But in saying this it is perhaps necessary to add a word of warning. The purpose can be explained, but *all* of the "how's" and "why's" should not be. The speechreader does not need to know how the various speech sounds are formed or how he identifies them. The beginning teacher sometimes feels that he should teach all that he knows. But to do so is a disservice to his students. They must not be trained to think about "how" they speechread. Such training can interfere with quick perception and apprehension. Save your explanation of how speech sounds are formed for your lessons on speech correction or speech development.

And finally, the teacher can help his students to help themselves by permitting them to ventilate their feelings and frustrations. Problems are easier to bear when they are shared with others and when one learns that they are not peculiar to himself. The hard-of-hearing often report that their families are unsympathetic. "You have a hearing aid, why can't you understand?" Other complaints are these: "There is no sense in my going to the theatre. I can't understand anything anyway." "People look annoyed when I ask them to repeat. I feel left out of conversations." "No one pays any attention when I have something to say." "As soon as people see my hearing aid, they begin to shout or avoid me." "Everyone mumbles in my family. They speak too fast for me to follow them." "My teacher always talks with her back to the board. She gets mad if I ask her to repeat. She thinks I'm just trying to get attention and could do better if I wanted to," and so on. Sometimes positive suggestions for amelioration can develop through group discussion, and even when this does not occur, the individuals feel better for having had a sympathetic ear.

A list of books is given below which, if read by teachers or by the normal hearing members of the family, may help them to empathize and to be of constructive help.

Canfield, N.: *Hearing, A Handbook for Laymen,* Garden City, New York, Doubleday, 1959.

Heiner, M.H.: *Hearing Is Believing.* Cleveland and New York, The World Publishing Co., 1949.

Murphy, G.E.B.: *Your Deafness Is Not You.* New York, Harper, 1954.

Morkovin, B., and Moore, L.M. (Eds.): *Through The Barriers of Deafness and Isolation.* New York, MacMillan, 1960.

Warfield, F.: *Cotton in My Ears.* New York, Viking Press, 1948.

Warfield, F.: *Keep Listening.* New York, Viking Press, 1957.

REFERENCES

1. Bunger, A.: *Speechreading—Jena Method,* 4th Edition, Danville, Illinois, Interstate Printers and Publishers, 1961.
2. Bruhn, E.: *The Mueller-Walle Method of Lipreading for the Deaf.* Lynn, Massachusetts, The Nichols Press, 1924.
3. Bruhn, M.E.: *The Mueller-Walle Method of Lipreading for the Hard of Hearing.* Washington, D.C., The Volta Bureau, 1955.
4. Kinzie, C.E., and Kinzie, R.: *Lipreading for Children, Grades I, II, III.* Seattle, Washington, 1929.
5. Morkovin, B.V., and Moore, L.M.: *Life Situation Speech-Reading Through the Cooperation of the Senses, A.V.K.R. Method.* Los Angeles, California, University of Southern California, 1948.
6. *New Aids and Materials for Teaching Lip-Reading.* Washington, D.C., American Society for the Hard of Hearing, 1943.
7. Nitchie, E.B.: *Lip-Reading Principles and Practise.* New York, Frederick A. Stokes Co., 1912.
8. Nitchie, E.H.: *New Lessons in Lip Reading.* Philadelphia and New York, Lippincott, 1950.

Chapter 6

MATERIALS FOR INSTRUCTION

1. SAMPLE LESSONS

1.1. Beginning Speechreading Material—Children

1.1.1 QUICK RECOGNITION EXERCISE.

Q.R.E.—visible initial consonants

*p*ay	*s*ay	*w*ay
*th*in	*f*in	*p*in
*sh*eet	seat	*m*eat

or

Q.R.E.—visible final consonants

li*v*e	lie*s*	li*m*e
pou*ch*	mou*th*	mou*s*e

1.1.2 OVERLEARNED SPEECH AT SCHOOL.

1. Go to your seat.
2. Get out your pencil and paper.
3. Put your name on the paper.
4. Do this again.
5. Go to the board.
6. Watch your spelling.
7. It is time for recess.
8. It is time for lunch.
9. Don't push.
10. Go to the office.
11. You are late.
12. Where is your book?
13. You did very well.

Contributed by Shirley Nelin

1.1.3 SIMPLE STORY.

My Friend

I have a friend.
I think she is my best friend.
Every day we play together.
She waits for me when I come home from school.
Then I take her for a ride on my bicycle.
She rides up in front in a basket.
Her hair blows in my face and makes me laugh.
When we get home we are hungry.
We have milk and cookies.
I drink my milk from a glass.
She laps her milk from a saucer.
Sometimes her nose gets in the milk.
It makes her sneeze.
My friend is a gray kitten.

1.1.4 COLLOQUIAL SENTENCES—CUED BY CLUE WORDS.

Clue Word	Sentences
dress	I like your blue dress.
pencil	Do you have an extra pencil?
musical instrument	My sister can play the piano.
rain	I like to hear the rain on the roof.
game	What game do you like best?
tardy	Don't be late for school.
gift	She brought an apple for her teacher.
story	Tell me a story.
weather	It is too warm to wear a sweater today.
schoolwork	I have to finish my homework before I can play.
ride	You will miss the bus if you don't hurry.
favorite	I like chocolate ice cream best.
circus	We saw some funny clowns at the circus.
bake	My mother and I baked a batch of cookies today.
	a. Do you like cookies?*

* Developmental sentences can be used, in addition to clue words, when necessary. The developmental sentences were contributed by Marilyn Lonsbury.

  b. I like to bake cookies.

  c. My mother helps me.

candy The new candy store on (name a street) sells my favorite candy—peanut brittle.

  a. Do you like candy?

  b. I like candy with peanuts in it.

  c. Where is the new candy store?

1.1.5 A QUIZ.

What Animal Am I?

Three clues are given for each animal; the last word in each sentence is a clue. Students may write or volunteer the answers. When used as a written exercise, write only the last word in each sentence.

I. What animal am I?
  1. I live on a *farm.*
  2. My coat is *wool.*
  3. I say *baa-baa.*
  What is my name?   *sheep*

II. What animal am I?
  1. I live in the *woods.*
  2. I have a *bushy tail.*
  3. I am very *sly.*
  What is my name?   *fox*

III. What animal am I?
  1. I have very soft *fur.*
  2. I have long *ears.*
  3. I live in a hole in the *ground* (or hutch).
  What is my name?   *rabbit*

IV. What animal am I?
  1. I am very *small.*
  2. I like to eat *cheese.*
  3. I ran up the *clock.*
  What is my name?   *mouse*

V. What animal am I?
  1. I am the only animal that can *fly.*

2. I have soft fur and *large ears.*
3. I like to live in a *cave.*
What is my name?   *bat*

VI. What animal am I?
1. I am a very good *swimmer.*
2. I am called an animal *engineer.*
3. I *build dams across a stream.*
What is my name?   *beaver*

VII. What animal am I?
1. I like to play and have *fun.*
2. Sometimes I look and act like *people.*
3. You can see me hang by my tail at the *zoo.*
What is my name?   *monkey*

VIII. What animal am I?
1. I like to live in the *house.*
2. I like to have you stroke my *fur.*
3. I can catch *mice.*
What is my name?   *cat*

1.2. *Beginning Speechreading—Upper Grade Level or Adults; Suitable for Adult Vocabulary*

1.2.1 QUICK RECOGNITION EXERCISE.

Visible Initial Consonants

*r*ead	*f*eat	*s*een
*ch*urch	*p*erch	*v*erge
*th*in	*w*in	*b*een

or

Visible Final Consonants

hoo*p*	whose	hoo*f*
ra*sh*	wra*th*	ra*m*

1.2.2 OVERLEARNED SPEECH.

Acknowledgements and Thanks in Phrases and Sentences

Many thanks.

It's been a pleasure.
Thank you for the very nice time.
The pleasure's all mine.
We're so glad you came.
It was nice of you to invite me.
It's just what I wanted.
You shouldn't have done it.
You were much too generous.
You are very thoughtful.
I'll be delighted to accept.
We are grateful for all your help.
I hope I can return the favor sometime.
It was a lovely party.
What a pleasant surprise.
I appreciate it.

Contributed by Elizabeth Wagman

1.2.3 SIMPLE STORY—A SERIES OF CLOSELY RELATED SENTENCES

My Car

I have a beautiful blue car.
It's not a new car.
I bought it last week.
The motor is very good.
The inside is very clean.
I plan to go on a trip in it this weekend.
I think I'll go to the zoo (or name a town, city, beach, or resort).
I went there about a year ago with friends.
It will be fun to drive my own car this time.
I hope the car will last a long time.

Contributed by Ronald Walker

1.2.4 COLLOQUIAL SENTENCES—CUED BY CLUE WORDS AND (WHEN NECESSARY) BY DEVELOPMENTAL SENTENCES

Clue Word Sentence

mail	Were there any letters for me today?
bargain	The house was cheap at $20,000.00.

resort	We spent our vacation at Palm Beach.
assist	Is there anything I can do to help you?
replica	The boy is the image of his father.
forecast	The paper said fair and warmer tomorrow.
travel	Would you rather fly or go by train?
farm	They bought a small ranch in Wyoming.
holiday	I hope you have a pleasant vacation.
talk	Speak up!
ill	I think she has the flu.
beau	She has a new boyfriend.
beagle	The boy has a new puppy.
absent	Why weren't you in class last week?

higher
prices

The cost of living is going up and people are paying more for food and clothing.
1. Prices are going up.
2. It costs more to live these days.
3. Food is higher.
4. Clothing is higher.

changing
weather

We can expect the weather to be changeable this time of the year.
1. It was warm yesterday.
2. Today it is cold.
3. The weather changes often this time of the year.

skirts

Women's skirt lengths seem to change about every ten years.
1. The skirts are short.
2. Now the skirts are getting longer.
3. What length will they be in ten years?

Contributed by Gayle H. Bishop

1.2.5 CONVERSATION FOR TWO—"WHEN FRIENDS MEET."
Topics: Lunch and Shopping

Shirley: Hello Barbara! What are you doing for lunch today?

Barbara: I'm trying not to think about it—I'm on a diet—again.

Shirley: Oh come on and have lunch with me. You can have a salad while I eat French fries.

Barbara: After lunch let's go over to (name a store). They are
            having a big sale.
Shirley: A sale on what?
Barbara: Just about anything—most everything is marked down
            50 percent.
Shirley: Are you looking for something special?
Barbara: Yes. We need a new sofa. The springs are broken in
            the old one.
Shirley: It sounds like your diet is a good idea.
Barbara: Ouch!
            Contributed by C. Freeman

1.3. Intermediate Speechreading—Children

1.3.1 Q.I.E.—Beginning Level.

        a. sauce   saws
        b. chirp   germ
        c. purse   purrs
        d. pies   buys   mice
        e. punch   bunch   munch

1.3.2 Story.

Saraphena the Witch

Clue Words.		kitten	(Sniffy)
soup	pot	spider	(Blackie)
country	animals	owl	(Big Eyes)

Exercise Sentences.

1. Saraphena loved to make soup.
2. Saraphena liked to make soup for her animal friends.
3. Her friends were a spider, an owl and a kitten.
4. They knew Saraphena could make the best soup.

Story Presentation.

Once upon a time there was a witch. Her name was Saraphena.
She was a very happy witch and she loved to make soup. She
made the best soup in the whole country. It was so good it made

your mouth water just to think of it. Everyone wanted to be invited to have some of Saraphena's soup. She made it in a big, black pot. The animals would sit and watch as she stirred and stirred and stirred. They watched as she put more good things into the pot. She would say, "Gaggle, waggle, laggle." (voice) Saraphena's pet kitten was named Sniffy. He said, "This is very good soup. I can tell by the way it smells." Saraphena's pet owl was called Big Eyes. He said, "I know this is 'specially good soup. I can tell because it is thick and has a beautiful color." Saraphena's pet spider whose name was Blackie said, "I am sure this is the best soup because it bubbles." Blackie was an expert bubble watcher. Saraphena said, "Maybe it is MAGIC." Do you think witches have magic?

Contributed by Roberta Evatt

This story can be adapted to a flannel board demonstration. Have cut-outs of a witch's hat, a black pot, a kitten, a spider, and an owl. Use the cut-outs as the story develops following the procedure in *Jimmy's Day*.

1.3.3 Topic Sentences.

Mary and John went to the circus to watch the funny clowns, and to eat lots and lots of popcorn.

Clue: Circus.
1. Have you ever gone to a circus?
2. You see clowns in a circus.
3. Clowns are funny.
4. Do you like popcorn?

Jimmy's little dog saw a squirrel and chased it up a tree, but the squirrel got away.

Clue: Animals.
1. Jimmy has a dog.
2. The dog saw a squirrel.
3. The dog chased the squirrel.
4. But he couldn't catch it.

My father bought us a cute little black puppy with curly hair, and a funny short tail.

Clue: *Puppy*.
1. We have a dog.
2. It is a puppy.
3. It has black curly hair.
4. It is so cute.
5. He wags his tail.

Our baby has two new teeth and she looks so funny when she smiles.

Clue: *Teeth*.
1. We have a baby.
2. She has two teeth.
3. The teeth just came in.
4. She smiles and smiles at us.
5. She looks funny.

Today would be a good day for flying kites, if only I had a kite.

Clue: *Kites*.
1. The wind is blowing.
2. What shall we do today?
3. (Let's fly our kites.) I wish I had a kite.
   Contributed by: M. Tamai and C. Freeman

1.3.4 Vocabulary Game or Contest—Add A Letter to "An."

All words end in *an*. One letter is added to make a word described by the teacher.

Procedure. Write *an* on the board. The teacher describes a word, and the student adds the letter to make the correct response.

Example. Teacher—Add a letter to "an" to make a word that is a boy's name. Answer: *Dan*.

1. Add a letter to "an," and you have a word meaning
   a male human being.   *man*
2. What letter added to "an" is a word which means "to
   move air?"   *fan*

3. Add a letter to "an" to make something we use when we cook.　　　*pan*

4. "An" with one letter is a word for a large truck used to move furniture.　　　*van*

5. Add a letter to "an" for a word meaning something we put food in.　　　*can*

6. What letter added to "an" is the name of a light brown color?　　　*tan*

7. Add a letter to "an" and the word means gone fast by foot.　　　*ran*

8. Add a letter to "an" to make a word which means "a girl's name."　　　*Jan*

1.4. Intermediate Speechreading Adult Vocabulary— Suitable for Upper Grade Level or Adult

1.4.1 Q.I.E.–BEGINNING LEVEL.

a. five　　fife
b. rose　　woes
c. myth　　pith
d. beam　　beep　　peep
e. rise　　rice　　wise

1.4.2 INTERMEDIATE STORY–ADULT VOCABULARY

"A BEELINE" FOR HOME

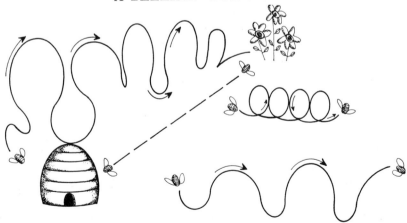

FIGURE 3. Beeline for Home.

Orientation.

When we say we make "a beeline" for home, we go directly home in as straight a line as possible. Scientists say the bee does this. Every movement in the flight of a bee has meaning. This is the story of a beeline and the flight of this insect.

Note that orientation is given before the clue words are written on the board. This procedure gives the student an opportunity to become "mentally set" and to anticipate the sequence of the story as the teacher lists the clue words.

Clue Words.

meandering	direction	wagging
straight	distance	scientists
dance	circle	signals

Exercise Sentences.
1. The bee flies to a flower.
2. The bee flies in a meandering way.
3. The bee flies straight home to the hive.
4. Then the bee dances for the other bees.
5. Somtimes it is a circle dance.
6. Sometimes it is a wagging dance.
7. The dancing bee is called a scout.
8. The circle dance and the wagging dance give information to the bees in the hive.
9. These bees are called workers.
10. The dances tell them where to find food.
11. Now scientists are sure bees "talk" to each other.

Note that these sentences stop short of the climax or the full presentation.

Story. *

The bee flies to a flower in a meandering way. When it comes home to the hive it flies in an almost straight line. If a person goes straight home, we say he makes a beeline for home. After

---

* The story and drawings are adapted from information in Compton's Pictured Encyclopedia, 1961 edition, p. 112.

a bee flies directly back to the hive, it tells the other bees where it has been. The bee gives this information in an interesting way. It performs a special dance which the other bees understand. The bee that performs the dance is called the scout. The other bees in the hive are called worker bees. The dance of the bee tells the direction in which they must fly to find food. There are two dances that tell how far the food is from the hive. We call them the circle dance and the wagging dance. A circle dance means the flowers are not far from home. But a wagging dance shows that the flowers are a long way from the hive. Do you believe a bee can count? Somehow it is able to tell just how far away the food supply is by the number of wags or circles the scout dances.

Some scientists believe the bee gives the direction to the food by the position of its body when it dances. A German scientist[*] put a microphone into a beehive. When the scout came back to the hive, it gave sound signals. The scientist heard these signals over the microphone. He got the surprise of his life. The bees were actually "talking" to each other. Some of the sounds were short and some were long. Some of the sounds were high and others were low. The scout bee "talks" while it dances. All of this information tells the worker bees where they can find food. The expression, "to make a beeline for home," comes from observing this interesting insect.

1.4.3 A Geography Game Related to the Story, "A 'Beeline' for Home."

The object of the game is to move in a beeline from one state to another, crossing *only one other* state, and to identify the state crossed.

Visual Aid. Use individual maps of North America, with the state boundaries marked but unnamed, or a large map with the states clearly defined for all students to see.

Procedure. The teacher gives four statements about each state to be identified. The student places his pencil on the map to

[*] Dr. Harold Esch of the University of Munich. *TIME MAGAZINE*, May 31, 1963, p. 54.

estimate the beeline between the two states mentioned. In defining the state, students must be careful to make the line cross only *one* state. One or two word answers are written by the students giving just enough information to show that they understand the statements. At the completion of the game volunteers go to the board and write briefly the information.

Example. The teacher uses a reduced voice.

Teacher Speechreads:	*Student Writes:*
1. Cross only one state in a beeline from Missouri to Minnesota.	1. Mo. to Minn.
2. You would cross a state best known for the production of corn.	2. produces corn
3. You could visit the state capital at Des Moines.	3. cap. Des Moines
4. Name the state you cross.	4. Iowa

1. Cross only one state in a beeline from Rhode Island to New Hampshire.
2. The Pilgrims arrived here in 1620.
3. The state is famous for an early American tea party.
4. Name the state you cross.   Answer: *Massachusetts*

1. Cross only one state in a beeline from South Dakota to Utah.
2. A large part of Yellowstone National Park is in this state.
3. This state is famous for its magnificent scenery.
4. Name the state you cross.   Answer: *Wyoming*

1. What state would you cross if you went in a beeline from Virginia to Delaware?
2. You would see the United States Naval Academy at Annapolis.
3. You could visit our National Capital.
4. Name the state you cross.   Answer: *Maryland*

1. Cross one state in a beeline from Nevada to Alaska.
2. You would see a beautiful blue lake formed by a volcano.

3. You would go through Crater Lake National Park.
4. Write the name of the state you cross. Answer: *Oregon*

1. Go in a beeline from Pennsylvania to Vermont.
2. The largest city in the nation is in this state.
3. It is called "The Empire State."
4. What is the name of the state? Answer: *New York*

1. Start in Michigan and go in a beeline to West Virginia.
2. You would cross a state that has given us seven Presidents of the United States.
3. Can you name three of these Presidents?
   (J. Garfield, U.S. Grant, W. Harding, B. Harrison, W. Harrison, W. McKinley, and W.H. Taft).
4. What state would you cross? Answer: *Ohio*

1. Cross only one state in a beeline from Louisiana to Hawaii.
2. You will cross the second largest state in the United States.
3. Six flag have flown over this state.
   (France, Spain, Confederate, Stars and Stripes, and Texas)
4. Name the state you cross. Answer: *Texas*

1. Cross one state in a beeline from Mississippi to Florida.
2. The capital of the state is Montgomery.
3. The popular name for this state is the Yellowhammer State.
4. What state do you cross? Answer: *Alabama*

1. Cross in a beeline from Iowa to Montana.
2. The famous Mt. Rushmore National Memorial is in this state.
3. A place in the state has become the geographic center of the United States.
4. Name the state you cross. Answer: *South Dakota*

1. Travel in a beeline from Florida to North Carolina.
2. You will cross a state that is famous for peaches.
3. This is the largest southern state east of the Mississippi River.
4. What state have you crossed? Answer: *Georgia*

1.4.4 Topic Sentences.

The Marine Corps, made up of men trained for war on land or sea, was authorized on November 10, 1775.

Clue: *Marine Corps.*
1. The Marine Corps had (or has) a birthday November 10th.
2. My brother was a soldier.
3. My father served in the Navy.
4. What is a Marine trained for?

September 17th has been designated as Constitution Day in the United States and should be observed by displaying the flag.

Clue: *Constitution Day.*
1. When is Constiution Day?
2. Do you have a flag?
3. When do you display your flag?

One of America's most famous sculptors created the famous figures on Mount Rushmore, South Dakota.

Clue: *Sculptor.*
1. Can you name an American sculptor?
2. Have you ever traveled in the midwest?
3. There is a famous sculpture in South Dakota.
4. The sculptor was Gutzon Borglum.

1.4.5 Skit.

Two Girls at a Dance

1st Girl:	You never know who will come to these dances.
2nd Girl:	Do you see anyone you know?
1st Girl:	That blonde girl in the corner looks familiar.
2nd Girl:	Wasn't she a redhead last week?
1st Girl:	I don't know. Look what's coming in the door.
2nd Girl:	Wow—tall, dark, and handsome.
1st Girl:	Remember, I saw him first.
2nd Girl:	All's fair in love and war.
1st Girl:	Now I know what that means. They're both the same.
2nd Girl:	Look, he's coming this way. What should I do?

1st Girl: Calm down.
2nd Girl: How can a girl keep calm at a time like this? I wonder which one of us he's going to ask to dance.
1st Girl: Isn't he dreamy?
2nd Girl: Shh! Here he comes. I've got goose bumps all over.
1st Girl: He walked right by us!!
2nd Girl: He's asking that blonde girl in the corner.
1st Girl: What's she got that we haven't?
2nd Girl: Him!

Contributed by Marion L. Sadowsky

1.5. Advanced Speechreading—Children

1.5.1 Q.R.E.—OBSCURE CONSONANTS.

cord   lord   sword
deck   less   ten

1.5.2 Q.I.E.—INTERMEDIATE LEVEL.

pot	pond	pod	bond	
feet	feed	feel	field	veal
run	rut	what	runt	won (one)

1.5.3 A TRUE STORY.

Easter Eggs Every Day

Introduction (full voice).

If you lived on a farm or ranch and raised a special kind of chicken, you could have Easter eggs every day. Can you imagine collecting eggs of different colors each morning? This could happen if you raised a special strain of chicken called Araucana (place the name on the board).

Part I   Clue Sentences.

1. Have you ever heard of the Araucana?
2. They are a special strain of chicken.
3. What are pastel colors? (Write pastel if necessary.)
4. Have you ever dyed Easter eggs?

5. Some chicken eggs do not have to be dyed to have color.
6. The colors are beautiful.

Story.

The hens that lay the beautiful eggs are called Araucanas. They are a special strain of chickens. They lay eggs of various pastel shades of color. The eggs are blue, light green, olive, pink, and grey. These eggs are not dyed as you dye Easter eggs. The colored eggs are laid naturally. There is nothing in the food given to the hens that determines the colors. Each hen lays eggs of only one color. In order to have several colors of eggs there must be several Araucana hens. The eggs are not only beautiful to see. They are good to eat too.
(Check student comprehension by letting volunteers give as much of the information as they can recall.)

Part II   Clue Sentences.

1. What is a name for one hundred years?
2. Clipper ships sailed the seas a long time ago.
3. Chile is a South American country.
4. Indians lived in Chile.
5. The Tinamou is a wild bird.
6. A new strain of bird is developed by cross-breeding.
7. What does abandoned mean?

Story.

What is the history of these birds? They have been known for about a century. In the days of the Clipper ships sailors visited southern Chile. When the sailors returned home they told stories of some strange wild birds. They said these strange birds laid eggs with colored shells! The sailors had seen the native Indians eating the eggs. The wild bird they had seen was the Tinamou. This bird is somewhat like a partridge. The early Spanish settlers went to South America and brought European chickens with them. When the Spanish left for home, they abandoned the chickens. The European chickens went back to the wild state. They bred with the Tinamou. After many generations of cross-

**Tinamou-The Wild Ancestor
of the Araucana**

FIGURE 4. Easter eggs—Tinamou.

breeding, an entirely new strain of chicken evolved. This chicken
is the Araucana. (Check comprehension as in Part I.)

Part III   Clue Sentences.

1. Have you ever seen a brown leghorn hen?
2. The Araucana are raised in the United States and Canada.
3. They are not easy to raise.

Story.

The Araucana looks like the brown leghorn. The hens are brown,
black, black and white, rust gold, or coppery green. These birds

are raised in several states, especially California, Minnesota, and Michigan. There are also breeding stock in Canada. The chickens retain many of their wild characteristics. They are difficult to raise. Araucanas are easily disturbed. They often die of nervous prostration. When they are frightened by loud noises they will fight and kill each other. The male bird has spurs on its feet. These become dangerous weapons in a fight. The Araucana may become more docile in time. They would be easier to raise if they were not so nervous. But the beautiful naturally colored eggs cannot be improved. Easter eggs happen every day where Araucana chickens live.

(Check comprehension on Part III.)

1.5.4 Cross Conversation—(Three in a Group).

Homework

A: 1. We have an awful lot of homework to do.
    2. Sometimes I can get my arithmetic done at lunch time.
    3. Do you ever go to the library to study?
    4. Next year we will have more to do.
    5. My mother always wants to help me.
    6. Is your brother in high school?

B: 1. I get some of my homework done in school.
    2. It takes me too long, and besides it is noisy in the lunch-room.
    3. Yes, I like to go there, but sometimes I spend too much time looking at the magazines.
    4. My father says we don't have half as much to do as he did.
    5. Mine doesn't explain the math the way our teacher does.
    6. I thought you just had a sister.

C: 1. Isn't it about time for lunch?
    2. It's not noisy if the librarian is on duty.
    3. I wish we didn't even have homework.
    4. We have plenty, I think.
    5. I like to have my brother help me.
    6. I have one of each, and they sure make me study.

1.6. Advanced Speechreading—Upper Grade Level or Adult Vocabulary

1.6.1 Q.R.E.—OBSCURE CONSONANTS.

guise	size	ties
hack	has	had

and/or

1.6.2 Q.I.E.—ADVANCED LEVEL.

shed	jell	jelled	Jan	shad	chat
chant	jet	shell	shelled	shine	chide
shield	child	shot	jot	John	shod

1.6.3 STORY—THE PORPOISE AND ITS BEHAVIOR.

Orientation.

The teacher uses full voice and gives basic descriptive information found in the beginning lesson.

Recent studies of the porpoise and its behavior have given new information about this interesting mammal. In this lesson on the porpoise you may learn something about the physical characteristics and mental ability of the mammal. Scientists are amazed at this intelligent giant of the animal world.

Clue Words.

scientists	brain	tests	detect
ability	apparatus	sonar	descent
trick	human		

Using reduced voice give the following "lead-in" sentences.

1. Scientists are observing the porpoise and its behavior.
2. The porpoise has the ability to think.
3. It can easily learn a trick.
4. The brain of the porpoise compares with yours.
5. Its voice apparatus is of great interest to scientists.
6. A porpoise can make human sounds.
7. Tests are being made on the hearing of the porpoise.
8. Do you know what sonar means?

9. It is a system of sending and receiving sounds.
10. A porpoise can detect objects by its sonar system.
11. It can make a very rapid descent.

Students volunteer the information after each sentence. The exact wording of the teacher is not required. The context is important.

Story. (Use reduced voice and give without interruption.)

Scientists in recent years have been very much interested in the behavior of this happy-go-lucky mammal. They know that a porpoise in captivity can solve problems. It is believed by some scientists that it may be superior to the chimpanzee in ability. In some cases a porpoise has learned a trick in one try. This same trick has taken a chimpanzee three hundred tries.

The Pacific Marineland maintains that it took a human two tries to learn the same trick. The porpoise has a brain structure comparable to yours. It has a complex voice apparatus. This animal is able to produce a series of twenty different sounds. It might conceivably learn human speech. The porpoise can hear very well. Tests have shown it has extremely acute hearing. (Note redundancy—this sentence is easier understood following the previous statement.) The sonar system of this animal is of great interest to science. By sending out sounds and receiving signals the porpoise can detect obstacles in a fraction of a second. A record has been made of the rapid descent and surfacing of the porpoise. A porpoise was observed surfacing from a depth of two hundred feet in less than two minutes. Scientists are deeply impressed with this mental giant of the animal world.

Class Participation. The participation by the class is in the form of questions and answers giving more information. Both questions and answers can be given by students, or the teacher can read questions and students give answers. Another variation is to have students give questions, and the teacher gives the answers. These are in written form on separate pieces of paper handed to students. Also vary with use of full or reduced voice.

Question 1 — How does the brain structure of the porpoise
(reduced   compare to the humans?
voice)

Answer 1 — The brain structure of the porpoise is 40 percent
(full   heavier with the same number of cells per cubic
voice)   centimeter.

Question 2 — How have some sounds made by the porpoise
            been described?

Answer 2 — The sounds have been described as squeals,
            whistles, the cheep of birds, the creaking of a
            rusty hinge, and impolite noises.

Question 3 — What has the porpoise been known to imitate?

Answer 3 — The porpoise has been known to imitate perfectly
            the laughter of the research scientists who were
            working with the animals.

Question 4 — Do the sounds made by the porpoise come from
            the throat?

Answer 4 — The sounds do not come from the throat. They
            come from the nasal sac.

Question 5 — How high in cycles per second can the porpoise
            hear?

Answer 5 — Tests have shown the porpoise can hear as high
            as 196,000 cycles per second. A human can hear
            up to 20,000 cycles per second.

Question 6 — How fast is the porpoise able to react to sounds?

Answer 6 — The porpoise is able to react to sounds less than
            a yard away under .001 second.

Question 7 — What is the meaning of sonar?

Answer 7 — Sonar is an apparatus that detects an object by
            means of high frequency vibrations. These vibra-
            tions are sent back by the object.

Question 8 — What have scientists observed about the ability of the porpoise to surface rapidly?

Answer 8 — Scientists have observed porpoises rising to the surface of the water from two hundred feet in less than two minutes—without the "bends."

1.6.4 HIDDEN NUMBERS—EXERCISE FOR QUICK RESPONSE.* Each sentence in the exercise has some number either given or implied. The teacher gives a sentence. The student replies by giving a complete sentence and uses a comparable but different number. For example: Teacher — Grandfather drove a span of horses. Student — Her grandfather drove two horses.
Her grandfather drove a pair of horses.

1. I found a dime on the sidewalk. (10¢)
2. How many lives is a cat supposed to have? (9)
3. The farmer sells alfalfa by the ton. (2000 lbs.)
4. The children in that family are triplets. (3)
5. The house is a mile from the bus. (5280 ft.)
6. We are going to see the Great Lakes next summer. (5)
7. The recipe for bread called for one pound of flour. (16 oz.)
8. I bought a yard of yellow ribbon. (36 in. or 3 ft.)
9. The young man became of age on his last birthday. (21)
10. Did you ever find a good luck clover? (4 leaf)
11. How many dwarfs were in the story of Snow White? (7)
12. We have had many presidents of the United States. (37)
13. We pay our taxes annually. (1)
14. Our car does not go far on a gallon of gas. (4 qts.)
15. Rome was not built in a day. (24 hrs.)
16. How many loaves of bread in a baker's dozen? (13)
17. February is the shortest month of the year. (28 days)
18. Can you reach an octave on the piano? (8 keys)
19. I always get hungry in the middle of the day. (12:00)
20. We served a gallon of ice cream at the party. (4 qts.)

* The exercise may be used as a contest. The class is divided into two sides. One student from each team competes in front of the class. The first to answer correctly scores for his team.

21. The child felt warm, but his temperature was normal. (98.6)
22. Can you change two bits? (.25)
23. Some plants live a century. (100 yrs.)
24. I like to hear a barbershop quartette sing old songs. (4)
25. A horse is measured by a hand's breadth. (4 in.)
26. How many degrees in a circle? (360)
27. When is life supposed to begin? (at 40)
28. The boat went aground in a fathom of water. (6 ft.)
29. She pays her club dues quarterly. (4)
30. The camel is a fleet footed quadruped! (4 legs)
31. The race was one furlong. (⅛ mi.)
32. The man's age was three score and ten. (70)

Contributed by Verla Peticolas—adapted.

2. QUICK RECOGNITION EXERCISES

2.1. *Visible Consonant Movements—Initial Position*

Define any unfamiliar word for vocabulary building.

Exercises			IPA		
1. pay	say	way	peɪ	seɪ	weɪ
thin	fin	pin	ɵɪn	fɪn	pɪn
sheet	seat	meet	ʃit	sit	mit
2. ripe	pipe	chime	raɪp	paɪp	tʃaɪm
saw	paw	thaw	sɔ	pɔ	ɵɔ
seat	wheat	feet	sit	hwit	fit
3. wild	child	mild	waɪld	tʃaɪld	maɪld
there	fair	wear	ðɛɚ	fɛɚ	wɛɚ
save	rave	shave	seɪv	reɪv	ʃeɪv
4. fill	chill	bill	fɪl	tʃɪl	bɪl
peak	weak	seek	pik	wik	sik
that	rat	bat	ðæt	ræt	bæt
5. read	feat	seen	rid	fit	sin
church	perch	verge*	tʃɝtʃ	pɝtʃ	vɝdʒ
thin	win	been	ɵɪn	wɪn	bɪn

* verge—v.i. to be on the edge of—or border.

	Exercises			IPA	
6. file	pile	while	faɪl	paɪl	hwaɪl
then	bent	cent	ðɛn	bɛnt	sɛnt
rocks	shocks	pox*	rɑks	ʃɑks	pɑks
7. bead	seed	weed	bid	sid	wid
that	fat	chat	ðæt	fæt	tʃæt
8. bell	sell	well	bɛl	sɛl	wɛl
pear	fair	rare	pɛɚ	fɛɚ	rɛɚ
jay	they	may	dʒeɪ	ðeɪ	meɪ
9. pack	sack	Jack	pæk	sæk	dʒæk
row	though	Joe	rou	ðou	dʒou
fill	chill	Bill	fɪl	tʃɪl	bɪl
10. food	root	mood	fud	rut	mud
peep	seep	weep	pip	sip	wip
thick	chick	pick	θɪk	tʃɪk	pɪk
11. pig	jig	wig	pɪg	dʒɪg	wɪg
ball	fall	Saul	bɔl	fɔl	Sɔl
Thor†	roar	more	θɔɚ	rɔɚ	mɔɚ
12. shot	pot	watt	ʃat	pat	wat
rye	my	thigh	raɪ	maɪ	θaɪ
veal	seal	meal	vil	sil	mil
13. rip	ship	bib	rɪp	ʃɪp	bɪb
said	shed	wed	sɛd	ʃɛd	wɛd
that	sad	vat	ðæt	sæd	væt

2.2. Visible Consonant Movements—Final Position

	Exercises			IPA	
1. sheep	sheath	chief	ʃip	ʃiθ	tʃif
lamb	latch	lass	læm	lætʃ	læs
2. cape	cave	cage	keɪp	keɪv	keɪdʒ
with	whiz	whip	wɪð	hwɪz	hwɪp
3. much	puff	mum	mʌtʃ	pʌf	mʌm
math	pass	match	mæθ	pæs	mætʃ

* pox—n. an illness—like chicken pox.
† Thor—n. a Norse god of thunder

	Exercises			IPA	
4. warm	wharf	roars	wɑɚm	hwɑɚf	rɑɚz
dash	lath	damp	dæʃ	læθ	dæmp
5. does	dove	dumb	dʌz	dʌv	dʌm
with	which	whip	wɪð	hwɪtʃ	hwɪp
6. birth	purrs	burp	bɝθ	pɝz	bɝp
mush	puff	pup	mʌʃ	pʌf	pʌp
7. peep	peach	piece	pip	pitʃ	pis
health	elf	help	hɛlθ	ɛlf	hɛlp
8. game	gave	gaze	geɪm	geɪv	geɪz
team	teeth	teach	tim	tiθ	titʃ
9. doors	torch	north	dɔɚz	tɔɚtʃ	nɔɚθ
move	boom	boos	muv	bum	buz
10. page	pave	pace	peɪdʒ	peɪv	peɪs
fourth	form	fours	fɔɚθ	fɔɚm	fɔɚz
11. rave	rage	race	reɪv	reɪdʒ	reɪs
bath	mash	map	bæθ	mæʃ	mæp
12. rough	rub	rush	rʌf	rʌb	rʌʃ
faith	face	fame	feɪθ	feɪs	feɪm
13. bus	puff	budge	bʌs	pʌf	bʌdʒ
tube	tooth	twos	tub	tuθ	tuz
14. sip	sieve	sis	sɪp	sɪv	sɪs
herb	earth	urge	ɝb	ɝθ	ɝdʒ
15. days	tame	Dave	deɪz	teɪm	deɪv
bath	badge	bass	bæθ	bædʒ	bæs
16. hoop	whose	hoof	hup	huz	huf
rash	wrath	ram	ræʃ	ræθ	ræm

2.3. Obscure Consonant Movements—Initial and Final Position

	Exercises			IPA	
1. gone	lawn	sawed	gɔn	lɔn	sɔd
lock	loss	lot	lak	las	lat

Exercises			IPA		
2. gall	salt	tall	gɔl	sɔlt	tɔl
like	line	lies	laɪk	laɪn	laɪz
3. kind	sign	dine	kaɪnd	saɪn	daɪn
knock	toss	tot	nak	tas	tat
4. cat	sad	dad	kæt	sæd	dæd
caulk	gauze	caught	kɔk	gɔz	kɔt
5. can't	sand	land	kænt	sænd	lænd
cog	cause	called	kɔg	kɔz	kɔld
6. got	sot	lot	gat	sat	lat
dike	ties	light	daɪk	taɪz	laɪt
7. keg	guess	get	kɛg	gɛs	gɛt
count	loud	sound	kaʊnt	laʊd	saʊnd
8. guise	size	ties	gaɪz	saɪz	taɪz
hack	has	had	hæk	hæz	hæd
9. cat	sat	tat	kæt	sæt	tæt
tyke	nice	nine	taɪk	naɪs	naɪn
10. cod	sod	dot	kad	sad	dat
yegg	yes	yet	jɛg	jɛs	jɛt
11. cord	lord	sword	kɔɚd	lɔɚd	sɔɚd
deck	less	ten	dɛk	lɛs	tɛn
12. car	czar	tar	kar	zar	tar
leg	lent	less	lɛg	lɛnt	lɛs
13. core	sore	door	kɔr	sɔr	dɔr
egg	ess	end	ɛg	ɛs	ɛnd
14. coil	toil	soil	kɔɪl	tɔɪl	sɔɪl
tack	lass	gnat	tæk	læs	næt
15. caw	law	saw	kɔ	lɔ	sɔ
deck	less	net	dɛk	lɛs	nɛt
16. kite	site	tight	kaɪt	saɪt	taɪt
lark	tars	tart	laɚk	taɚz	taɚt

2.4. *Visible Vowel Movements*

	Exercises			IPA		
1.	talk	take	took	tɔk	teɪk	tʊk
	wipe	whip	roam	wɑɪp	hwɪp	roʊm
2.	rim	wrap	rube	rɪm	ræp	rub
	man	meat	moan	mæn	mɪt	moʊn
3.	real	well	roll	ril	wɛl	rol
	ten	town	tune	tɛn	tɑun	tjun
4.	foot	fad	fin	fʊt	fæd	fɪn
	weep	rap	rope	wip	ræp	rop
5.	rice	ruse	raise	rɑɪs	ruz	reɪz
	let	load	lot	lɛt	loʊd	lɑt
6.	birth	bath	mouth	bɜ·θ	bæθ	mɑʊθ
	rod	wheat	went	rad	hwit	wɛnt
7.	kit	coat	cat	kɪt	kot	kæt
	fame	farm	foam	feɪm	fɑɚm	foʊm
8.	week	work	walk	wik	wɜ·k	wɔk
	right	route	win	rɑɪt	rut	wɪn
9.	mad	moon	mean	mæd	mun	min
	cute	caught	kite	kjut	kɔt	kɑɪt
10.	look	lake	lock	lʊk	leɪk	lɑk
	roil	while	rut	rɔɪl	hwɑɪl	rʌt
11.	tin	tan	tune	tɪn	tæn	tjun
	shout	shoot	chain	ʃɑʊt	ʃut	tʃeɪn
12.	boil	bad	boot	bɔɪl	bæd	but
	wood	want	weed	wʊd	want	wid
13.	rink	rag	work	rɪŋk	ræg	wɜ·k
	doll	deal	tool	dal	dil	tul
14.	soil	sad	suit	sɔɪl	sæd	sut
	time	team	term	tɑɪm	tim	tɜ·m
15.	pick	pack	poke	pɪk	pæk	pok
	boys	base	boos	bɔɪz	beɪs	buz
16.	deer	tear	door	dɪɚ	tɛɚ	dɔɚ
	six	sacks	soaks	sɪks	sæks	soʊks

3. QUICK IDENTIFICATION EXERCISES

3.1. Beginning Level*

1. sauce	saws			
2. fife	five			
3. chirp	germ			
4. rose	woes			
5. myth	pith			
6. mope	pope			
7. chose	shows			
8. fox	fogs			
9. purse	purrs			
10. beach	(beech)	peach		
11. mirth	birth	(berth)		
12. pies	buys	mice		
13. beam	beep	peep		
14. punch	bunch	munch		
15. rise	rice	wise		
16. rime	ripe	wipe		
17. wave	rave	waif		
18. robe	roam	rope		
19. sheep	cheap	(cheep)	jeep	
20. muss	bus	buzz	pus	
21. birch	perch	merge	purge	

3.2. Intermediate Exercises

1. foil	voile	void			
2. pot	pond	pod	bond		
3. word	wort	whirl	world		
4. shine	child	chide	shield		
5. pock	mock	bog	bock		
6. shirt	shirred	churn	churned		
7. sight	(site)	sign	signed	sighed	
8. shot	shod	jot	John		
9. feet	feed	feel	field	veal	
10. sheet	sheen	shield	cheat	gene	(Jean)

* Homophones having the same sound pattern but different spelling are in parentheses in these exercises.

11.	fat	fad	fan	vat	van	fanned	
12.	bound	mound	pound	pout	bout	bowed	mount
13.	run	rut	what	runt	won	(one)	
14.	fault	vault	fought	fall	faun	(fawn)	
15.	shad	chat	shall	chant	Jan		
16.	seat	seed	seen	(scene)	seal	zeal	sealed
	also:	seek	sea	(see)	zee		
17.	bird	burn	burl	pearl	(purl)	pert	
18.	fen	fed	fend	fell	vet	vent	vend
19.	June	jute	chewed	shoot	(chute)	chewed	
20.	fight	fine	find	(fined)	file	filed	
21.	wed	wen	when	well	wet	wend	went
	weld	red	wren	rend	rent		
22.	pone	boat	bode	bone	bowl	moat	moan
	mode	mole	pole	boned	bold	bolt	mold
	molt	poled	bowled	polled	mowed	mown	

3.3. Advanced Level

1.	fag	fang	fog				
2.	then	that	than	thine			
3.	ninth	tenth	death	lath			
4.	gaff	calf	calve	golf			
5.	sack	sang	sank	sock			
6.	shag	shack	shank	check	shock	jog	jag
7.	ledge	lash	latch	lodge	dash	dodge	notch
8.	set	send	sent	sell	sat	sand	sal
	sight	(site)	sign	signed	sod	sot	sol
9.	wreck	wag	whack	rack	(wrack)	rank	rang
10.	shed	jell	jelled	Jan	shad	chat	chant
	shed	jet	shell	shelled	shine	chide	shied
	child	shot	jot	John			
11.	Tom	top	lob	knob	time	type	dime
	lime	tam	dam	dab	lamb	tab	tap
12.	peg	peck	beg	beck	pack	pang	bag
	back	bang	pike	pock	bock	bog	
13.	fat	fad	fan	fanned	vat	van	fen
	fend	vend	fell	felled	fine	fight	find
	filed	file	vied	vine	vile	fond	

14. pet	pen	bet	bed	bell	belt	pelt
bend	bent	bat	ban	band	(banned)	met
men	mend	meld	melt	meant	mat	man
mad	pat	pan	pad	pal	pant	panned
manned	pine	pied	pile	pined	piled	pint
bine	bide	bile	bind	bite	mine	might
mile	mind	(mined)	pot	pod	pond	bond
15. debts	dense	tense	lens	dens	tens	nets
lends	lets	less	lass	lands	lads	tines
dines	nines	lines	dice	lice	dies	(dyes)
nice	loss	toss	tots	lots	dots	knots
dolls						

4. BEGINNING SPEECHREADING

4.1. Overlearned Speech—Familiar Sentences

4.1.1 INTRODUCTIONS.

1. I'm happy to meet you.
2. I'm sorry, I didn't catch your name.
3. I've heard so much about you.
4. Where did you say you lived?
5. Are you sure we haven't met before?
6. I hope we'll meet again.
7. My name is _____.
8. How do you do.
9. How are you?
10. How do you spell your name?
11. Did you come with someone?
12. It was so nice to meet you.
   Contributed by Kathleen Peters.

4.1.2 BELIEF AND DISBELIEF.

1. I don't believe it.
2. I tell you, it's the truth.
3. It just can't be so.
4. Like it or not, it's true.
5. You can't really mean it!

6. I swear it's the truth!
7. Where did you hear *that?*
8. If she says it, I believe it.
9. It simply can't be true!
10. I *know* it's the truth.
11. Oh, come now!
12. I never heard of such a thing!
13. It's really true.
14. You must be kidding.
15. It couldn't be true.
16. I'm telling the truth.
17. Don't hand me that.
18. Things like that just don't happen.
19. I believe it.
   Contributed by Elizabeth Raus.

4.1.3 SORROW OR SYMPATHY.

1. Sorry to hear that.
2. Tough luck!
3. I am just as sorry as I can be.
4. That's too bad!
5. Isn't that a shame.
6. That's the worst thing I've ever heard.
7. It shouldn't happen to a dog!
8. How sad!
9. I wish I could help.
10. Is there anything I can do?
11. How did *that* happen?
12. You've had more than your share.
13. It never rains but it pours!
14. It just doesn't seem fair.
15. Tell me all about it.
   Contributed by L. T. Wagman.

4.1.4 RAIN.

1. It looks like rain.
2. Take an umbrella.
3. It's pouring!

4. It must have rained all night.
5. We need rain.
6. I like to walk in the rain.
7. Be sure to wear your raincoat.
8. Did you hear the rain last night?
9. Don't get your feet wet.
10. The game was rained out.
11. I hope it doesn't rain.
12. Look at it rain!
13. Why does it have to rain today?
14. It's raining cats and dogs.
15. This rain is for the birds.
16. Get in out of the rain.

4.1.5 THE JOB.

1. I have a new job.
2. That man is a slave driver.
3. The hours are good, but the pay could be better.
4. It is back to the old grind on Monday.
5. Where do you work?
6. Do we get paid this Friday?
7. How much overtime will you get if you work Saturday?
8. He takes his work too seriously.
9. I think I am due for a raise.
10. He has been with the firm for twenty-five years.
11. He is always switching jobs.
12. I am looking for a position where I can travel.
13. Some day I'm going to quit this job.
14. How much do they pay for mileage?
15. How long have you worked for the company?
16. He holds down two jobs.
    Contributed by Artie L. Sims—adapted.

4.1.6 BASEBALL.

1. Take me out to the ball game.
2. I love baseball.
3. Three strikes and you're out.
4. He pitched a curve.

5. He's going to steal second.
6. Throw him out!
7. He missed it by a mile.
8. Boy, did he hit that one.
9. It went all the way.
10. He got a free base.
11. He's home free.
12. Batter up!
13. There's a long fly ball into center field.
14. Going, going, gone!
15. That's the end of the ball game.
16. We'll win next time.

Contributed by Conrath Leatherman.

4.2. Overlearned Speech—Familiar Phrases

This instruction is based on programmed learning principles.*
The following expressions stress words in the Thorndike list of
the most frequent five hundred words.†

1. It's about time.
2. after all
3. I'm against it.
4. a long time ago
5. good afternoon
6. all I know about it
7. all of them
8. if you like
9. It always happens.
10. Do you have any?
11. I didn't say anything.
12. around ten o'clock
13. He'll be back.
14. What became of them?
15. Where have you been?
16. I believe so.
17. the best way
18. He knows better.
19. between you and me
20. both of them
21. Bring it here.
22. funny business
23. Glad to meet you.
24. Guess who it was.
25. They came early.
26. Can you do it?
27. He has a new car.
28. I don't care.
29. Is there any chance?
30. Here's your chance.

* Appreciation is expressed to James R. McDearmon, Ph.D., Washington State University, Pullman, Washington, for permission to reproduce his materials and his method of utilizing them.
† Edward L. Thorndike and Irving Lorge, *The Teacher's Word Book of 30,000 Words*, Columbia University, New York, 1959.

31. Are they coming?
32. They're having company.
33. Did you know that?
34. That's different.
35. I'm glad of it.
36. I don't know about it.
37. Leave it open.
38. going down
39. a pretty dress
40. Don't drop it.
41. each one
42. Take either one.
43. That's the end
44. Do you have enough?
45. this evening
46. every single one
47. It has everything.
48. the whole family
49. How do you feel?
50. Fill it up.
51. Can you find it?
52. He's feeling fine.
53. The food was good.
54. a friend of mine
55. He gave it away.
56. Give it to me.
57. Have they gone yet?
58. It's a good thing.
59. about finished
60. That's hard to do.
61. I have to go.
62. We heard about it.
63. Can you hear me?
64. hello
65. Help me with this.
66. I'm over here.
67. Are you going home?
68. what an idea
69. if it's important
70. Are you interested?
71. How are you feeling?
72. How are you?
73. just a minute
74. I knew about it.
75. What do you know?
76. last night

4.3. Simple Stories

4.3.1 At the Beach.

1. We went to the beach yesterday.
2. We took our supper with us.
3. We took supper in a big basket.
4. We went swimming before supper.
5. The sun was warm.
6. The sand was warm.
7. The water was cool.
8. We splashed and swam.
9. It was cool when we came out.
10. We built a big fire.
11. We ate our supper by the fire.
12. It was a wonderful day.

13. We had fun at our picnic at the beach.
Contributed by Ann Pilkenton.

4.3.2 Dogs.

1. We have two dogs.
2. One is a small dog.
3. His name is Joe.
4. Joe likes to fight.
5. Our other dog is a big dog.
6. His name is Pete.
7. Pete does not like to fight.
8. When we got Pete he was just a puppy.
9. Joe was already a grown dog, but not very big.
10. Pete grew up and now he is much larger than Joe.
11. But he still thinks Joe is the boss.
12. When it is time to eat, Joe chases Pete away from his own food.
13. Pete is afraid to fight back.
14. All Joe has to do is give a little growl.
15. Then Pete runs like a scared rabbit.
16. He doesn't seem to know that Joe should be afraid of him.
17. I wish Pete would get brave some day and growl back at Joe.
Adapted from story contributed by Luella Oliver.

4.3.3 Cat.

Do you have a cat?   We have a big grey cat.
We got her when she was a kitten.   She has green eyes.
She loves to sleep on my bed. She curls up at the foot of my bed.
I brush her fur every night   She likes this.
Then she begins to purr.
She makes so much noise she keeps me awake.
I think she is very happy.

4.3.4 Guinea Pigs.

We have three fat guinea pigs.
They are very fat.
They are fat because they eat so much.
No wonder they are called "pigs."

Our three guinea pigs eat a whole box of lettuce every day.
Every time we come to the door they think it is time to eat.
They eat more than our dog.
The guinea pigs squeek at night because they think they are
hungry.
They squeak so much it bothers our dog.
She chases them around the yard.
I wonder how they stay so fat!
Contributed by Sherman R. Holdridge.

4.3.5 VACATION.

We are going to have a vacation.
It will be in July this year.
We think it would be fun to go to a ranch in Wyoming.
There are so many things to do.
The children can ride horseback every day.
My husband likes to fish.
He can fish and will not have to clean them.
They do that for him at the ranch.
I plan to rest, read, and enjoy someone elses cooking.
There is one problem for me.
It is too easy to put on weight.
Oh well, I'll lose weight in June and August!

4.3.6 SLEEPLESS.

Last night I couldn't sleep.
I tried everything.
I went to bed at ten o'clock.
At eleven I started counting sheep.
One, two, three, four, five.
That didn't work.
At twelve o'clock I tried to think of something pleasant.
A vacation in San Francisco would be fun.
That didn't work.
I thought about buying new furniture.
At one o'clock I recited poetry.
"Wynken, Blynken and Nod one night
Sailed off in a wooden shoe
Sailed on a river of crystal light
Into a Sea of dew."

That didn't work.
I looked at the clock.
It was three A.M.
I began to feel drowsy.
Suddenly I heard a loud "Mommy" coming from my son's room.
I looked at the clock.
It was six o'clock.
I couldn't get up.
    Contributed by Beverly Ellman.

4.4. *Colloquial Sentences Cued by Clue Words*

The following materials consist of a series of unrelated colloquial sentences. A word that is a clue to the meaning of the sentence is given in full voice, followed by the sentence given in reduced voice. Usually a "clue word" is all the help that the speechreader needs. If, however, it proves to be insufficient, the instructor will often make use of clue sentences, i.e. sentences that establish the less visible words through association of ideas. See Methods Chapter, pp. 230–233. In order to illustrate this technique clue sentences as well as clue words have been provided for the first series of sentences.

4.4.1 CLUE WORDS–COLLOQUIAL SENTENCES.

1. I didn't get up in time for breakfast, and now I'm starved.
   Clue Word: *Hungry*
   1. I'm so hungry
   2. I missed my breakfast.
   3. I overslept.
   4. I am very hungry.

2. The baby is crying because he wants to go outside.
   Clue Word: *Unhappy*
   1. The baby has been sick.
   2. He has to stay in the house.
   3. Babies often cry when they have to stay indoors.

3. We had breakfast this morning at the Pancake House.
   Clue Word: *Breakfast*
   1. What did you have for breakfast?
   2. I like pancakes and syrup.
   3. Do you ever eat breakfast at a restaurant?

4. My father and I went deep sea fishing last week.
   Clue Word: *Fishing*
   1. My father likes to fish.
   2. I like to fish in the ocean.
   3. Where did you go last week?
   Numbers 3 and 4 were contributed by Patricia Rabel.

5. We will need a new car before we leave for our vacation next month.
   Clue Word: *Car*
   1. Our car is old.
   2. We should buy a new car.
   3. We need a new car now.

6. The lawn is drying up in this hot weather and needs to be watered.
   Clue Word: *Lawn*
   1. The weather is hot.
   2. The grass is dry.
   3. I hope we will have rain.

7. I stayed up late last night reading a very good book.
   Clue Word: *Book*
   1. Do you like to read?
   2. I have a good book.
   3. A good book will keep you up late.

8. My arithmetic and memory are so bad my checking account never balances.
   Clue word: *Checkbook*
   1. Do you have a checkbook?
   2. Do you ever make a mistake?
   3. My math is poor.
   4. I forget to write down a check.
   5. Then I am in trouble!

9. Let's stop after class for a sandwich, a glass of milk and a piece of apple pie.
   Clue Word: *Food*
   1. I'm starved.
   2. Let's get a sandwich.

3. I'm thirsty.
4. Do you like to drink milk?
5. What is your favorite pie?

Sentences contributed by: Luella Oliver, Susie Titus, Patricia Rabel, Alta Taylor, Shirley Nelin, Conrath Leatherman, and Gloria Feld.

4.4.2 CLUE WORDS—COLLOQUIAL SENTENCES.

size	1. Our dog is a large boxer.
home	2. We live in an apartment house.
forgot	3. I left my homework in my desk.
appetite	4. It makes me hungry to ride my bicycle.
choice	5. I can't decide if I want a hamburger or a hot dog.
frightened	6. I was scared to death.
autumn	7. When do the football games begin?
exercise	8. How many push-ups can you do?
sport	9. My brother wants to be a baseball player.
money	10. Baseball mitts are expensive.
crowd	11. We had to stand up on the bus going home.
fib	12. Have you ever told a little white lie?

4.4.3 CLUE WORDS—COLLOQUIAL SENTENCES.

sleepy	1. I can hardly keep my eyes open.
age	2. Is your brother four or five years old?
sharp	3. Be careful of that knife!
beach	4. The children like to play in the sand at the seashore.
absent	5. He has been out of school for two weeks.
pain	6. I have a toothache.
noise	7. What was that?
telephone	8. Call me when you get home.
visit	9. My grandmother is coming to see us.
gift	10. What would you like for your birthday?
trouble	11. What's the matter?
hungry	12. I like a big breakfast every morning.
dinnertime	13. Wash your hands before you come to the table.
tight	14. My shoes are too small; I need a new pair.

4.4.4 CLUE WORDS—COLLOQUIAL SENTENCES.

help	1. Can you sweep the floor for mother?
play	2. John can jump rope.
can't	3. That's too hard for me.
easy	4. Mary knows the answer.
accident	5. The milk spilled all over the floor.
vacation	6. No school this summer!
work	7. Please erase the chalk board.
clean	8. Please pick up the trash on the floor.
change	9. Put away your math and get some art paper.
try	10. Say this sentence one more time.
share	11. Would you like some of my candy?
visitor	12. My grandmother is coming to see me tomorrow.
new	13. Mother bought me two dresses.
direction	14. How do I get to your house?

Contributed by Gayle H. Bishop.

4.4.5 CLUE WORDS—COLLOQUIAL SENTENCES.

bake	1. Can you make a pie?
mail	2. Send me a postcard when you go on your vacation.
congratulations	3. She will be seven years old tomorrow.
east	4. Have you ever watched the sun rise?
money	5. I think I should have more allowance.
timid	6. Are you afraid of a mouse?
stuffed	7. I ate too much for lunch.
frown	8. Why are you scowling?
building	9. They are putting up a new house across the street.
ouch!	10. I just hit my funny bone.
babies	11. Our mother cat had four kittens.
allergy	12. Some flowers make me sneeze.
windy	13. We flew our kites after school.
mouse	14. What do you think our cat brought home in her mouth?

Contributed by Marguerite Davis.

4.5. *Games and Quizzes*

4.5.1 WHAT AM I?

This is an exercise for visual memory and familiarity in recognizing numbers.

Procedure. Draw from dot to dot as it is dictated by the teacher. The teacher gives one, two, three, or more numbers at one time, depending on the ability of the pupils. Read across from left to right for each group:

I am found in the water.

1 – 21 – 9 – 26 – 8 – 13   3 – 11 – 27 – 24 – 29 – 7
30 – 4 – 17 – 25 – 12 – 22   2 – 20 – 15 – 10 – 19 – 5
6 – 18 – 28 – 14 – 23 – 16   31 – 32

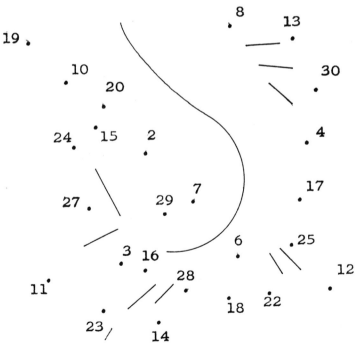

FIGURE 5. What am I?—Fish.

4.5.2 WHAT AM I?

I am found in a swamp.

1 − 56 − 20 − 30 − 42 − 50   59 − 31 − 17 − 33 − 24 − 47
8 − 3 − 38 − 48 − 22 − 51   32 − 12 − 41 − 25 − 11 − 45
29 − 10 − 52 − 37 − 49 − 15   57 − 58 − 16 − 28 − 6− 44
53 − 23 − 55 − 35 − 13 − 46   7 − 40 − 5 − 2 − 4 − 39
26 − 43 − 36 − 14 − 34 − 21   54 − 27 − 9 − 18 − 19 − 60

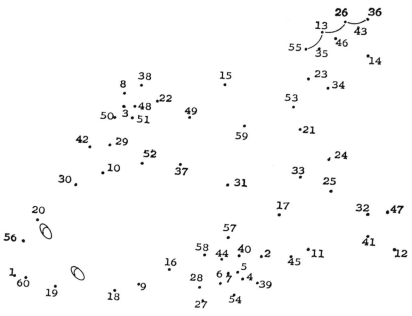

FIGURE 6. What am I?—Frog.

4.5.3 CLOCK GAME.

Make individual clocks from paper plates; use a staple to fasten the cardboard hands. Pupils indicate understanding by setting clocks.

1. The time is five o'clock.
2. The time is 6:30.
3. The time is four o'clock.
4. The time is 7:25.
5. The time is 3:45.
6. The time is 2:35.
7. The time is twelve o'clock.
8. The time is 1:30.
9. The time is 6:20.
10. The time is 11:55.
11. Twelve minutes past three o'clock
12. A half-hour past 4:00.
13. Twenty-five minutes before 1:00.
14. 11:35.
15. Seventeen minutes before 12:00.
16. Sixteen minutes after 7:00.
17. Twenty-three minutes after 3:00.
18. 6:26.
19. 9:32 (more voice).
20. 5:37.
21. midnight
22. high noon
23. breakfast time
24. bed time
25. this class is over
26. come to school
27. coffee break
28. lunch
29. time to get up
30. time for a nap

Contributed by Francine Hokin Katz.

4.5.4 QUIZ ON FAMILIAR SPEECH.

I. What do you say?

1. . . . When you answer the telephone?
2. . . . When you have been to a birthday party?
3. . . . When you wish to leave the table?
4. . . . When you are introduced to someone?
5. . . . When you have dialed the wrong telephone number?
6. . . . When you have interrupted a conversation?
7. . . . When you are invited to a ball game?
8. . . . When you ask someone to do a favor for you?

II. What would you use?

    1. . . . to cut paper?
    2. . . . to press clothes?
    3. . . . to move a rowboat?
    4. . . . to chop a tree?
    5. . . . to scrub the floor?
    6. . . . to find a telephone number?
    7. . . . to open a locked door?
    8. . . . to fly across the United States?

III. Where would you go?

    1. . . . if you wanted to buy a toy?
    2. . . . if you wanted a loaf of bread?
    3. . . . if you needed gasoline for the car?
    4. . . . to see people threshing corn?
    5. . . . to see the Yankees play ball?
    6. . . . to get an ice cream cone?
    7. . . . to see the Soap Box Derby?
    8. . . . if you had one hundred dollars?

IV. What goes with . . . . ?

    1. . . . a knife and fork?   (List answers if nec-
    2. . . . red and white?   essary to set responses
    3. . . . hop and skip?   mentally.)
    4. . . . ball and bat?
    5. . . . stop and look?
    6. . . . sun and moon?
    7. . . . ready and set?
    8. . . . healthy and wealthy?

V. What color is . . . . ?

    1. . . . the sky on a clear day?
    2. . . . fresh snow on the ground?
    3. . . . a ripe lemon?
    4. . . . cabbage growing in the field?
    5. . . . a palomino horse?
    6. . . . a polar bear?

7. . . . a ripe strawberry?
8. . . . our state flower?

4.5.5 THREE WORD SQUARES.

This is a game of vocabulary building. A three-block square is drawn on the board. The students are told to watch for the last word in the sentence dictated by the teacher. The instructor gives a sentence or asks a question in a reduced voice. A student volunteers to write the last word horizontally in the first line of the square, using one space for each letter. The word may be filled in vertically by the teacher or the student. The next word will then be easier to anticipate. A clue to the meaning of the word should be written beside the line just before the sentence is dictated.

I.

child   1. Another name for a small child is *tad.*
lifetime   2. What is your *age?*
moisture 3. This morning the ground was covered with *dew.*

```
T  A  D
A  G  E
D  E  W
```

II.

animal   1. Do you have a *dog?*
time   2. The school bell will ring this afternoon at *one.*
jewel   3. Another name for jewel is *gem.*

```
D  O  G
O  N  E
G  E  M
```

III.

weather 1. The weather has been hot and *dry.*
grain   2. My favorite kind of bread is *rye.*
O.K.   3. He always says O.K. when he means *yes.*

```
D  R  Y
R  Y  E
Y  E  S
```

IV.

sheep	1. The father of a lamb is called a *ram*.
time	2. That happened a long time *ago*.
passed	
scrub	3. My mother washed the floor with a *mop*.

R   A   M
A   G   O
M   O   P

Contributed by Drake M. Rogers.

4.6. Conversations and Skits for Two

4.6.1 TIME. Slips are read alternately.

Slip A:

1. Can you tell time?
2. Or course I can. It is fifteen minutes after two right now.
3. I set my watch by school time.
4. Do you come to school on the first bus?
5. I get to school in time to play for awhile.
6. Can you come to my house after school?
7. That's OK, we'll have an hour to play catch (ball, games, or . . .).

Slip B:

1. Yes, I can. Can you?
2. That's wrong. My watch says twenty minutes after two right now.
3. I set my watch by the radio this morning.
4. No, that bus is too early. I leave on the eight thirty bus.
5. I get to school just when the bell rings at five minutes to nine.
6. Sure, but my mother says I have to be home by four thirty.
7. Good, see you later.

4.6.2 WHAT TIME DO YOU GET UP?

Encourage the students to add their own comments after completing the script.

Slip A:

1. What time do you get up in the morning?
2. My mother has an alarm clock, but it makes too much noise.
3. I like to sleep late on Saturday.
4. Next Saturday we are going fishing, so we will have to get up at four o'clock.
5. Whenever I get up early I am sleepy all day.

Slip B:

1. Oh, whenever my mother calls me. Do you have an alarm clock?
2. Our alarm clock rings every morning at seven good and loud.
3. I don't because it is the only day I can play.
4. That's too early for me.
5. What time did you get up today? I just saw you yawn.

4.6.3 "Let's Go Swimming."

Procedure. Prepare two copies of the "Let's Go Swimming" conversation. The two students who will give the exercise should have some time to practice together before presenting it to the class. Each has his script only.

1. Boy! The weather is beautiful.
2. Let's go swimming!

1. Did you bring a bathing suit?
2. No, I didn't.

1. That's OK. I'll loan you one of mine.
2. Fine. We can save time that way.

1. I just ate lunch.
2. Then we'll have to wait an hour before we go in.

1. Good. It's dangerous to swim before your food is digested.
2. I know. I once got a cramp in my stomach.

1. I won't let that happen to me.
2. It sure frightened me.

1. What did you do?
2. I was lucky. I was swimming at the pool and I was in the shallow end.

1. Were you able to get up out of the pool?
2. Just barely made it.
1. I'll bet it hurt.
2. It really did. Now when I go swimming, I always wait an hour after eating.

Contributed by Kenneth Nibur.

5. INTERMEDIATE AND ADVANCED SPEECHREADING

5.1. Stories

First is the flannel board story for children or adults.

5.1.1 JIMMY'S DAY.

The story is told with a flannel board and cut-outs to illustrate the plot and action.

Visual Aids. These include cut-outs of the following:

1 sun—yellow	6 Indian head bands—
5 curlers—pink	feathers assorted colors
2 cowboy hats—brown	1 bear head—black
and black	1 chief headdress—
1 Confederate hat—grey	colored feathers
1 Union hat—blue	1 bow and arrow
1 nurse hat—white	1 father's hat

Procedure. Show the cut-outs. Write the words on the board as they are shown. As the story develops, the cut-outs are placed on the flannel board.

Presentation.

1. One sunny morning Jimmy woke up early. He jumped out of bed. He put on his cowboy hat and galloped into the kitchen.
2. Mother was still in her curlers. She gave him breakfast. He had orange juice, cereal, and milk.
3. Jimmy went outside. He met another cowboy. The two cowboys rode the range together.
4. The other cowboy decided to be a bank robber. So Jimmy had to fight him. He put the robber in jail.

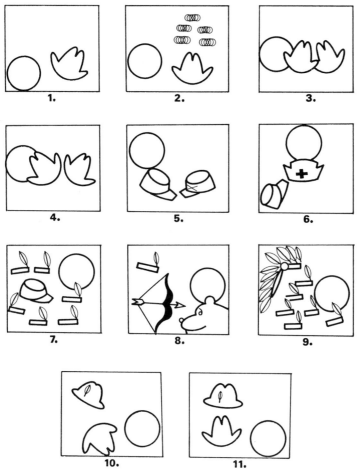

FIGURE 7. Jimmy's Day.

5. Then Jimmy rode out of town. He met a Confederate soldier. Quick as a wink he put on a Union cap. Then the battle was on.

6. Jimmy was shot and had to go to the hospital. A beautiful nurse made him well again. The sun was high in the sky.

7. Jimmy heard there was trouble out West. There were Indians on the warpath. He rode right into an ambush. The whole whooping, hollering tribe rushed at Jimmy. He fought them single-handed.

8. After he won the war he decided he'd rather be an Indian. A big, black bear was bothering the Indian tribe. Jimmy said, "I will save my tribe from the mean old bear." And so he did. He shot him right between the eyes with his bow and arrow.

9. All the Indians gathered around him. They shouted, "Be our chief, oh brave Indian." Jimmy said, "Ugh! Ugh! O.K."

10. The sun was going down. Jimmy saw his daddy coming home. He put on his cowboy hat and galloped down the sidewalk to meet him. "Hi, Daddy," he said. "Hi, Jimmy," said Daddy, "What have you been doing today?" "Nothing much," said Jimmy.

11. Daddy took Jimmy's hand. They walked into the house together.

Test comprehension of the story with a class participation exercise. Ask a volunteer to choose cut-outs and place them on the flannel board. The student tells in his own words one of the sequences of the story.

Contributed by Lois Douglass.

5.1.2 THE STORY PICTURE—VISUAL AID.

To the Teacher. A story picture structures, defines, and limits the situation. Used as a visual aid and story, such a picture can and usually does invite a free and easy exchange of comments and impressions.

Visual Aid. A picture of five young people in and around an old model car is used.

Procedure.

I. A careful inspection of the picture is indicated. (It is recommended that the teacher hold it and walk about the room.)

II. Hold it high enough and to one side. Point to a given object or activity. Remove the picture from view; then talk in a subdued voice. (Students cannot simultaneously look at the picture and the teacher.)

III. Encourage the exchange of comments.

FIGURE 8. Story picture. Old car photograph.

IV. Recapitulate without voice. Remember to include the added comments of your students.

Presentation.

These boys are very industrious. Do you suppose they will succeed in getting this automobile in good working condition? These boys look as if they know what they are doing. They are probably very good mechanics. Does it pay to fix an old car like this? It is worthwhile for them to fix it. Working on this automobile gives these boys good experience. This is one of the best ways to learn. There are far more parts on the floor than must belong inside this car. Would the parts for such an old car be easily available? Where would they find the parts for this car? What do you suppose the painting of the wolf's head stands for? What do you think is most important to these boys, the car or the girls?

Note. If the vocabulary from the students should include obscure words, such as "rear axle," then write this on the board. Repeat without voice the highlights of the conversation.

Variation. After talking about this picture put it out of sight. Ask questions about the details given in the presentation. This is a good check on the students' powers of observation. (Use a reduced voice.) How many people are there in this picture? What does the smaller girl have in her hand? What did you see on the window sill of the house? Which boy is not wearing shoes? What does the other girl have in her hand?

Contributed by Bernice Parker.
Picture from *The Saturday Evening Post.*

5.1.3 THE SEA HORSE.

Suggested visual aids. These include pictures of sea horses, the head of a horse, a kangaroo showing pouch, a monkey showing prehensil tail, pipefish, and a ruler.

Orientation—with full voice. One of the most interesting and delightful creatures in the ocean is the sea horse. In Florida two species live compatibly together. One is a giant in comparison to the other. The larger sea horse grows to be five or six inches long. The smaller one is called the pygmy sea horse, and it is about an inch long. Sea horses have dozens of children and are very unusual parents. This story is mostly about the smaller species.

Clue Words—Part I.

pipefish	giant	colors	coral	sand	camouflage
waters	pygmy	red	green	natural	protects

Exercise Sentences.

1. The sea horse is not a horse.

2. It is a fish.
3. Sea horses live in warm waters.
4. What is a giant?
5. What is a pygmy?
6. Sea horses live among coral.

Story—Part I.

The sea horse is a fish. It belongs to the pipefish family. Sea horses live in warm waters all over the world. The giant sea horse grows to be five or six inches long. The pygmy sea horse grows only an inch in length. They are different colors. You will find orange and red sea horses where there is orange and red coral. You will find green sea horses among the seaweed. Some of them are the color of sand. We call this a natural camouflage. It is the way nature protects these tiny fish.

Questions for Part I.

1. Does the sea horse belong to the horse family?
2. Where are sea horses found?
3. What is camouflage?

*Clue Words—Part II.**

scales   tail   animal   bony   plates   whinny

Clue Words—Part III.

deposits   ten   dozen   hundred   grow   acts

Exercise Sentences.

1. The mother sea horse gives the eggs to the father sea horse.
2. He carries the eggs in his pouch.
3. It takes about ten days for them to hatch.
4. The baby sea horses grow very fast.

Story—Part III.

The mother sea horse does not raise her babies! She deposits the eggs in the pouch of the father sea horse. The father sea horse carries the eggs for about ten days. Then the pouch opens

---

* The remainder of Part II will be found in the Methods Chapter.

and out comes the babies. A pygmy sea horse will send out as many as three dozen babies. The giant sea horse produces several hundred babies in a few hours. The babies never go back to the pouch. They grow very fast and are full grown sea horses in a few months. There are very few families in the animal world where father acts as mother!

Questions—Part III.

1. How does father sea horse help raise the babies?
2. Do sea horses have many babies?
3. Do animal fathers usually take full care of the babies?

Recapitulation.

The sea horse is a small (colorful) fish found in warm waters all over the world. It looks something like a horse and an insect and has a tail like no other fish. It sucks up tiny sea animals for food. It can make a very low sound. Father hatches the babies! This is unusual in the animal world. It is mother who plays. While father takes care of the young, she is off to greener seaweed!

5.1.4 THE GREAT SEAL OF THE UNITED STATES. This is adapted from Department of State Publication #6455. The story may be given with clue words and/or clue sentences depending on the ability of the group. Questions should be asked following the presentation of each part.

Orientation—(Introduce with full voice.)

Have you ever seen the great seal of the United States? You have if you have ever closely examined a one-dollar bill. Both sides of the seal appear on the "greenback" of a bill. It is possible you have not carefully examined one because most of us have such a brief acquaintance with a dollar bill! The seal may be familiar to most Americans, but many do not know the significance of the design. The story of the seal began July 4, 1776.

Part I—Clue Words.

Congress   design   leaders   years   symbolic   result

Clue Sentences.

1. The Congress of the United States is an important part of our government.
2. Congress appoints committees and passes resolutions.
3. The first Congress wanted an official seal to represent our new country.
4. Who were some of the leaders of our country in 1776? (Allow for answers.)
5. What is a symbol? (full voice if necessary): A symbol is something that suggests something else by association, i.e. a lion is symbolic of courage, a dove is a symbol of peace.

Story—How it Began.

The United States became a country on July 4, 1776. On that same day Congress appointed a committee of men. This committee was to prepare a design for a Great Seal. Three of the men were leaders for our independence. They were John Adams, Thomas Jefferson, and Benjamin Franklin. It took these men and others who worked with them six years to prepare the seal. Congress approved the design in 1782 and passed a resolution accepting it. The design was symbolic of the new country. The Great Seal expressed what the founding fathers firmly believed.

Part II. Ask the students to take out a one-dollar bill and examine the seal.

Clue Words

pyramid	Annuit Coeptis—L	numerals
eye	Novus Ordo Seclorum—L	

Clue Sentences.

1. Why do you think a pyramid was used on the seal?
2. There is a large eye over the pyramid.
3. What kind of numerals are those on the bottom of the pyramid?

Story—The Back of the Seal.

The pyramid on the left hand circle is symbolic of strength and duration. Nothing man-made has been stronger or more enduring than the pyramids of Egypt. Count the steps of the pyramid. (Wait.) There are thirteen. Thirteen is symbolized in many ways on the seal. Each use of thirteen represents the thirteen original states. Above the pyramid is an eye. This represents the eye of Providence. Our founding fathers were God-fearing men. They believed our progress must always be under His watchful eye. The Latin words "Annuit Coeptis" mean, "He has favored our undertakings." This was another expression of the faith of the founding fathers. The Latin words "Novus Ordo Seclorum" mean "a new order of the ages." They are symbolic of the beginning of a new life in the world. What do the Roman numerals stand for? (Write on the board.)

$$M = 1000 \qquad L = 50 \;)$$
$$D = 500 \qquad XX = 20 \;) \qquad \text{—a total of 1776}$$
$$CC = 200 \qquad VI = 6 \;)$$

This adds up to the year when the United States began as an independent nation. Look closely at the design. The dollar bill is one of the few places where you will see the reverse side of the seal. This side has never been used officially as a seal.

Part III—Clue Words.

eagle	bundle	shield	stars
turkey	talon	bar	E Pluribus Unum
olive branch	military readiness		

Clue Sentences.

1. The eagle is our national bird.
2. Why do you think an olive branch was put on the seal?
3. What is the bundle the eagle holds in its talon?
4. Can you give me another name for talon?
5. A shield is used for protection.
6. Have you ever seen the words *E Pluribus Unum* before? (on the back of all United States coins)

Story—The Front of the Seal.

In 1782 Congress chose the eagle to be our national bird. This was the same year the seal was adopted. Benjamin Franklin did not want the eagle to represent our country. He believed the turkey was the truly American bird. He said the eagle was a lousy bird (and he meant it literally). Can you imagine the awkward turkey on all our official documents (papers) and decorations? The eagle seems a much better symbol for strength and courage. The olive branch in the right claw of the eagle is a symbol of peace. How many leaves are on the olive branch? A bundle of arrows in the left talon are symbolic of military readiness. The shield has thirteen stripes to represent the States. Holding the stripes together is a bar which is a symbol for Congress. It represents the body of our government which holds together the states. Each of the thirteen stars stand for a state. A banner is in the eagle's beak. On the banner are the Latin words "E Pluribus Unum." What do they mean? (allow for answers.) One out of many. One out of many states. One nation out of many in the world. This completes the symbolism of the great seal of the United States.

5.1.5 OUR AMERICAN HERITAGE—GADGETS AND TOOLS.

Procedure. Orientation to the story is given with full voice. Pictures or drawings of the articles are given to each student. One drawing is discussed at a time; the teacher asks the students to guess each object. First, the name of the object is given with reduced voice. If no one can read the name, it should be given again with full voice. The name is then written on the board.

Orientation.

What are gadgets? (allow for suggestions). Gadgets are tools, implements or devices we use to make work easier or perhaps more interesting. You will be given drawings of ten gadgets to identify. All of them were in common use in American households between 1850 and 1900. Some are used today as conversation pieces. As you look at the drawings remember that they are not in true proportion.

Picture 1

Clue Words.

dessert   table   cracked   hollow

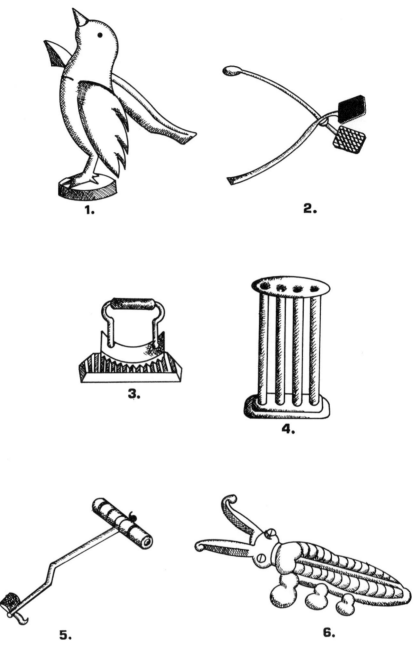

FIGURE 9. Tools and gadgets.

Exercise Sentences.

1. This is a picture of a nutcracker.
2. This was useful and ornamental.
3. Do you ever serve nuts for dessert?
4. This nutcracker was passed around the table for everyone to use.
5. Children loved to operate the gadget.
6. Can you figure out how it worked?

Story.

This is a nutcracker. It was a useful and ornamental gadget. It was placed on the table when nuts were served as dessert. How do you think the nut was cracked? The wing was raised. This made the head of the bird tip forward on a hinge. Then a nut was placed in the hollow of the wing. By pressing down on the wing, the bird cracked the nut for you!

Picture 2

Clue Words.

baked   fire   held   handles

Exercise Sentences.

1. Number two is a picture of a waffle iron.
2. How do you think the waffles were baked?
3. Sometimes they were baked over an open fire.
4. The waffle iron was held by the very long handles.

Story

This was a waffle iron. The waffles were baked over a fire in the fireplace. Sometimes the waffle iron was used out-of-doors. Then they were baked over a camp fire. The iron probably had to be turned from side to side as the waffle baked. The iron was held over the fire by the long handles. They were necessary to protect the hands.

Picture 3

Clue Words.

flutes   ruffles   parts   ridges   rocked

Exercise Sentences.

1. This is called a fluting iron.
2. What are flutes?
3. This iron was used to make pleats in ruffles.
4. It was a great improvement on the old-fashioned way of ironing one pleat after another.
5. The fluting iron had two parts—the iron and a separate base.
6. There were ridges on the iron and the base.

Story

Number three is called a *fluting iron*. The fluting iron gave a ruffle a professional touch. The flutes or pleats were ironed into a ruffle. It was done this way: The ruffled cloth was placed on the base. Then the hot iron was rocked back and forth over the material. This made even flutes in the cloth. It must have taken a long time to iron a dress with several ruffles!

Picture 4

Clue Words.

homes   fat   smell   scented   berries

Exercise Sentences.

1. Number seven is a mold for making candles.
2. In the early days of our country candles were made in the homes.
3. They were made from fat.
4. They did not always smell good!
5. Sometimes the candles were scented.
6. Children gathered nice smelling berries to add to the candles.

Story.

This is a picture of a candle mold. It was an item found in almost all homes in the early 1800's. The candles were made from animal fat. Sometimes a perfumed candle was made. For special occasions a bayberry candle was used. Bayberries were crushed and added to the tallow. This gave a delightful fragrance to a burning candle. The candle mold was a "modern" improvement over hand-dipped candle making.

Picture 5

Clue Words.

dentist   modern   instrument   hook   jerks   torture

Exercise Sentences.

1. Number five was a dentists' tool.
2. In the 1800's this was a modern tool.
3. Do you know how this instrument was used?
4. The hook went around the tooth to be pulled.
5. Then what do you think happened?
6. Aren't you glad you can go to the dentist today instead of more than one hundred years ago?

Story.

Number five was not a gadget. This was a tool. In the 1800's this tool was a modern instrument. It was used by dentists. It was a tooth extractor. (Point to parts described) The hook went around the tooth and was turned tight. How do you think the tooth was extracted? Do you suppose the dentist gave several firm jerks? Maybe he used a sawing motion to make the tooth loose! Today we would think of this tool as an instrument of torture.

Picture 6

Clue Words.

muddy   dirty   tight   iron   cricket

Exercise Sentences.

1. Number six is a bootjack.
2. Bootjacks have been used a long time.
3. They are still used today.
4. Bootjacks helped a person pull off muddy, dirty or tight boots.
5. They were made of wood or iron.
6. The one in this picture is made to look like a cricket.

Story.

Number six is a picture of a bootjack. Not too many years ago this gadget was a common article in American homes. The bootjack was placed near the fireplace or near the door of the house. They were made of wood or iron. Some bootjacks were made to look like crickets. It was an ornament too. It became a cricket on the hearth! This is how a boot was pulled off (point to drawing): The heel of one shoe was placed between the forked part of the jack. Then by stepping on the back of the bootjack with the other foot a person could easily pull off his boot. Today the old-fashioned bootjack cricket is manufactured for a door stop and a conversation piece.

5.2. Topic Sentences*

The Steamship Titanic was struck by an iceberg and sank on its maiden voyage in 1912.

Clue Word.

shipwreck

1. In 1912 there was a shipwreck.
2. A famous steamship sank.
3. It was on its first trip.
4. A first trip by a ship is called a maiden voyage. (Return to the original topic sentence)

In 1918 the United States government inaugurated its air mail service between Washington, D.C. and New York City, and within two years the service extended across the country.

Clue Word.

airmail

1. The United States began to fly mail in 1918.
2. The first airmail service began in the East.
3. How long does it take to fly mail from coast to coast?
4. By 1920 mail was flown across the country. (Return to the original sentence)

* See pp. 232–233 in Methods Chapter for procedure.

A very small part of the state of Washington is attached only to Canada, but since it is south of the 49th parallel it belongs to the United States.

Clue Words.

A United States border
 1. Washington is a northwestern state.
 2. Washington borders the United States and Canada.
 3. The northern border of the United States is the 49th parallel.
 4. A very small part of Washington is a peninsula.
 5. It is attached only to Canada. (Return to the original sentence)

Tiger sharks sometimes weigh two tons, but the biggest one ever caught on a fishing pole weighed 1,780 pounds.

Clue Words.

Tiger sharks
 1. Tiger sharks grow to be very large.
 2. They sometimes weigh as much as 4,000 pounds.
 3. How many tons are there in 4,000 pounds?
 4. Do you have a fish pole? (Return to the original sentence)

Los Angeles, California is the largest city in the world by area, but Tokyo, Japan, has the most people.

Clue Words.

Large cities
 1. There are many large cities in the world.
 2. Some of the large cities are Tokyo, London, New York, Chicago, and Los Angeles.
 3. Some are large and sprawling.
 4. Others are smaller in space but greater in population. (Return to the original sentence)

Yesterday, when I made my first pie, I followed the recipe carefully, but it was an awful failure because when I served it all of the filling ran out.

Clue Word.

Pie

  1. Yesterday I made a pie.
  2. It was the first one I ever made.
  3. I measured everything carefully.
  4. It was a failure.
  5. The filling ran out.

Companies spend much money for television commercials, which are sometimes so offensive they make us mad, but we do remember the product.

Clue Words.

Television commercials

  1. Do you watch television?
  2. There are many commercials on television.
  3. Some of them are obnoxious.
  4. Companies do this on purpose.
  5. Do you remember these commercials?

The Soap Box Derby began in 1930 in Dayton, Ohio and is a sports event for youngsters who race in their own homemade cars.

Clue Words.

Soap Box Derby

  1. There are many sports events.
  2. The Soap Box Derby is especially for children.
  3. This is a small car race.
  4. The cars are made by the children.
  5. Did you ever make a car when you were a child? (Back to the original sentence)

The famous cherry trees in Washington, D.C. were a gift to this country from the Japanese in 1909.

Clue Words.

cherry trees

  1. Spring is a beautiful time of the year.

2. Are the wild flowers in bloom?
3. The flowering trees are blooming now.
4. What is your favorite flowering tree?
5. Have you ever seen the cherry trees in bloom in Washington, D.C.?
6. Where did they come from? (Back to the topic sentence)

This week we celebrate Flag Day which commemorates the adoption of the Stars and Stripes by the Continental Congress, but was not made a national Flag Day until 1949.

Clue Words.

Flag Day

1. June is the month of roses.
2. June is the month of brides.
3. June is also the time for graduation.
4. We celebrate a holiday in June.
5. June 14th is Flag Day.
6. When did Flag Day become a national observance? (Back to topic sentence)

New Year's Day had its origin in Roman times when sacrifices were made to the two-faced god Janus who looked back on the past and forward to the future.

Clue Words.

New Year's Day

1. We celebrate New Year's Day on January first.
2. This is a very old celebration.
3. Who were the first people to observe New Year's Day?
4. The month of January was named for a Roman god.
5. The Roman god Janus was two-faced! (Back to topic sentence)

The Marathon race was given this name after the Battle of Marathon when a messenger ran twenty-two miles to Athens to announce the victory to the Greeks.

Clue Words.

Marathon Race

1. Have you ever seen an automobile race?
2. One of the most famous horse races is the Kentucky Derby.
3. Children like a three-legged race.
4. How did the Marathon race get its name?
5. The battle of Marathon prompted the Marathon race.

Ice-breakers are strong ships used for breaking paths or channels through the ice so that other ships can proceed.

Clue Words.

Ice-breakers

1. Ice-breakers are strong ships.
2. They are a special kind of ship.
3. They make paths through the ice.
4. The ice-breakers chop the ice so a channel is made.
5. Then other ships can pass through the opening.
6. These strong ships are used whenever it is necessary to free other ships.
7. When the ice is broken, regular ships can proceed in icy waters. (Back to topic sentence)

   Sentences contributed by Shirley Nelin, Nancy Algotson, Alta Taylor, and Eileen Kelleher.

5.3. Speechreading Instruction Based Upon Programmed Learning Principles, Phase Two*

1. Start with reading material with very simple vocabulary. Reader's Digest Reading Skill Builders, 3rd Grade Level, are excellent. Read it. Then re-write it as though you were saying it.
2. From your new script read a few words aloud slowly, with the student carefully observing your lip movements. Repeat if necessary.

* James R. McDearmon, Ph.D., Director Speech and Hearing Clinic, Washington State University, Pullman, Washington.

3. Reread with reduced voice, this time in smaller word groups containing one, two, or three words each. The student repeats aloud each word group after the teacher attempting to tell exactly what words were spoken in the group. The number of words in a group is always varied so that the student must watch closely to determine exactly what words are formed.

4. If the student misses a word group, immediately repeat it aloud slowly for him to watch, then again with reduced voice. This is most important to avoid frustration in the student.

5. The same procedure is continued with sentences or parts of sentences. A few words are read aloud then broken down into small word groups that are read with reduced voice which the student attempts to read and repeat precisely.

6. After a group of sentences (the number depending on the ability of the student) is taught in this way, all previously used sentences are reviewed in similar manner. Each presentation of a sentence utilizes different word groupings. With each review, word groupings tend to be made longer and presented more rapidly.

7. The flexibility of this method permits a maximal percentage of successful responses. The following suggestions will increase the likelihood of successful responses where any difficulty is experienced.

   (a) Increase the frequency of reviewing.

   (b) Reduce the number of words presented at one time aloud to the student.

   (c) Present only one word at a time aloud; then present the same words again two or more at a time.

   (d) Repeat the sentence or part of the sentence aloud several times before presenting it with reduced voice.

   (e) Present with silent lip movements one word at a time for the student to repeat, before presenting the same words in groups.

   (f) Make the lip movements as slow and distinct as necessary, but without distortion of natural movement.

8. As the student's memory for a passage and his skill in lip reading becomes stronger, the teacher gradually eliminates the "crutches" in the following ways:

   (a) He decreases the amount of reviewing.

   (b) He increases the number of words presented at one time to the students; later, he eliminates reading aloud old material; finally, he eliminates reading aloud new material.

   (c) He increases the average number of words in a group presented with reduced voice.

   (d) He increases his distance from the student.

   (e) He increases the speed of his lip movements.

   (f) He gives practice in reading the lips at increasingly difficult angles or with increasingly difficult distractions (such as the hand near, but not covering the mouth).

9. Should a passage become memorized, its use is discontinued until memory has faded sufficiently.

10. When the student first arrives at the level of skill where he can read new sentences not first read aloud to him, word groups must be extremely small and presented very slowly. However, speed is gradually developed at the new level of ability.

5.4. Games and Quizzes

5.4.1 THE ONLY STATE—A CONTEST. This contest can be used for beginning speechreaders by writing a clue on the board before the question is asked. Each question has two parts. Two contestants for each of the nine questions compete in front of the class. The two-part question enables each of the students to have a chance to win.

Clue Words for beginners if necessary.

oceans   1. a) What is the only state touched by two oceans?   Alaska
             b) Name the oceans.   Arctic and Pacific

border   2.   a) What is the only state bordered by one state?   Maine

b) What state borders it?   New Hampshire

invaded   3.   a) What is the only state to be settled or invaded by the Vikings?   Minnesota

b) About what year was it?   1,000 A.D.

languages   4.   a) What is the only state to have two official languages?   New Mexico

b) What are they?   Spanish and English

camels*   5.   a) What is the only state to have a monument to camels?   Arizona

b) Why were camels brought to Arizona?   a Civil War experiment

flag   6.   a) What is the only state whose flag was designed by a school boy?   Alaska

b) Who was he?   Bennie Benson thirteen years old.

sea   7.   a) What is the only state to have a land locked sea?   California

b) What is its name?   The Salton Sea

flag   8.   a) What is the only state whose flag was originally designed for a king?   Hawaii

b) Who was the king?   King Kamehameha I

---

* Camels were brought to Arizona to transport freight and supplies to California. The experiment was a failure and the camels were abandoned. The monument is near Quartzite, Arizona.

bordered   9. a) What is the only state bordered by eight
                          other states?   Tennessee
                      b) Can you name at least four (5 or 6) of
                          the bordering states?
                          Alabama   Kentucky   Virginia
                          Mississippi   Arkansas   Missouri
                          Georgia   North Carolina

5.4.2 MULTIPLE CONNOTATIONS. All words have a number
of connotations.

Procedure. The words are written on the board. The teacher
gives various meanings for one of the listed words. The student
writes the word so described. For review the teacher gives one
of the words and asks for a volunteer to recall three or four
meanings for the word.

game	bank	fast	check	
catch	bay	rest	crab	chop

  I. What word means these things?   (check)
     1. a written order for money
     2. a sudden stop
     3. a design in a piece of cloth
     4. a break or a chink in a piece of stone or wood
     5. a mark used to signify examination

 II. What word means these things?   (bay)
     1. a window
     2. a sound made by an animal
     3. a shrub
     4. an inlet of the sea
     5. a ship's hospital

III. What word describes these things?   (bank)
     1. the slope of a hill
     2. to cover a fire
     3. a storage place for money
     4. an elevation under the sea
     5. the incline of an airplane

IV. What word means these things? (catch)
   1. to capture
   2. to receive
   3. to understand
   4. a momentary stoppage
   5. please or charm

V. What word means these things? (chop)
   1. to cut up with a knife
   2. a sharp jab or blow in boxing
   3. a quick stroke in golf
   4. a way to buy meat
   5. to cut off someone speaking

VI. What word means these things? (fast)
   1. to go without food
   2. to be firmly attached (fixed)
   3. speed—rapid action
   4. to be dissipated
   5. a mooring rope

VII. What word means these things? (crab)
   1. a crustacean
   2. someone with a bad disposition
   3. a variety of apple
   4. a kind of grass
   5. the sidewise motion of an airplane

VIII. What word means these things? (game)
   1. a contest
   2. animals
   3. to be lame
   4. plucky, a good sport
   5. something of amusement

IX. What word means these things? (rest)
   1. a sleep
   2. a short pause
   3. a shelter
   4. the remainder—what is left
   5. a musical symbol for silence

5.4.3 FOUR AND FIVE WORD SQUARES. These are games for vocabulary building. See Three Word Square for procedure. Use the clue words only if needed.

I

beat   1. What word means to punish with a switch?
animal   2. What is another name for a rabbit?
flower   3. This flower is sometimes called a flag.
annoyance   4. What do you call someone who bothers you?

$$\begin{array}{cccc} W & H & I & P \\ H & A & R & E \\ I & R & I & S \\ P & E & S & T \end{array}$$

Contributed by Joan Carleton.

II

refined ore   1. What do you call a piece of silver or gold?
scratch out   2. What word means to rub out a mistake?
city   3. Can you name a Florida winter resort?
plant   4. What is the name of a tree that grows in the mountains and whose leaves quake?
tilts   5. What word describes the position of a famous tower in Pisa, Italy?

$$\begin{array}{ccccc} M & E & T & A & L \\ E & R & A & S & E \\ T & A & M & P & A \\ A & S & P & E & N \\ L & E & A & N & S \end{array}$$

Contributed by Mildred Erskine.

5.4.4 FIND THE TWIN—A GAME OF SYNONYMS. A dual purpose is served in this game: practice in speechreading and development of vocabulary through the recognition of synonyms.

Procedure. Write the long word on the board. This gives the student time to think of a possible synonym. With reduced voice give a sentence containing the word. Then with greatly reduced or no voice give a second sentence which contains the shorter word synonym. Have a student volunteer to give the synonym as soon as he recognizes it. Have him write the synonym on the board and give the context of the sentences which were dictated.

Example. Write the word "prosecute" on the board. The synonym "sue" is found in the letters of "prosecute." Give the sentence, "Do you think Perry Mason will *prosecute* my case?" Then give, "The driver who struck our car was going to *sue* us."

evacuate	We will evacuate the building if there is a fire.
vacate	Because of the fire we had to vacate the building.
encouraged	Both parties encouraged their members to vote.
urged	Everyone was urged to do his civic duty.
rapscallion	Tom Sawyer was a young rapscallion.
rascal	Another young rascal was Huckleberry Finn.
indolent	An enthusiastic reader is never indolent.
idle	If you like to read you will never be idle.
container	The container was made of glass.
can	I buy vegetables frozen or in a can.
splotches	What are the splotches on the child's face?
spots	The spots on the child's face may be chicken pox.
curtail	The government has been asked to curtail expenses.
cut	This will mean a cut in pay for some employees.
passage	The highway went through a passage in the mountains.
gap	The highway was constructed through a gap in the mountains.

slithered	The snake slithered through the grass.
slid	The reptile slid down the grassy slope of the river.
appropriate	Do you have an appropriate costume for the Halloween party?
proper	Be sure to wear the proper mask with your costume.
contemplate	I do not contemplate any action just now.
plan	I do not plan to do anything about it just now.
participate	Are you willing to participate in the work?
part	I shall be glad to do my part of the work.
capable	The senator is a capable leader.
able	He is an able politician.

Sentences suggested by Virginia Fraser.

5.4.5 Acres of Words. This is a vocabulary game that may be used as a contest, with two students competing for each word described by the teacher. One student from each team stands in front of the class. If neither contestant can give the answer, any member of either team may respond.

Procedure. The word *acre* is written on the board. The teacher explains that one letter is added to each *acre* to make the word described. The letters in *acre* are mixed to create each new word. The letter to be added is placed on the board beside the word *acre*. The new word is then defined, and the first student to respond with the correct word wins a point for his team.

Example. Teacher—Rearrange the letters in *acre* and add the letter *v*. The word means, "to wish very much for something" (qualify if necessary with another description). Answer: *crave*

1. Acre and h, is a word meaning to stretch out or extend.

reach

2. Acre and m, is the rich part of milk.   *cream*
3. Acre and s, is a word meaning to frighten or alarm. *scare*
4. Acre and b, means to support, give strength to something
   by supporting it.   *brace*
5. Acre and n, is the name of a long-legged bird, one found
   where there is water.   *crane*
6. Acre and g, is the name of a girl, or it means beautiful
   movement.   *Grace*
7. Acre and t, is a large box used for packing fruit, oranges
   and apples.   *crate*
8. Acre and k, describes a sound made by a rusty gate when
   it closes.   *creak*
9. Acre with l, is a word for transparent, or the way we speak
   of the sky without clouds.   *clear*
10. Acre and f, you have a short humorous drama, a funny
    show.   *farce*
11. Acre and r, is the name of a reptile, a kind of snake. *racer*
12. Acre and t, is a very small amount, just a vestige.   *trace*

Contributed by Cora Sydnor.

5.5. Cross Conversations and Skits

5.5.1 SALE DAY.

Scene. Two saleswomen are discussing the beginning of a new day—a sale day.

1. Are you ready? Here they come.
2. What a mob!

1. Have you ever noticed how fast they can tear through a counter of merchandise?
2. Yes,—like puppies digging for a bone.

1. The counters don't look strong enough to hold them.
2. I just hope my feet are strong enough to hold me all day.

1. There must be an easier way to earn a living.
2. Do you see that customer in the red polka-dot dress?

1. Yes. She comes in the store frequently, doesn't she?
2. Every sale day. She never buys a thing, and what a pest.

1. Don't look now, but here she comes.
2. Oh, no! Heaven save us!

1. Well, I think I'll take an early coffee break. See you later.
2. And I thought you were my friend. Oh, well,—May I help you?

Contributed by Roberta Evatt.

5.5.2 THE LIBRARY.*

1. "I'd like to return these."

2. "Why you just checked them out last night."
3. "Did you read them all?"

4. "Every one!"

5. "You're a fast reader."
6. "You must be able to skim well."
7. "Would you like to check out some more?"

8. "Yes, I would."
9. "Have you any books on travel?"

10. "What kind of travel—by air, boat, or train?"

11. "No, space travel."
12. "I like science fiction."

13. "Well we have a whole shelf of books on that subject— *right* over *there*."

14. "Fine, I'll look them over, pick out the best ones, and have them back tomorrow."

15. "Tomorrow's Wednesday and we're closed all day."

* From the Arthur Speechreading Film Test. Information concerning the films may be obtained from Robert H. Arthur, Ph.D., Director of Audiology, L.A. County-U.S.C. Medical Center, 1200 N. State Street, Box 25, Los Angeles, California 90033.

16. "Are you closed in the evening too?"

17. "Yes, we won't open again until Thursday."

18. "In that case I'll take a few more books."
19. "I won't have to hurry with these I borrow tonight."

5.5.3 THE RESTAURANT.*

1. "Good evening, may I help you?"

2. "Yes, I would like two hamburgers and an order of French fries."

3. "Do you want your hamburgers all the way?"

4. "All the way? What's that?"

5. "With lettuce, tomato, pickle, and onions."

6. "That'll be fine."

7. "Would you like something to drink?"
8. "We have milk, tea, and coffee."

9. "A cup of coffee please."

10. "Black or with cream?"

11. "Cream please."

12. "I'll get your order right away."
13. "Will there be anything else sir?"
14. "Would you like some dessert?"

15. "Nothing else thank you. I'm full."
16. "You make a mighty fine hamburger."
17. "How much do I owe you?"

18. "That will be a dollar ten."

19. "Thank you very much. Just keep the change."

20. "What change!"

* From the Arthur Speechreading Film Test.

5.5.4 A PARTY.

A:

1. Did you know our class has been invited to a party?
2. It's Saturday night for a barbeque and dancing at Joan's house.
3. What are you going to wear?
4. We'll have good food and plenty, too.
5. There's only one thing about the party I don't like.
6. Unless you-know-who takes me home, I have to call my father to come and get me.
7. After you get it, can you have the car?

B:

1. Oh, good, when and where?
2. Let's take our new records. I love to (name a popular dance).
3. Oh, the usual. I have a new blue sweater I think I'll wear.
4. I wonder how many hot dogs and soft drinks we can have.
5. Well, what is that?
6. I know. I can hardly wait until I get my driver's license.
7. By that time I hope I have my own.

C:

1. I hope it is going to be a beach party.
2. There's a new record out by . . . (name a recording group).
3. I have a new pants outfit I want to wear.
4. Maybe we should bring extra soft drinks. The boys sure can drink gallons of it.
5. The same old story—how do we get home?
6. I flunked the first driver's test, and now I'm scared to try again for that license.
7. I'm saving for mine—but it looks a long way off—not enough money.

5.5.5 TOPICS FOR SIMULTANEOUS CROSS CONVERSATIONS. Several conversations may be prepared, one for every two students.

Each pair of speechreaders has a different script. This is a simultaneous exercise with all talking at the same time against the confusion of surrounding voices.

Suggested topics are shopping, sports, travel, gardening, vacations, hobbies, movies, space travel, professions, weather, cooking, and the title, "If I had a million dollars."

Procedure.

The students should all be facing each other in a circle. Each pair of speechreaders talks across the circle using full voice. Make separate conversations so that one student may not know in advance the response of his partner. Limit the time of this exercise to a few minutes.

Variation.

A single topic can be assigned to all students. A more natural conversational situation is the result, but it is a more difficult procedure. The teacher should monitor the talking to avoid monopoly by any one speaker in a pair.

Chapter 7

SPEECHREADING TESTS

A number of tests of speechreading have been developed which are very helpful in evaluating the beginning skill of the various members of a speechreading group, and, of course, can also be used at the end of a training period to assess the progress that has occurred. They are organized into two sections: those designed for use with both children and adults and requiring a language recognition level comparable to a third grade reading level, and those designed specifically for children and incorporating a vocabulary commensurate with a third grade or lower reading level. Within these two broad categories the tests are presented roughly in order of difficulty of language construction and level of abstraction from the easiest to the more difficult.

1. TESTS DESIGNED FOR BOTH CHILDREN AND ADULTS

There are three tests which appear to fall within this category. They are those of Barley, Keaster, and Utley.

1.1. Barley Speechreading Test—CID, Everyday Sentences

1.1.1 DESCRIPTION AND COMPARATIVE DATA. A group of sentences has been developed at Central Institute for the Deaf to represent "everyday American speech."[*] They were prepared in accordance with the specifications laid down by a Working Group (Chairman, Dr. Grant Fairbanks) of the Armed Forces— National Research Council Committee on Hearing and Bio- Acoustics—CHABA. They consist of ten sets of ten sentences each or a total of one hundred sentences. Following are several specifications enumerated by the group.[*]

[*] Davis, H., and Silverman, S.R. (Eds.): *Hearing and Deafness, revised edition.* New York, Holt, Rinehart, and Winston, 1960, pp. 548–552.

1. The vocabulary is appropriate to adults.
2. The words appear with high frequency in one or more of the well-known word counts of the English language.
3. Proper names and proper nouns are not used.
4. Common nonslang idioms and contractions are used freely.
5. Phonetic loading and "tongue-twisting" are avoided.
6. Redundancy is high.
7. The level of abstraction is low.
8. Grammatical structure varies freely.
9. Sentence length varies . . .
10. Sentence forms are . . . declarative, rising interrogative, imperative and falling interrogative.

In examining the CID Everyday Sentences, it was noted that, because of their content (everyday colloquial speech) and their high face validity, they might serve admirably as a test of speechreading. Accordingly, one of the authors of this text, Mrs. Margaret Barley, constructed such a test by selecting sentences from each of the ten subgroups. Since the Utley Sentence Test had been selected as the criterion for validation, it was used as a pattern. Care was taken to include sentences of comparable length, and each form contains approximately the same number of words as the comparable forms of the Utley Test.

On two occasions data have been collected regarding performance of individuals on the Barley-CID Everyday Sentences Test. These data were then compared with similar data obtained on the same populations with the Utley Sentence Test.

In Fall 1966 a total of 132 individuals were given the Barley Test Form A, followed or preceded by the Utley Test Form B. Forty-nine of the subjects were college students, and the remainder, eighty-three, hard-of-hearing adults. The college students were evaluated statistically as one group; the hard-of-hearing were broken down into five subgroups corresponding to the speechreading classes in which they were enrolled. The tests were administered live, without voice, and were presented by one speaker. Normal facial expression was used. A rate appropriate to silent speechreading was employed—within the normal range, but somewhat slower than "average conversational rate."

Care was taken to insure comparable seating arrangement and lighting conditions for the two test presentations. No more than twenty subjects were tested at any one session. The data are summarized below. They indicate that the Barley Test, Form A, is a valid test of speechreading as judged by the criterion test, Utley Test, Form B. Results obtained with the two tests were very similar. There were no significant differences between means or variance for any of the six subgroups.

In the Fall of 1967 additional data were obtained. The experimental population consisted of five adult speechreading classes with a total enrollment of ninety-three. Subjects were given three tests—Barley-CID Sentences Test, Form A; Barley-CID Sentences

TABLE 7-I
COMPARISON
BARLEY-CID EVERYDAY SENTENCES TEST—FORM A
VS
UTLEY SENTENCE TEST—FORM B

Group	Test	N	Range	Median	Mean	S.D
College Students	Barley A	49	16–116	72	70	22.1
	Utley B	45	17–104	64	62	
Pasadena City Center*	Barley A	25	19–112	65	57	26.5
	Utley B	12	27–72	52	53	
Scripps Home	Barley A	19	17–111	54	61	25.6
	Utley B	14	15–98	58	58	
Alhambra Lutheran	Barley A	19	8–108	42	49	25.7
	Utley B	15	4–79	45	42	
Pasadena High School	Barley A	6	78–118	91	96	14.8
	Utley B	10	63–107	80	86	
Episcopal Home	Barley A	14	33–116	70	68	25.8
	Utley B	12	12–93	63	62	

* S.D. Barley Form A. for total hard-of-hearing groups (83) was 25.3.

TABLE 7-II
COMPARISON MEANS AND VARIANCE
BARLEY-CID EVERYDAY SENTENCES TEST-FORM A
VS
UTLEY SENTENCE TEST-FORM B

	Hypothesis Equal Means (t test) Accepted at:	Hypothesis Equal Variance (F test) Accepted at:
College Students	.05	.01
Pasadena City Center	.05	.01
Scripps Home	.05	.01
Alhambra Lutheran	.05	.01
Pasadena High School	.05	.01
Episcopal Home	.05	.01

Test, Form B; and the Utley Sentence Test, Form A. The order of giving the tests was randomized, and the experimental controls and conditions described above were employed.

The mean scores and standard deviations obtained with the Barley-CID everyday Sentences Test are presented below.

	Form A	Form B
N	92	86
Range	14–109	7–113
Mean	59.2	60.2
S.D.	25.4	27.1

Seventy one of the subjects took both Form A and Form B. The data yielded a high correlation of .87 which would indicate that the two forms test the same thing and are interchangeable.

High correlations were also found between both forms of the Barley CID Everyday Sentences Test and the Utley Sentence Test, Form A. They were the following: Barley A versus Utley A ($N = 80$), $r = .79$; Barley B versus Utley A ($N = 76$), $r = .83$.

1.1.2 PRESENTATION AND METHOD OF RESPONSE. Each sentence is presented only once. No voice is used. The examinee writes down what he thinks the speaker said.

1.1.3 SCORING. Form A contains a total of 125 words, and Form B, a total of 117 words. One point is given for each correct word.

1.1.4 INTERPRETATION OF SCORES. Evaluation of scores can best be made through a comparison with the data obtained on the experimental populations.

1.1.5 SCRIPTS.

Barley Speechreading Test—CID Everyday Sentences

Form A

Number of Words	CID List	Sentences
2	A.5	1. Good morning.
3	A.9	2. Here we go.
4	B.5	3. Where are you going?

3	C.2	4. Everything's all right.
6	C.7	5. Pass the bread and butter please.
6	C.10	6. There's a good ball game this afternoon.
4	D.1	7. It's time to go.
6	E.10	8. How do you spell your name?
9	E.5	9. I don't want to go to the movies tonight.
6	E.3	10. I'll catch up with you later.
4	E.4	11. I'll think it over.
3	E.8	12. Stop fooling around.
9	F.3	13. We live a few miles from the main road.
9	H.3	14. Let's get out of here before it's too late.
6	G.1	15. I'll see you right after lunch.
2	I .6	16. What's new?
5	J .6	17. Call me a little later.
8	I .9	18. I'll take sugar and cream in my coffee.
8	A.6	19. Open your window before you go to bed.
7	A.2	20. Here's a nice quiet place to rest.
5	G.10	21. The phone call's for you.
10	B.2	22. Why should I get up so early in the morning.
___		
125		

Barley Speechreading Test—CID Everyday Sentences

Form B

Number of Words	CID List	Sentences
2	C.4	1. That .right.
4	I .10	2. Wait just a minute.
8	D.6	3. Did you forget to shut off the water?
9	J .7	4. Do you have change for a five dollar bill?
8	J .9	5. I'd like some ice cream with my pie.
3	I .4	6. The show's over.
7	C.1	7. Everybody should brush his teeth after meals.
6	B.6	8. Come here when I call you.
7	B.10	9. Do you want an egg for breakfast?

2	B.4	10. It's raining.
9	A.4	11. It would be much easier if everyone would help.
2	D.10	12. I'm sorry.
3	C.2	13. Everything's all right.
2	E.9	14. Time's up.
7	F.6	15. Where have you been all this time?
3	F.9	16. Where is he?
5	G.7	17. It's no trouble at all.
2	G.8	18. Hurry up!
6	H.2	19. Let's get a cup of coffee.
4	H.7	20. How do you know?
7	H.6	21. She'll only be gone a few minutes.
11	I .8	22. How come I should always be the one to go first?

117

1.2. The Keaster Film Test of Lip Reading

1.2.1 DESCRIPTION AND COMPARATIVE DATA. This test was constructed by Jacqueline Keaster[*] when she was an assistant professor in the Department of Otolaryngology, State University of Iowa Medical School. Her original test consisted of six forms of ten sentences each, available in both black and white and color. Each form was presented by a different speaker (three males and three females). The film was later made available to the John Tracy Clinic for use in their experimental studies and was administered by them to 408 college students.[10] Analyses of these data proved the test to be reliable and showed that it provided a basis for quantitative discriminations among speech-readers. Since it was deemed desirable to have two forms, the sentences were graded with respect to difficulty, and the original film was cut apart and reassembled into Forms A and B, each consisting of thirty sentences. The equivalence of the two forms was verified through giving them to 173 additional college students. Coefficients of reliability for male subjects ($N = 52$)

[*] Miss Keaster is currently Director of the Hearing and Speech Clinic, Children's Hospital, Los Angeles, California.

were these: Form A, .90 and Form B, .92. For female subjects (N = 121) the coefficients of reliability were these: Form A, .89 and Form B, .89. Coefficients of this size indicate a high degree of reliability.

The revised forms of the test are referred to in the literature as simply "A Film Test of Lip Reading."[10,12] But since there are many filmed tests of speechreading, this designation can be ambiguous. To avoid confusion we have elected to follow the common practice of referring to a test by author name, e.g., Keaster Film Test of Lip Reading. To indicate the revision in form we shall refer to the forms as John Tracy Clinic Form A and John Tracy Clinic Form B.

1.2.2 PRESENTATION AND METHOD OF RESPONSE. Each sentence is presented only once. No voice is used. The examinee writes down what he thinks the speaker said.

1.2.3 SCORING. Each form contains a total of 188 words. One point is given for each correct word.

1.2.4 INTERPRETATION OF SCORES. Evaluation of scores can best be made through a comparison with the data obtained on the experimental population.[12]

TABLE 7-III
MEAN LIP READING SCORES[12]
COLLEGE STUDENTS—NORMAL HEARING

Subjects*	N	FORM A		FORM B	
		Mean	*S.D.*	*Mean*	*S.D.*
Male	52	84.71	33.20	94.87	34.19
Female	121	102.02	32.80	109.84	29.40

* Data were analyzed separately with respect to sex because females were found to be the better speechreaders.

1.2.5 SCRIPTS.

Keaster Film Test of Lip Reading
John Tracy Clinic Form A*

1. How are you?
2. Do you have a piece of paper?

* Appreciation is extended to Dr. Edgar L. Lowell, Administrator and Director of Research, John Tracy Clinic, for permission to reproduce these forms. The film can be obtained by writing to him at the John Tracy Clinic, 806 West Adams Boulevard, Los Angeles, California 90007.

3. What hours do you work?
4. Do you have a pencil?
5. Do you like to go to the movies?
6. How far is it to the post office?
7. How much time have you?
8. How far is it from here to Chicago?
9. Where do you work?
10. Did you enjoy the baseball game?
11. The train leaves at five o'clock.
12. Do you have an umbrella?
13. What is your favorite television program?
14. This is a cold day.
15. Have you any children?
16. How much snow did we have last night?
17. Did you finish high school?
18. Do you have chains on your car?
19. Have you ever lived in the west?
20. I'm going south for my vacation.
21. How many miles did you drive your Ford?
22. Did you get my letter?
23. What does the paper say about the weather?
24. I think it is going to snow.
25. The bank closes at two-thirty.
26. The snow is five inches deep.
27. Isn't this a beautiful day?
28. It was a perfect day for a football game.
29. You had a long distance call while you were gone.
30. It rained most of the night.

Keaster Film Test of Lip Reading
John Tracy Clinic Form B

1. What time is it?
2. Do you have a dog?
3. What time did you have breakfast this morning?
4. Do you have a new car?
5. What kind of a dog do you have?
6. Have you read the newspaper this morning?

7. Where is your home?
8. How are your family?
9. Are you going home for vacation?
10. Do you like to shop?
11. Do you think it will rain this afternoon?
12. Would you like to go to the show with us?
13. What is your occupation?
14. Do you like to watch television?
15. What are your hobbies?
16. What kind of a car do you drive?
17. What day of the week is this?
18. Do you drink your coffee black?
19. My watch is slow.
20. Have you any brothers or sisters?
21. The wind is blowing from the northeast.
22. My watch doesn't keep good time.
23. What shall we do tonight?
24. Did you drive or come by train?
25. Can you have lunch with me on Friday?
26. I have an appointment at three o'clock.
27. Are your parents living?
28. I'll meet you at three o'clock.
29. You could drop me a postcard to let me know.
30. Do they allow children in that building?

1.3. Utley Film Test—"How Well Can You Read Lips?"*

1.3.1 DESCRIPTION AND COMPARATIVE DATA. This is probably the best known and most widely used test of speechreading ability. It consists of three parts. Part I is a Sentence Test and consists of two forms, A and B. Part II is a Word Test and also has two forms, A and B. Part III is a Story Test and consists of six short stories or scenes. They are based on interests and experiences that were believed to be common to children of intermediate school age. Each story is followed by five questions which are based on the conversations in the story. The film can

---

* Dr. Jean Utley Lehman is currently a professor at California State College at Los Angeles, where she directs education of the deaf program. Appreciation is extended to her for permission to reproduce her test materials.

be rented or purchased from the DeVry Corporation, 1111 Armitage Avenue, Chicago 14, Illinois.

The test was given to 761 deaf and hard-of-hearing individuals, age range from eight to twenty-one years, enrolled in one large state residential school, four public elementary day schools, two public high schools, two conservation of hearing classes, and one Society for the Hard-of-Hearing. It has not been found possible to standardize a test of speechreading in the sense of establishing norms with respect to age or some other common variable. (See Chapter 4.) In lieu of this, the data were organized into tables showing raw scores and percentile ranks. From the tables, which accompany the film, it is possible to judge the relative proficiency indicated by a given score.

The tests require an aural recognition vocabulary comparable to that of approximately the third grade reading level. The sentences consist of common colloquial and idiomatic expressions. The words were taken from Thorndike's list of the one thousand most frequently used words. Each tenth word was extracted from the list. Familiarity was the only criterion used in establishing the list. The coefficient of correlation between Forms A and B of the Sentence Test is .866; between the two forms of the Word Test, .663. The index of reliability, or coefficient of validity for the whole test is .971.

1.3.2 Evaluation of Sentence Test—Experimental Study. The Utley Test has been criticized in the literature as being excessively difficult.[6,8] There is reason to believe, however, that the difficulty, at least with respect to the sentence tests, is in the filmed version and not in the content. Scores made by college students when the test presentation was "live" have been found to be uniformly better than one would anticipate from the experimental data. It was noted that in the filmed version the speaker used very little jaw movement and maintained the same smiling countenance regardless of the content of the message. Moreover, not enough time elapsed between the presentation of the cue card indicating the number of the sentence and speaking of the sentence itself. Unless the viewer were alert, his eye focus might not have shifted rapidly enough from the cue card to the talker's lips.

To test the hypothesis that the method of presentation rather than the test content, per se, was responsible for the reported difficulty, Jeffers and Barley[9] gave Sentence Test Form A "live," followed by Sentence Test Form B filmed to a group of college students and to four groups of hard-of-hearing adults. Two talkers were used, one for the college students and one for the hard-of-hearing adults. Both talkers were experienced teachers of speech-reading and spoke in such a manner as to provide optimal viewing conditions. (See Chapter 2, "Ideal Viewing Conditions.") Care was taken to insure adequate jaw as well as lip movement and to provide facial expression appropriate to the content. The data are presented below in Table 7-IV. From an examination of them

TABLE 7-IV
COMPARATIVE DATA—LIVE VS FILMED VERSION
UTLEY SENTENCE TEST OF LIPREADING ABILITY
FORMS A AND B

College Students—Speaker I	
Utley Form A—Live	N = 31; Mean, *80.82*; S.D. 18.264; Range 36–115
Utley Form B—Filmed	N = 31; Mean, *39.13*; S.D. 19.368; Range 19–61
Hard-of-Hearing—Speaker II	
Utley Form A—Live	N = 88; Mean *72.41*; S.D. 19.32; Range 38–109
Utley Form B—Live	N = 96; Mean *68.79*; S.D. 21.17; Range 23–113.
Utley Form B—Filmed	N = 83; Mean *21.8*; S.D. 14.76; Range 3–79

it can be readily observed that the live presentation constituted a much easier task for the subjects than the filmed presentation—this, despite the fact that the "live" version was given first to all groups and, hence, should have served as practice for the filmed version. Note, also, that Form B was given "live" to the hard-of-hearing groups just two weeks prior to their being tested on the same filmed form; yet their scores were dramatically better on the "live" presentation. The college students did twice as well on the "live" version as on the filmed version, and the hard-of-hearing groups, three times as well.

The college group was found to be comparable to Utley's

experimental population on the filmed version. For her population (N, 761) the mean score was 34 with a range of from 0 to 89 and a standard deviation of 17.5. The hard-of-hearing population's mean score, on the other hand, was less than that of the original experimental population. In other words, the college students were better speechreaders than the hard-of-hearing adults used in this study and comparable in skill to Utley's subjects. A possible explanation is the difference in age and presumably in eyesight and perhaps in cognitive factors as well for the two groups. The college students were for the most part in their early twenties while the bulk of the hard-of-hearing population was over sixty years of age (age range: 50–89 years; mean age: 75.2 years).

It was concluded that the purported difficulty of the Utley Sentence Tests is due not to test content but to difficulties inherent in the filmed version. It is suggested that it is a useful test for the diagnosis of lipreading ability providing it is given "live" and presented in such a way as to provide optimal viewing conditions. Substantiation for this view is obtained from the relative high correlation (Spearman Rank Order Correlation Coefficient of .64) between scores on the "live" and filmed versions. Sixty-eight of the hard-of-hearing subjects took both versions of the test. A correlation as high as this indicates that the live version is testing the same skill as the filmed version.

The Utley Sentence Test can be considered by itself to constitute a test of speechreading and is perhaps as good a test of speechreading skill as the test as a whole. Respectable correlations were found by Utley between it and the Word Test and Story Test portions (.778 and .749, respectively), and between it and the complete test (.984).

1.3.3 PRESENTATION AND METHOD OF RESPONSE—SENTENCE TEST "LIVE". Each sentence is said only once. The testee responds by writing down what he thinks he has seen. Five practice sentences are given before the test. No voice is used. The speaker is to use a fairly slow though normal rate of speech, normal rhythm and stress and ample, but not exaggerated, lip and jaw movement. Facial expression appropriate to the content is employed.

1.3.4 SCORING AND INTERPRETATION OF SCORES—SENTENCE TEST. There are two ways of scoring the Sentence Test. The first one, used by Utley, is to allow one point for each correct word. Homophenity of words is not considered. A convenient way to record the scores is to place the number of words correct at the left of each sentence. The highest possible score would be 125 for either Form A or Form B.

Test scores can best be interpreted in terms of comparative data. If the test is given in its filmed version, the following data obtained by Utley on 761 hearing handicapped subjects, age range eight to twenty-one years, apply.

Filmed Version

	Form A	Form B
Range	0–84	0–89
Mean	33.629	33.804
S.D.	16.355	17.535

If, however, the sentence tests are given "live," the data can perhaps be best interpreted with reference to the scores made by the college students, referred to earlier. The data from the college students are selected for this purpose in preference to that from the hard-of-hearing adults because their scores on Form B, Filmed, are closer to Utley's data (Mean 39.13; S.D., 19.358; Range, 19–61). While no data were obtained for Form B, Live, on the college students, the data for Form A can be used in interpreting scores made on either test because of the high coefficient of correlation between the two forms of .866.

Live Version

	Range	Mean	Standard Deviation
Form A	36–115	80.82	18.264

Score—Number Words Correct	Interpretation
110 and above	Excellent
100–109	Good
65–99	Average
Below 65	Poor

The second way of scoring the test was developed by the Audiology Clinic of Northwestern University. In this method the number of sentences correct is recorded. A sentence is scored correct if the content is perceived with reasonable accuracy. Word for word speechreading is not required. The value judgments given below are based on our data from our college students who scored, as noted before, on the filmed version very close to the scores made by Utley's experimental population. They are somewhat more rigorous than those employed at Northwestern.

SCORE		INTERPRETATION
Number Sentences Correct	Percent Correct	
28–31	90–100%	Excellent
24–27	78–87%	Good
15–23	52–74%	Average
Below 15	Below 49%	Poor

1.3.5 SCRIPTS.

Practice Sentences

1. Good morning.
2. Thank you.
3. Hello.
4. How are you?
5. Goodbye.

Utley Sentence Test, Form A

1. All right.
2. Where have you been?
3. I have forgotten.
4. I have nothing.
5. That is right.
6. Look out.
7. How have you been?
8. I don't know if I can.
9. How tall are you?
10. It is awfully cold.

11. My folks are home.
12. How much was it?
13. Good night.
14. Where are you going?
15. Excuse me.
16. Did you have a good time?
17. What did you want?
18. How much do you weigh?
19. I cannot stand him.
20. She was home last week.
21. Keep your eye on the ball.
22. I cannot remember.
23. Of course.
24. I flew to Washington.
25. You look well.
26. The train runs every hour.
27. You had better go slow.
28. It says that in the book.
29. We got home at six o'clock.
30. We drove to the country.
31. How much rain fell?

Utley Sentence Test, Form B

1. What happened?
2. It is all over.
3. How old are you?
4. What did you say?
5. O.K.
6. No.
7. That is pretty.
8. Pardon me.
9. Did you like it?
10. Good afternoon.
11. I cannot help it.
12. I will see you tomorrow.
13. You are welcome.
14. You are all dressed up.

15. What is your number?
16. I know.
17. It is cold today.
18. I am hungry.
19. I had rather go now.
20. What is your address.
21. What does the paper say about the weather?
22. It is around four o'clock.
23. Do you understand?
24. They went way around the world.
25. The office opens at nine o'clock.
26. None of them are here.
27. Take two cups of coffee.
28. Come again.
29. The thermometer says twenty above.
30. It is your turn.
31. It is hard to keep up with the new books.

2. TESTS DESIGNED FOR CHILDREN

The tests presented in this section are by Butt, Craig, Costello, and Cavender.

2.1. Butt, Children's Speechreading Test*

2.1.1 DESCRIPTION AND COMPARATIVE DATA. This test is intended for young children who have not yet learned to read. The child indicates comprehension through motor action. It consists of two portions, Test A, an informal checklist for children under three years, and Test B, for children three years of age and over. The beginning items can be understood by a one-year-old child; a mental age of three years is considered to be adequate for successful performance of all test items. Test items were evaluated with respect to developmental age. (See Table 7-V, below.)

---

* Dolores S. Butt, Ph.D. is assistant professor of speech at the University of New Mexico, Albuquerque, New Mexico.

TABLE 7-V

COMPARISON OF TEST QUESTIONS OF THE CHILDREN'S SPEECHREAD-
ING TEST WITH LANGUAGE ITEMS OF CERTAIN INTELLIGENCE
TESTS AND LANGUAGE DEVELOPMENT STUDIES

Language Skill	Age in Months	Authorities
A: Speechreading checklist items for children under three		
1. Attends readily to speaking voice	1.3	Bayley
	2.0	Cattell
2. Understands gestures	9.0	Buhler
3. Responds to "bye-bye"	10.0	Gesell, Thompson, and Amatruda
4. Adjusts to command	10.0	Gesell, Thompson, and Amatruda
5. Responds to inhibitory words	12.0	Gesell and Thompson
6. Comprehends simple verbal commissions	12.0	Gesell and Thompson
7. Says "hello," "thank you," or equivalent	18.0	Gesell and Thompson
8. Comprehends simple questions	18.0	Gesell
9. Understands a command with gesture: "Sit down."	21–23	Buhler
"Throw me the ball."	21.0	Stutsman
"Give me that."		Buhler
B: Test questions of the children's speechreading test		
10. Object identification:		
Names one object	17.4	Bayley
Names three objects	21–24	Gesell
Identifies object by name, 4 out of 6:	24.0	Terman and Merrill
kitty, button, cup, thimble, train, spoon.		
Names 4 out of 5 objects:	21.6	
chair, auto, box, key, and fork.		
11. Picture identification:		
Names pictures in a book	18.7	Bayley
Example: baby	22.5	Shirley
dog	19.0	Shirley
dog on picture card	15.0	Gesell
picture vocabulary, 15 out of 18 cards	42.0	Terman and Merrill
12. Refers to self by name	24.0	Ilg and Ames
13. Body parts:		
Points to 3 of these:	24.0	Terman and Merrill
hair, eyes, mouth, hand		
Points to all of above	30.0	
Points to 2 of these:		
nose, eyes, mouth, hand	20.0	Cattell
Points to all of above	22.0	
14. Follows simple directions		
Example: "Give me the kitty."		
"Put the spoon in the cup."	24–42	Terman and Merrill
15. Number concepts:		
Concept of one	30	Cattell
Counts three objects	48	Ilg and Ames
16. Color naming:		
Can be taught basic colors	48–60	John Tracy Clinic Course
Knows red, green, yellow, and blue	60.0	Ilg and Ames
17. "Action-agent" test		
Example: "Who sleeps?"	30–35	Stutsman
18. Comparison of objects	42.0	Terman and Merrill

* Taken in part from McCarthy (1946).

All seventy items were found to discriminate satisfactorily between subjects who perform well and subjects who perform poorly on the test as a whole. The reliability of the test was evaluated by means of the Kuder-Richardson Formula. The coefficient of reliability was found to be .95, significant at the .001 level.

A total of 130 subjects (age range, 2–9 years; median, 6 years), selected at random from nursery schools and primary departments of ten schools for the deaf were given the test. Degree of hearing loss was found to be related to speechreading ability in a sub-group of twenty children, all of whom had severe hearing losses (at least 50% bilaterally acquired before the acquisition of speech), but no other handicaps. As a group, totally deaf children had a lower speechreading score than hard-of-hearing children.

2.1.2 PRESENTATION AND METHOD OF RESPONSE.

Test Form A. Responses are elicited in playing with and observing the child.

Test Form B. Sit about four feet from the child in a well-lighted room. Attract the child's attention to your face before presenting each item. Speak to the child naturally but in an inaudible voice. Present the spoken material from the front view the first time; then repeat once or twice with your face slightly turned so the child sees a three-quarter view. If the child tires, allow him to rest. Child responds with the appropriate motor action.

TABLE 7-VI

MEANS AND STANDARD DEVIATIONS FOR HEARING HANDICAPPED CHILDREN, AGE 3–9 ON THE CHILDREN'S SPEECHREADING TEST

Age in Years	N	Mean	Standard Deviation
3	9	28	24
4	19	26	19
5	23	35	20
6	25	39	22
7	31	40	19
8	17	52	16
9*	4	37	20

* 9 year olds do not represent a random selection because only slow students of this age are retained in the primary departments of schools and day classes for the deaf.

2.1.3 SCORING. Each correct answer receives one point. Correct answers are credited even if the child seems to be guessing. Give the entire seventy items of Test B.

2.1.4 INTERPRETATION OF SCORES. Evaluation of scores can best be made through a comparison with the data obtained on the experimental population. The total possible score is 70.

CHILDREN'S SPEECHREADING TEST

Dolores S. Butt

Name...................... Speechreading Test Score.....
School.................... Test Date..................
Examiner.................. Birthdate..................
Years of Training.............Age............. Sex........
Hearing: Right...... Left.... Mental Age........ IQ......

Age and Cause of Hearing Loss ....

Test A: Informal Checklist for Children Under Three Years

Normal age of
appearance

2 months	1. Does child attend to face? ....
10 months	2. Does child respond to gesture?..... (Pat-A-Cake, Bye-bye, etc.)
12 months	3. Does child inhibit on command? (no-no with gesture) ....
18 months	4. Does child understand simple questions? (Where's Daddy?) ......
21 months	5. Will child follow simple commands? (Give it to me; Come; Look; etc.) ......
24 months	6. Can he speechread his own name? The names of others? ......
24 months	Objects? (milk, shoe, etc.) ...... Or concepts? (up, hot, good boy, etc.) ......

(no norms)

7. Can he repeat the words he speechreads? (Hello, Mama, etc.) . . . . . .

8. Can he answer questions? (What is your name? How are you?) . . . . . .

TEST B

Test Materials. The examiner can obtain these materials from a toy store.

1. Toys, durable, realistically colored, and in correct proportion: 3″ baby doll, 1″ baby doll, doll bed, table, and chair, doll shoe, car, airplane, bus, train, gun, top, toy wrist watch, button, bell, cellophane wrapped candy, toy cup, fork, and spoon, child's toothbrush, 1″ rubber ball, ½″ rubber ball, cow, chicken, pig, horse, fish.

2. Blocks: five 1″ counting blocks of uniform color.

3. Color chips: 1″ colored paper squares: yellow, blue, black, white, red, and brown.

4. Ten picture cards 8½″ x 11″ that can be constructed from colored pictures in children's books or magazines. Each picture must be realistic and easily recognized by a child:

Card (a) baby, kitten, flower
　　　(b) mother, father, boy, girl
　　　(c) bird, dog, hammer, spoon
　　　(d) television set, motor boat, house, bed
　　　(e) girl putting on her shoes; boy eating at the table; girl or boy swimming
　　　(f) child playing with a ball; child taking a bath; girl jumping rope
　　　(g) child in bed; child reading a book; child playing with blocks
　　　(h) apple, water faucet and glass of water, pie, butter
　　　(i) an orange; milk carton and glass of milk; loaf of bread and a piece of bread; a vegetable
　　　(j) banana, cookies, cooked meat, soup

5. Paper dolls with clothes. Boy and girl dolls should be mounted on separate 8½″ x 11″ cards, and the clothing should be cut so it can easily be placed in position: Two dolls with pants, shirt, dress, pajamas, hats, and shoes.

Part I.   Identification of Objects

Place objects in random order on the table. Encourage child to watch your face while you name the object three times, then allow child to indicate the correct object. Replace object after each task. It is helpful to keep each set of objects in a separate box.

Present: fish, shoe, ball, train

. . . . . .1. Show me the fish.   . . . . . .2. Show me the ball.
. . . . . .3. Show me the shoe.

Present: top, airplane, baby, gun

. . . . . .4. Show me the airplane.   . . . . . .5. Show me the top.
. . . . . .6. Show me the gun.

Present: chair, toothbrush, button

. . . . . .7. Show me the chair.   . . . . . .8. Show me the button.
. . . . . .9. Show me the toothbrush.

Present: fork, table, car, bus

. . . . . .10. Show me the table. . . . . . .11. Show me the car.
. . . . . .12. Show me the bus.

Present: candy, watch, bell, hat

. . . . . .13. Show me the bell.   . . . . . .14. Show me the candy.
. . . . . .15. Show me the watch.

Part II.   Numbers

Place five blocks on the table. Demonstrate the first task by saying, "four," and scooping four blocks toward you. Replace the blocks, repeat the word "four" and indicate for the child to push the correct number toward you.

. . . . . .16. one   . . . . . .17. three   . . . . . .18. two

Part III.   Picture Identification

Present Test Card (a) and say,

. . .19. See baby? Where is baby?   . . .20. Where is the flower?

Present: Test Card (b)

. . . . . .21. Where is mother?   . . . . . .22. Where is father?
. . . . . .23. Where's the boy?   (or daddy)

Present: Test Card (c)

. . . . . .24. Point to the bird.   . . . . . .25. Point to the dog.
. . . . . .26. Point to the hammer

Present: Test Card (d)

. . . . . .27. Point to the T.V.   . . . . . .28. Point to the boat.
                (or television)
. . . . . .29. Point to the home.
                (or house)

Part IV.   Color Identification

Place color squares on table three at a time. Say the name of one color and reach your hand out to receive it. Change color cards for each item.

Present: blue, yellow, and white.   . . . . . .30. blue
Present: black, white, and brown.   . . . . . .31. white
Present: yellow, red, and brown.   . . . . . .32. brown

Part V. Actions.   Present Test Card (e)

. . . . . .33. Who put on her shoes?
. . . . . .34. Who eats her supper? (or dinner)

Present Test Card (f)

. . .35. Which one plays ball?   . . .36. Which one takes a bath?

Present Test Card (g)

. . . . . .37. Who goes to bed? Who sleeps in bed?
. . . . . .38. Who reads a book?

Part VI.   Foods

Present Test Card (h) to child. Allow him to examine it and proceed.

......39. Show me the apple. ......40. Where is the water?
......41. Point to the pie.

Continue with Card (i)

......42. Show me the orange......43. Where is the milk?
......44. Where is the bread?

Card (j)

....45. Show me the banana......46. Where are the cookies?
....47. Show me the meat.

Part VII.   Descriptive Words

Place on the table a large ball and a small ball, a 3″ baby doll and a 1″ baby doll.

....50. Where is your mouth? ....51. Where are your eyes?
....52. Where is your nose?   ....53. Show me your teeth.
....54. Show me your arm.   ....55. Where are your feet?

Part IX.   Animal Names

Place the animals on the table in random order. Include: chicken, pig, sheep, cow, horse. Replace after each item.

......56. Give me the cow. ......57. Give me the horse.
......58. Give me the pig. ......59. Give me the chicken.

Part X.   Clothing

Place on the table a paper doll mounted on 8½″ x 11″ card. Use a boy or a girl doll according to the sex of the child. Place the doll's clothes beside test card. Demonstrate the first item. "Put on his (her) pajamas." Replace each piece before proceeding with the next item.

Part XI.   Simple Directions

Place these objects on the table: chair, bed, baby, cup, table.
......64. Put the baby to bed. Put her in bed. Go to bed, baby.

...... 65. Put the spoon in the cup. Put it in the cup.
...... 66. Put the fork on the table. Put it on the table.

Part XII.   Activities

Stand up and gesture for the child to stand. Say, "Stand up."
"Do what I do." "Can you hop? Hop and encourage the child
to perform this action as a demonstration. Avoid gesturing with
the actual test items to follow.

...... 67. Can you jump? Jump.
...... 68. Can you walk? Walk. Walk to the door.
...... 69. Open the door. Go open the door. Open it.
...... 70. Come here. Come.

2.2. *Craig Lipreading Inventory**

2.2.1 DESCRIPTION. The Craig Lipreading Inventory consists
of a word recognition test and a sentence recognition test. Each
test has two forms making it possible to compare scores when
the test is given without voice and with voice. The vocabulary
was selected from words presented in kindergarten and the first
grade. The vocabulary contains enough items so that the lack
of a few word concepts will not markedly affect the speechreading scores. The tests were designed to differentiate among speechreaders from the end of the first grade through the tenth grade.

2.2.2 PRESENTATION AND METHOD OF RESPONSE. The tests are
given "live".† Students are to be tested in groups of six, with
each child seated exactly eight feet from the speaker. Each
item is presented twice permitting each child to have a full view
and a three-quarter face view of the speaker. When giving the
word test, the speaker precedes each word with the phrase, "show
me."

Multiple choice response forms are provided, with four pos-

* William N. Craig, Ph.D. is an associate professor in the School of Education, University of Pittsburgh, Pittsburgh, Pennsylvania.
† The filmed version may be obtained from WRS Motion Picture Laboratory,
210 Semple Street, Pittsburgh, Pennsylvania, 15213.

CRAIG LIPREADING INVENTORY

Word Recognition

NAME:_____

AGE: _____   DATE: _____   SCHOOL :_____

EX.	fish	table	baby	ball
1.	kite	fire	white	light
2.	corn	fork	horse	purse
3.	two	zoo	spoon	shoe
4.	cup	jump	thumb	drum
5.	hair	bear	pear	chair

FIGURE 10. Craig Lipreading Test.

WORD RECOGNITION   PAGE 2.

6.	yoyo	hello	Jello	window
7.	doll	ten	nail	suit
8.	pig	pie	book	pear
9.	two	toe	tie	toy
10.	flower	finger	fire	feather
11.	six	sing	sit	kiss

WORD RECOGNITION

12.	table	apple	woman	rabbit
13.	fire	tie	fly	five
14.	four	frog	fork	flag
15.	grapes	airplane	tables	cups
16.	goose	tooth	shoe	school
17.	desk	sled	leg	nest

WORD RECOGNITION   PAGE 4.

18.	dog	sock	star	car
19.	wing	sing	ring	swing
20.	three	teeth	key	knee
21.	duck	rug	truck	gun
22.	moon	school	spoon	boot
23.	ear	hair	eye	egg

WORD RECOGNITION   PAGE 5.

24.	horse	house	ice	orange
25.	goat	gate	kite	girl
26	dish	duck	desk	dog
27.	cat	cake	gun	coat
28.	nail	nut	nest	ten
29.	man	bat	milk	bird

WORD RECOGNITION			PAGE 6.
30.	egg	cake	key	car
31.	eight	egg	cake	gate
32.	pencil	picture	mitten	pitcher
33.	wet	dress	nest	desk

CRAIG LIPREADING INVENTORY

SENTENCE RECOGNITION   NAME: _____

1.

a drum is on a chair.	a coat is on a table.
a drum is on a table.	a coat is on a chair.

2.

a sock and a ball are on the floor.	a sock and a shoe are on the floor.
a top and a shoe are on the floor.	a top and a ball are on the floor.

3.

a woman is flying a kite.	a boy is making a kite.
a boy is flying a kite.	a woman is making a kite.

SENTENCE RECOGNITION

4.

a girl is jumping.

a girl is sitting.

a boy is jumping.

a boy is sitting.

5.

a boy stuck his fork in an egg.

a boy stuck his thumb in a shoe.

a boy stuck his fork in the pie.

a boy stuck his thumb in the pie.

6.

a cow and a pig are near the barn.

a cow and a sheep are near the gate.

a cow and a pig are near the gate.

a chicken and a pig are near the gate.

SENTENCE   RECOGNITION   PAGE 3.

7. a man is throwing a stick to the dog.

a man is throwing a ball to the dog.

a baby is throwing a ball to the dog.

a baby is throwing a stick to the dog.

8. an airplane has white wings.

a bird is in the nest.

an airplane is over the house.

a bird has white wings.

9. a light is over a door.

a light is over a table

a picture is over a door.

a picture is over a table.

SENTENCE RECOGNITION   PAGE 4.

10.

a horse is standing by an old car.

a boy is standing by a new car.

a horse is standing by a new car.

a horse is standing by a new wagon.

11.

a boy is putting a dog in a chair.

a boy is putting a dog in a sled.

a boy is putting a nail in a chair.

a boy is putting a nail in a sled.

12.

a big fan is on a desk.

a big fan is on the bed.

a little fan is on a desk.

a big shoe is on the desk.

SENTENCE RECOGNITION   **PAGE 5**

13.

an owl is looking at the mouse.

a cat is looking at the moon.

an owl is looking at the moon

a cat is looking at the mouse.

14.

one bird is in the sky.

three stars are in the sky.

three birds are in the sky

one star is in the sky

15.

a whistle and a spoon are on the chair.

a whistle and a ball are on the table.

a knife and a spoon are on the table.

a whistle and a spoon are on the table

SENTENCE RECOGNITION   PAGE 6.

16.

| a frog is hopping away from a boat. | a frog is hopping away from a cow. |
| a rabbit is hopping away from a cow. | a rabbit is hopping away from a boat. |

17.

| Bread, butter and grapes are in a dish. | Bread, meat and grapes are in a dish. |
| Bread, meat and apples are in a dish. | Jello, meat and grapes are in a dish. |

18.

| The woman has long hair and a short dress. | The woman has long hair and a long dress. |
| The woman has short hair and a long dress. | The woman has short hair and a short dress. |

SENTENCE RECOGNITION

19.

the boys are jumping behind the school.

the boys are swinging behind the tree.

the boys are jumping behind the tree.

the boys are swinging behind the school.

20.

a cat is playing with a ball.

a squirrel is playing with a nut.

a cat is playing with a nut.

a squirrel is playing with a ball.

21.

a man has his foot on a chair.

a man has his hand on a truck.

a man has his foot on a truck.

a man has his hand on a chair.

SENTENCE RECOGNITION   PAGE 8.

22.

	a woman is washing a chair.		a woman is carrying a chair.
	a woman is washing a shirt.		a woman is carrying a shirt.

23.

	a man is eating an apple.		a man is picking an apple.
	a woman is eating an apple.		a woman is picking an apple.

24.

	a girl is blowing a feather.		a girl is blowing a flower.
	a girl is cutting a flower.		a girl is cutting a feather.

TABLE 7-VII
WESTERN PENNSYLVANIA SCHOOL FOR THE DEAF
N = 164 (Preschool 101, Nonpreschool 63)

	Preschool	Nonpreschool
Lipreading Words	62.5%	68.0%
Lipreading Sentences	52.5%	61.5%

sible responses for each word and for each sentence. The possible responses are pictured as well as written to insure that reading ability will not affect test score.

2.2.3 SCORING. One point is given for each word or each sentence corectly identified. The highest possible score for the word recognition test is 33, and for the sentence test it is 24.

2.2.4 INTERPRETATION OF SCORES. Evaluation of scores can best be made through a comparison with the data obtained on the experimental populations.

CRAIG LIPREADING INVENTORY
Word Recognition
Correction Key—Form A

1. White
2. Corn
3. Zoo
4. Thumb
5. Chair
6. Jello
7. Doll
8. Pig
9. Toy
10. Finger
11. Six
12. Woman
13. Fly
14. Frog
15. Grapes
16. Goose
17. Sled
18. Star
19. Sing
20. Three

TABLE 7-VIII
AMERICAN SCHOOL FOR THE DEAF
N = 79 (Preschool 50, Nonpreschool 29)

	Preschool	Nonpreschool
Lipreading Words	68.0%	69.0%
Lipreading Sentences	62.0%	63.0%

21. Duck
22. Spoon
23. Ear
24. Ice
25. Goat
26. Dog
27. Cat

28. Nut
29. Milk
30. Cake
31. Eight
32. Pencil
33. Desk

CRAIG LIPREADING INVENTORY
Word Recognition

Correction Key—Form B

1. Fire
2. Purse
3. Two
4. Drum
5. Bear
6. Yo-Yo
7. Suit
8. Book
9. Two
10. Feather
11. Sing
12. Apple
13. Five
14. Four
15. Cups
16. Shoe
17. Leg

18. Sock
19. Swing
20. Knee
21. Rug
22. Moon
23. Hair
24. House
25. Kite
26. Dish
27. Gun
28. Ten
29. Bird
30. Car
31. Egg
32. Picture
33. Nest

CRAIG LIPREADING INVENTORY
Sentence Recognition

Correction Key—Form A

1. A coat is on a chair.
2. A sock and a shoe are on the floor.
3. A boy is flying a kite.
4. A girl is jumping.
5. A boy stuck his thumb in the pie.

6. A cow and a pig are near the gate.
7. A man is throwing a ball to the dog.
8. A bird has white wings.
9. A light is over the door.
10. A horse is standing by a new car.
11. A boy is putting a nail in the sled.
12. A big fan is on a desk.
13. An owl is looking at the moon.
14. Three stars are in the sky.
15. A whistle and a spoon are on the table.
16. A frog is hopping away from a boat.
17. Bread, meat and grapes are in the dish.
18. The woman has long hair and a short dress.
19. The boys are swinging behind the school.
20. A cat is playing with a nut.
21. A man has his foot on a truck.
22. A woman is carrying a chair.
23. A woman is eating an apple.
24. A girl is cutting a feather.

CRAIG LIPREADING INVENTORY

Sentence Recognition

Correction Key—Form B

1. A coat is on a table.
2. A top and a ball are on the floor.
3. A boy is making a kite.
4. A boy is sitting.
5. A boy struck his fork in an egg.
6. A cow and a pig are near the barn.
7. A baby is throwing a ball to the dog.
8. An airplane has white wings.
9. A picture is over a table.
10. A horse is standing by a new wagon.
11. A boy is putting a dog in a chair.
12. A big shoe is on the desk.
13. A cat is looking at the moon.
14. Three birds are in the sky.

15. A knife and a spoon are on the table.
16. A frog is hopping away from a cow.
17. Bread, meat and apples are in a dish.
18. The woman has short hair and a short dress.
19. The boys are swinging behind the tree.
20. A squirrel is playing with a ball.
21. A man has his hand on a chair.
22. A woman is carrying a shirt.
23. A man is picking an apple.
24. A girl is cutting a flower.

2.3. Costello Test of Speechreading[*]

2.3.1 DESCRIPTION. The Costello Test of Speechreading was designed to measure word and sentence recognition skill when the visual perceptual information varied among the various items from words easily identified in speechreading, such as "mouth," to words quite difficult to perceive, such as "yes." Vocabulary used in both the word and sentence tests was selected from kindergarten lists in order that all words would be familiar to the subjects. With only familiar concepts and vocabulary used, the test purported to measure the skill of speechreading and not vocabulary or language development.

In the final form of the word test, the level of difficulty varied from the first ten words (Group I), recognized 89 percent of the time by college students with normal hearing, to the last ten words (Group V), which were recognized only 18 percent of the time. The sentences in the sentence test were selected in a similar manner.

TABLE 7-IX
MEAN PERCENTAGE OF RECOGNITION BY COLLEGE STUDENTS (47)
FOR THE WORD TEST

Group I	Group II	Group III	Group IV	Group V
89	69	47	34	18

[*] Dr. Mary Rose Costello is at the present time Audiologist in charge of Children's Division in the Department of Otolaryngology, Henry Ford Hospital, Detroit, Michigan.

TABLE 7-X
MEAN PERCENTAGE OF RECOGNITION BY COLLEGE STUDENTS (33)
FOR THE SENTENCE TEST

Group I	Group II	Group III	Group IV	Group V
70	45	39	31	13

Since only beginning (kindergarten level) vocabulary is included, the test can be used with quite young children.

2.3.2 PRESENTATION AND METHOD OF RESPONSE—WORD TEST. The test is given without voice and with the testee seated opposite the examiner and at a distance of about six feet. The testee responds by repeating each word said by the examiner. The procedure is as follows:

Examiner: "I'm going to say some words. You tell me what I say. First let's practice."
Practice words are *arm, eye, light*. If necessary, these words are repeated and any errors pointed out.

Examiner: "Now we will begin." Number one (in full voice) followed by the word without voice, etc.

2.3.3 SCORING. One point is given for each word interpreted properly. The maximum score is 50.

2.3.4 INTERPRETATION. Evaluation of scores can best be made through comparison with the data obtained on the experimental population.

TABLE 7-XI
COMPARISON OF THE DEAF AND HARD-OF-HEARING
ON THE WORD TEST
(Age Range 9–14 Years)

Group	N	Mean	S.D.	T-score	Significance
Deaf	36	18.86	7.46	2.863	Significant*
H.-of-H.	34	23.95	7.40		

* 2.659 required at the .01 level.

2.3.5 SCRIPT.

Word Test with Speech Reading

1.	five	18.	go	35.	laugh
2.	wash	19.	girl	36.	foot
3.	home	20.	shoot	37.	school
4.	room	21.	street	38.	fast
5.	smoke	22.	live	39.	star
6.	ball	23.	drink	40.	shut
7.	horse	24.	bed	41.	cow
8.	stop	25.	yes	42.	read
9.	farm	26.	fish	43.	shirt
10.	look	27.	thought	44.	door
11.	church	28.	mouth	45.	milk
12.	work	29.	lamp	46.	teeth
13.	warm	30.	house	47.	day
14.	store	31.	one	48.	flag
15.	chair	32.	first	49.	ten
16.	sock	33.	blue	50.	late
17.	think	34.	road		

SCORE ——————————————

2.3.6 PRESENTATION AND METHOD OF RESPONSE—SENTENCE TEST. There are two parts to the sentence test, each consisting of twenty-five sentences. The test is given without voice and with the examinee seated opposite the examiner and at a distance of about six feet. A doll house is used which contains the objects and figures mentioned in the sentences. Each sentence is given only once. The examinee responds by using these materials to act out the meaning of the sentences. For example, "Mother gave the baby a bath." Correct oral responses are also accepted. Before the test, practice is given in the recognition of a number of words represented in the home scene. Objects are indicated and named, and the proper names are presented in writing. The child is asked to point to the object or figure named. For example, *Bob, Jane, Mother*, etc.

2.3.7 SCORING. One point is given for each sentence that is interpreted correctly. The total possible score for the test is 50.

2.3.8 INTERPRETATION OF SCORES—SENTENCE TEST. Evaluation of scores can best be made through comparison with the data obtained on the experimental populations. See Table 7-XII.

TABLE 7-XII
COMPARISON OF THE DEAF AND HARD-OF-HEARING
ON THE SENTENCE TEST
(Age Range 9–14 Years)

Group	N	Mean	S.D.	T-score	Significance
Deaf	36	12.22	10.31	2.557	Significant*
H.-of-H.	34	21.00	11.42		

* 2.364 required at the .02 level; interpreted at the .05 level.

2.3.9 INTERPRETATION OF SCORES—Total Test. See Table 7-XIII.

TABLE 7-XIII
COMPARISON OF THE DEAF AND HARD-OF-HEARING
ON THE TOTAL SPEECHREADING TEST

Group	N	Mean	S.D.	T-score	Significance
Deaf	36	15.54	8.45	3.295	Significant*
H.-of-H.	34	22.47	9.16		

* 2.625 required at the .01 level; interpreted at the .02 level.

2.3.10 SCRIPT.

Practice Words Prior to
Speech Reading Sentence Test

Bob	clock	car
Jane	another boy	ball
Mother	table	lamp
Father	dog	couch
baby	cat	flowers
television	fire	pocketbook
bath	stove	truck

Sentence Test with Speech Reading*

1. What time is it?
2. Mother gave the baby a bath.
3. Mother swept the floor.
4. The dog went to sleep in front of the fire.

* Dr. Mary Rose Costello, author.

5. How many people do you see?
6. Mother put some flowers on the living room table.
7. What does Bob like to play with?
8. The baby was very sick so mother put him to bed.
9. Bob went outside to play with his dog.
10. The television was broken.
11. Mr. Brown drove the car to work.
12. The cat washed his face.
13. Where is the girl in the blue dress?
14. They all went to church on Sunday.
15. Mother made the baby's bed.
16. Jane helped mother clean the house.
17. Mother couldn't find her pocketbook.
18. Jane brushed her teeth and washed her face.
19. Mother was angry at Jane because she tore her dress.
20. Bob and another boy had a fight.
21. Mrs. Brown burned her hand on the stove.
22. Father gave Bob a new truck.
23. Bob looked at a show on television.
24. The dog shook hands with Bob.
25. Jane was ten years old.

SCORE_____

Sentence Test Part II with Speech Reading*

1. What is the boy's name?
2. The baby woke up and cried.
3. How many rooms are in the house?
4. When Mr. Brown came home he was very tired.
5. Whose dress is blue?
6. What day is it?
7. There was something the matter with the car.
8. How old do you think Bob is?
9. Bob and Jane washed the dishes.
10. The clock stopped.
11. Mother told Bob to take a bath.
12. The baby pulled the lamp off the table.

* Dr. Mary Rose Costello, author.

13. Who is sitting on the floor?
14. Jane went to the kitchen and got a drink of water.
15. What color is Bob's suit?
16. The ball rolled under the table.
17. Jane was happy because it was her birthday.
18. Mrs. Brown sat down on the couch and read the paper.
19. Bob got his books and went to school.
20. Bob fed the dog and the cat.
21. The cat climbed up on the chair and went to sleep.
22. The flowers smelled sweet.
23. Jane cried when she cut her finger.
24. The baby's face and hands were dirty.
25. Father said his new hat cost five dollars.

SCORES_____

2.4. *Cavender Test of Lip Reading Ability**

2.4.1 DESCRIPTION. Cavender[3] constructed four sentence type tests, all of which appear to be of equal merit. Only one of them is reproduced herein. The tests were designed for use by public school hearing therapists in testing hard-of-hearing children. Vocabulary was selected from the three-fourths most important vocabulary for the first three grades as determined by Gates. Visibility was computed by the method established in the New York W.P.A. Lipreading Project. Test III consists of ten practice sentences and forty-five test sentences.

2.4.2 PRESENTATION AND METHOD OF RESPONSE. Presentation is "live" and without voice. Each sentence is given twice. The testee responds by underlining the one word that occurred in the sentence from a choice of five words on his multiple choice response blank. Criteria for the selection of the answer words for the multiple choice response were that (a) they must be neither the first nor the last word of the sentence, (b) they must be important to the meaning of the sentence, and (c) they must have approximately the same visibility as the rest of the sentence.

*Appreciation is extended to Betty Jane Cavender for permission to reproduce her test.

2.4.3 SCORING. One point is given for each word underlined correctly.

2.4.4 INTERPRETATION OF SCORES. Scores can best be evaluated by a comparison with those made by the experimental population. The test was given to 141 pupils with normal hearing; grades six through twelve, age range, eleven to eighteen years. The mean score was 21.2; standard deviation, 6.44; range, 2–37.

Test III

Example Sentences

1. Will you play ball with me?
2. May I have a piece of pie?
3. The clown was very funny.
4. Watch that ship sail off.
5. Do you like apple pie?
6. Did you hear the band play?
7. The baby lamb wanted its mother.
8. Will you wash that jam off?
9. The baby laughed and laughed.
10. What time is it now?

Part I

1. The farmer's wife found three mice.
2. We burned the leaves last night.
3. Did he get the groceries?
4. Don't frighten the baby.
5. Can you come when I call you?
6. He has his ax.
7. How sick is your dog?
8. Please push the swing.
9. We marched with the band.
10. The car keys are gone.
11. Is his neck clean?
12. Will you have lunch with me now?
13. Is the gate closed?
14. Watch while they show you their play.
15. Did the dog bite you?

Part II

1. My brother found the puppy.
2. I threw his old shoes away.
3. How high did the kite go?
4. I want you to meet my friend.
5. The ground is frozen.
6. He took his own nickel.
7. Do you have a gold ring?
8. Does that bump hurt?
9. Wash your face after you play.
10. What did you eat on the picnic?
11. Can you cook a dinner?
12. May I have that piece of pie?
13. He is going down the street.
14. Show them the baby lamb.
15. This cat caught five mice.

Part III

1. Did she paint that picture?
2. How far can you swim?
3. The kitten killed the hen.
4. Put the knife on the table.
5. What do we get from cows?
6. Did I kick the kitty?
7. Who wants a drink now?
8. I knew that question.
9. Wipe that mud off your shoes.
10. I always cut the grass.
11. A king rules this country.
12. Watch that girl throw the ball.
13. He cracked nuts for the cake.
14. Throw me that ball.
15. Who won that race?

Answer Sheet, Test III

Directions: Underline the word used in each sentence.

(Example 1)　house　ball　Paul　catch　bawl

(Example 2) slice peas bees bite piece
(Example 3) down show clown book loud
(Example 4) gym ship glider boat chip
(Example 5) apple happen cherry peach ample
(Example 6) pat new pan band orchestra
(Example 7) lap lion lamb leopard lamp
(Example 8) wash what's take set watch
(Example 9) paper girl boy baby maybe
(Example 10) type dime class day time

Directions: Underline the word used in each sentence.

1. caught found vowed saw fouled
2. purred raked bird collected burned
3. get head buy hen remember
4. vine hurt wake frighten fried
5. cup obey come hear gum
6. has gas lost broke ask
7. sink big sick old sing
8. bush stop butch push get
9. barged marched rode played marsh
10. geese ease tires lights keys
11. dig neck shirt paper deck
12. coke touch game Dutch lunch
13. gate door cane ate window
14. Joe joke show teach do
15. hurt pint chase bite mine
16. caught vowed fouled found saw
17. old brown oat hold brown
18. guide kite plane balloon kind
19. bean help bead tell meet
20. crown cream ground crowd water
21. look lost took used nook
22. oat new cone gold class
23. bump bum cut sore pump
24. hands vase fades self face
25. do eat keen heat have
26. cook serve hook hung fix

27. bees slice kind piece peas
28. in down doubt up town
29. paper new baby maybe black
30. can trap dog can't cat
31. main buy paint bait like
32. cat will do can canned
33. killed guilt caught chased hilt
34. dive knife milk life cards
35. head get hen learn catch
36. ink king miss feed kick
37. drink rest trick test ring
38. missed due had knew two
39. snow dirt but bun mud
40. gun hunt cut water mow
41. kick ink child woman king
42. boy girl curl man eel
43. tons eggs corn nuts does
44. me her pea him bee
45. one what won ran lost

REFERENCES

Tests of Speechreading

1. Barley, M.: CID everyday sentences test of speechreading ability. Unpublished material, 1964.
2. Butt, D.S., and Chreist, F.M.: A speechreading test for young children. *The Volta Review*, 70:225–244, 1968.
3. Cavender, B.J.: *The Construction and Investigation of a Test of Lip Reading Ability and a Study of Factors Assumed to Affect the Results.* Unpublished M.A. Thesis, Indiana University, 1949.
4. Costello, M.R.: *A Study of Speech Reading as a Developing Language Process in Deaf and in Hard of Hearing Children.* Unpublished Doctoral Dissertation, Northwestern University, 1957.
5. Craig, W.N.: Effects of preschool training on the development of reading and lipreading skills of deaf children. *Amer Ann Deaf, 109:* 280–296, 1964.
6. Di Carlo, L.M., and Kataja, R.: An analysis of the Utley Lipreading Test. *J Speech Hearing Dis*, 16:226–240, 1951.
7. Evans, L.: Factors related to listening and lip reading. *The Teacher of the Deaf*, 58:417–423, 1960.

8. Heider, G.M.: The Utley Lip Reading Test. *The Volta Review, 49:* 457–458, 488, 499, 1947.

9. Jeffers, J.: *A Re-evaluation of the Utley Lipreading Sentence Test.* Paper presented at the 1967 Convention of the American Speech and Hearing Association, Chicago, Illinois.

10. Lowell, E.L.: Pilot studies in lip reading. *John Tracy Clinic Research Papers VIII,* Los Angeles, John Tracy Clinic, February, 1958.

11. O'Neill, J.J., and Stephens, M.C.: Relationships among three filmed lipreading tests. *J Speech Hearing Res,* 2:61–65, 1959.

12. Taaffe, G.: A film test of lip reading. *John Tracy Clinic Research Papers II,* Los Angeles, John Tracy Clinic, November, 1957.

13. Utley, J.: *Development and Standardization of a Motion Picture Achievement Test of Lip Reading Ability.* Unpublished Ph.D. Thesis, Northwestern University, 1945.

14. Utley, J.: Factors involved in the teaching and testing of lip reading ability through the use of motion pictures. *The Volta Review, 48:* 657–659, 1946.

15. Utley, J.: "A Test of Lip Reading Ability," *The Journal of Speech Disorders, 11:*109–116, 1946.

16. Utley, J.: *Teacher's Lesson Manual* (to accompany the 16 mm motion picture, "How Well Can You Read Lips?"). Chicago, De Vry Corporation. (1111 Armitage Avenue, Chicago 14, Illinois.)

ADDENDUM BIBLIOGRAPHY

Language Age References For Various Items of the Children's Speechreading Test (Butt and Chreist)

Bayley, N.: Mental growth during the first three years: An experimental study of sixty-one children by repeated testing. *Genet Psychol Monogr, XIV*:1–92, 1933.

Buhler, C.: *The First Year of Life.* New York, Day, 1930.

Cattell, P.: *The Measurement of Intelligence of Infants and Young Children.* New York, Johnson Reprint, 1966.

Gesell, A.: *The Mental Growth of the Preschool Child: A Psychological Outline of Normal Development from Birth to the Sixth Year, Including a System of Developmental Diagnosis.* Macmillan, 1925.

Gesell, A., Thompson, H., and Amatruda, C.S.: *The Psychology of Early Growth.* New York, Macmillan, 1938.

Ilg, F.L., and Ames, L.B.: *Child Behavior.* New York, Harper, 1955.

Correspondence Course for Parents of Little Deaf Children, Designed to Be Used with Preschool Children from Two to Five Years of Age. Los Angeles, John Tracy Clinic, 1954.

Stutsman, R.: *Mental Measurement of Preschool Children.* Yonkers-on-Hudson, World Book, 1931.

Terman, L.M., and Merrill, M.A.: *Measuring Intelligence: A Guide to the Administration of the New Revised Stanford-Binet Tests of Intelligence.* Boston, Houghton Mifflin, 1937.

NAME INDEX

Arthur, R.H., 204, 205

Barber, C.G., 45, 59, 62
Barley, M., 329, 338
Bell, A.G., 4, 81, 82
Bell, A.G. (Mrs.), 91, 92
Bell, A.M., 5, 82
Bernero, R.J., 147
Black, J.W., 123
Bode, D.L., 4
Brannon, J.B., 153
Brauckmann, K., 108, 109
Bruhn, M.E., 95, 99
Bunger, A.M., 108
Butt, D.S., 343
Byers, B.W., 146–148

Cavender, B.J., 126, 136, 374
Conklin, E.S., 125, 151, 152
Coscarelli, J.E., 21, 124, 133, 134, 154–156
Costello, M.R., 129, 133, 134, 141, 142, 160–162, 166–168, 369
Craig, W.N., 34, 125, 133, 134, 137, 174, 351
Cranwill, S., 148
Cushing, F., 81

Daniloff, R., 50
Davidson, J.L., 131, 136, 140, 142, 160, 161, 165, 166

Edwards, A.L., 115
Eisman, B., 141, 142
Elkin, V.B., 140, 142
Evans, L., 125, 133, 134, 137, 138, 144, 166, 174

Fisher, C.G., 57, 62
Fries, C.C., 33
Frisina, D.R., 34, 130, 137, 147, 148
Fuller, S., 5, 81, 82, 84, 85, 96

Goetzinger, C.P., 149, 174, 175
Greenberg, H.J., 4
Greenberger, D., 86

Hardick, E.J., 149
Heider, F., 114, 115, 123–126, 130, 144, 145, 163, 164
Heider, G., 114, 115, 123–126, 130, 144, 145, 163, 164
Hill, F.M., 81
Hough, E.L., 85
Howe, S.G., 80
Hubbard, M., 81, 83, 91
Hutton, C., 123

Irion, P.E., 149

Jeffers, J., 338

Kates, S.L., 168, 169
Keaster, J., 333
Keeler, S.W., 86
Kinzie, C.E., 103, 104, 107
Kinzie, R., 103, 104, 107
Kitson, H.D., 116, 153, 156–158, 175
Kodman, F., 153

Levy, J., 141, 142
Lieberman, L., 146–148
Lippit, J., 81
Lloyd, L., 204
Lowell, E.L., 123, 129, 130, 133, 134

Mann, H., 80
McDearmon, J.R., 211
Moll, K., 50
Moore, L.M., 111
Moores, D., 101
Morkovin, B.V., 111
Mueller-Walle, J., 99

SUBJECT INDEX

A

Abstract inductive reasoning, 27, 139, 165, 167

A.G. Bell Association for the Deaf, 84

Affricates, 53

American Association for Teaching Speech to the Deaf, 84, 91

American Hearing Society, 89

Analysis and diagnosis of learning difficulties, 238

Ancillary
  to synthetic ability and flexibility, 27, 31, 159
  to training and language proficiency, 23, 34, 128–132
  to visual perceptual proficiency, 22, 25, 128–132

Association, training in, 204

Automatic speech, *see* Overlearned speech

A V K R, 111

B

Bad instructional practices
  loading sentences, 85, 95, 101, 102
  mirror practice, 84, 87, 88, 90, 91, 94, 100, 101
  part to whole, vi, 84, 85, 96, 103, 106
  teaching the what and hows, 47, 84, 87, 94, 101, 108, 195, 196, 246
  using no voice, 107

Barley Speechreading Test—CID everyday sentences
  and CID sentences, 328, 329
  and experiments with, 329, 331
  interpretation of scores, 331
  presentation and scoring, 331
  scripts for, 331–333

Beginning speechreading materials, 205–225

Bilabial plosives, 51

Martha E. Bruhn
  add a phrase technique, 101, 102
  exercise story, 102, 227, 229
  Mueller-Walle method, 99–103
  part to whole, 103
  personal history, 99
  school and texts, 99, 100

C

Cavender Test of Lip Reading Ability
  answer sheets for, 376–378
  description of, 374
  interpretation of, 375
  presentation and response for, 374
  scoring of, 375
  scripts for, 375, 376

Children's Speechreading Test—Butt
  description and comparative data for, 343
  interpretation of, 346
  presentation and response for, 345
  scoring of, 346
  scripts for, 346–351

Chronological age, 115, 123, 124, 125

Clarke School, 81, 85

Closures
  conceptual, 22, 25–27, 30, 158, 159, 204
  conjectural, 22, 27, 156, 158
  perceptual, 22, 25, 26, 30, 150, 151, 153, 158, 159, 204
  revision of, 30, 31, 158, 159

Coefficient of correlation, 118–121

Colloquial sentences—clue words
  discussion of, 216, 217
  materials, 216, 217, 249, 250, 252, 253, 285–288

Composite skill, 148, 167, 184